MODERN MILITARY HEROES

UNTOLD STORIES OF COURAGE AND GALLANTRY

NARELLE BIEDERMANN

ECHO BOOKS

First published in 2006 by Random House.

This second edition has been published by Barrallier Books Pty Ltd, trading as Echo Books.

Barrallier Books registered office: 35-37 Gordon Avenue, West Geelong, Victoria 3220, Australia.

www.echobooks.com.au

National Library of Australia Cataloguing-in-Publication entry
Creator:
Biedermann, Narelle, author.

Title:
Modern military heroes : untold stories of courage and gallantry / Narelle Biedermann.

Edition:
Second edition

ISBN:
9780994491169 (paperback)

Notes:
Includes bibliographical references.

Subjects:
Soldiers--Australia--Biography.
Sailors--Australia--Biography.
Australia--History, Military--Biography.
Heroes--Australia--Biography.

Dewey Number:
355.0092

Cover design and book preparation by Tim Millhouse

Cover photograph: *Three Australian soldiers evacuate one of the thousands of Rwandans wounded during the massacre at the Kibeho Displaced Persons camp in Rwanda, April 1995. The soldier in the centre is Trooper Jon Church, who was to lose his life just over a year later in the Black Hawk training accident. (Defence Public Affairs photograph)*

I dedicate this book to my sister-in-law, Kirsty Jones,
the most courageous woman I know

CONTENTS

What these men did nothing can alter now. The good and the bad, the great-ness and the smallness of their story will stand. Whatever of glory it contains nothing can now lessen. It rises, as it will always rise, above the mists of ages, a monument to great-hearted men; and for their nation, a possession forever.

Charles Bean
'The AIF in France During the Allied Offensive, 1918',
The Official History of Australia in the War of 1914–18.

Acknowledgements

My thanks go to Ian Gordon at Echo Books, for agreeing to work with me to get this book back into print – these stories are too important to just let disappear; Kara Dubois, John Cadogan and Kim Smee from Radio 2UE, for being the catalyst to returning these important stories into the public consciousness; Warrant Officer Class 2 Bruce "Stumpy" Payne, Jo Harding, and Major Andrew Gisinger, for trusting me enough to go into bat for me; Major Tony Duus, Captain Jason Logue, Captain Gabrielle Parker, Lieutenant Natalie Boulton RAN, and Mrs Caroline Chalker, for their enthusiastic support of the first edition of this book; Dean Alston (The West Australian newspaper), for his generous offer of his poignant and meaningful cartoon; John Crawley, Editor, Flying Safety Spotlight, for his assistance with photographs; and to everyone else who asked me, "Where can I get a copy of that book?"

To my husband Tom, my handsome man, thank you for all you did to support me in writing the book and encouraging me to find a way to get the story back out there. I love you; truly, madly, deeply. To my beautiful girls, Mikaelie and Riley, be who you are meant to be and love who you are. This book is about ordinary people who have done something extraordinary, and like them, you too should always take the chance and never be afraid to fail – I will always be there to catch you if you fall.

Additionally, I would like to formally acknowledge those heroic people who agreed to be in this book. I know that for many of you, talking about the events and your decoration was difficult, and I am still very appreciative of your time. I trust that this book is something that you and your family can be proud of.

In Memoriam

Let us always remember the men who lost their lives
on the evening of 12 June 1996
on board Black Hawk 1 and Black Hawk 2.

Special Air Service Regiment

Captain Timothy James Stevens
Sergeant Hugh William Ellis
Corporal Mihran Avedissian
Corporal Michael John Bird
Corporal Andrew Constantinidis
Corporal Darren John Smith
Corporal Brett Stephen Tombs
Lance Corporal Gordon Andrew Callow
Lance Corporal David Andrew Johnstone
Lance Corporal Darren Robert Oldham
Trooper Jonathon Gaius Sanford Church
Trooper David Frost
Trooper Glen Donald Hagan
Trooper Timothy John McDonald
Signaller Hendrick Peeters

5th Aviation Regiment

Captain John Berrigan
Captain Kelvin James Hales
Corporal Michael Colin Baker

FOREWORD

Australia has a proud and distinguished military history. From the shores of Gallipoli and the battlefields of the Western Front in World War I, to the skies over Europe, the deserts of North Africa and the islands of the Pacific in World War II, right through to Korea, Vietnam and our commitment today in Iraq, Afghanistan, Timor-Leste and the Solomon Islands, Australian military personnel have served our country with honour, and have been consistently recognised for their bravery, skill, and compassion.

Being an Australian soldier, sailor, or airman or airwoman is about teamwork. It's about being trustworthy and using your initiative. Men and women of the Australian Defence Force (ADF) show courage, endurance and empathy. And, perhaps above all else, being an Aussie serviceman or servicewoman is about mateship – displaying a sense of selfless sacrifice and of loyalty – to the very end. There is no doubt that Australia's modern military personnel are serving with great distinction in the fine tradition of those who went before, and they continue to serve in a manner that would make their forebears proud.

Nowhere is this more clearly represented than in the pages of this book. In *Modern Military Heroes* Narelle Biedermann shares with us the inspiring – and in some cases, harrowing – stories of amazing men and women of the ADF, whose strong commitment to their peers, their country and the task at hand meant they were willing, without question or hesitation, to risk their lives in the hope that they might be able to save others. In the ADF we try very hard to provide our men and women with the very best training, preparation and leadership available, but each of these stories details remarkable people going far above and beyond what could reasonably have been expected of them.

Of course, in the tradition of the unassuming, humble Aussie heroes of the past, they don't consider themselves to be heroes, nor their actions heroic. If you ask them, they were only doing their job, only doing the same thing many others would have done in their position. They even had doubts about accepting their awards – some believing their actions didn't measure up to Australian military heroes of the past; some not wanting to be recognised when their peers were not; some not wanting a fuss to be made when they believe they could have done more. But after reading their stories, you will see they are heroes. You will see they each greatly deserve the honours they received.

Narelle Biedermann has done a magnificent job in reminding us all that true Australian military heroes exist, and not only in history books; they are currently serving Australia here at home and all over the world, working and training hard to protect our nation and our national interests. As Chief of the Defence Force I am particularly privileged to introduce this book, which so aptly depicts the values and courage of some of our modern ADF heroes. They have done us very proud.

Air Chief Marshal Angus Houston, AO, AFC
Chief of the Defence Force
June 2006

INTRODUCTION

The hero is commonly the simplest and obscurest of men.

Henry David Thoreau
From 'Walking', 1862

STORIES OF THE BRAVE HAVE FASCINATED AND ENTHRALLED people throughout the ages, and tales of courage and gallantry abound in the lore that follows in the wake of battles. Hardly any war or skirmish is without a story of a heroic deed or action to accompany its telling. We have all read, or read about, the hundreds of men, and the occasional woman, who have single-handedly taken on large numbers of enemy soldiers, or run the gauntlet of enemy troops to kill their leader, or rushed into 'no-man's-land' to rescue a wounded comrade without any outward fear for his or her own life.

Consider the story of American medical corpsman Donald Ballard, who was awarded the highest American military decoration, the Medal of Honor, for his actions in the Quang Tri Province, South Vietnam in 1968.

During the violent and bloody clash, Ballard noticed one of the soldiers from his company fall to the ground, wounded. Without hesitation he ran across the fire-swept terrain to reach the soldier where he lay. While he was treating the soldier's wounds, Ballard directed four marines to carry the soldier to a position of relative safety away from the battle so that he could receive further medical help in preparation for evacuation.

As the marines prepared to move the wounded man, an enemy

soldier popped up from his concealed position nearby and, after hurling a hand grenade that landed in the midst of their group, started firing at them all. Ballard shouted a warning to the marines carrying the stretcher and then threw himself on top of the grenade to protect his comrades from the deadly blast that was to follow. However, the grenade failed to detonate. When Ballard realised what had just happened, he calmly got up and continued to treat the increasing numbers of casualties around him.

Ironically, because the grenade failed to detonate and he survived the incident, Ballard was initially not nominated for the Medal of Honor but for a lesser decoration. Dozens of American soldiers have been awarded the Medal of Honor posthumously for throwing themselves on top of grenades to protect their comrades, but Ballard's story is unique because by some fortuitous stroke of fate, 'his' grenade didn't explode. Ballard, and the dozens of other soldiers around the world who have carried out the same deadly action to protect the lives of others, clearly knew that this act would mean their own death and yet they still did it, seemingly without hesitation. Reading about such an act makes you ask yourself: would I do the same thing under the same circumstances?

Some experts suggest that at a crisis point, like a live grenade landing nearby, we are faced with a choice between going forward into certain death (throwing your body onto the grenade) or doing whatever it takes to survive (fleeing the scene and protecting yourself from its imminent blast). The fact that Ballard survived is a miracle but his story reminds us that making the choice to die in battle does not necessarily mean that you *will* die. The 13 outstanding stories in this book highlight that it is that choice made by the individual that signifies the depth of their courage, bravery or gallantry.

Courage, by definition, is the quality of being brave. It refers to the ability of an individual to face danger, difficulty, uncertainty or pain without being overwhelmed by fear or being deflected from a chosen course of action. Bravery can be understood as extreme courage in the face of danger or difficulty, while gallantry refers to bravery, particularly in war or in a situation of great danger. I chose the stories that follow in this book purely as acts of courage, bravery and gallantry in the modern Australian Defence Force (ADF).

The human body is supported by a multitude of emotions that ebb and wane continuously throughout life, and people respond to these emotions in clear and generally predicable ways. For example, when we experience happiness, the response is usually a feeling of well-being, a smile or laughter. The battlefield, both modern and in days gone by, exacts an overwhelming environment on the soldier in which he is challenged by emotions that are far from pleasant and not regularly experienced in everyday life. Fear, an emotion commonly felt by warriors in battlefields, is entirely natural and is vital in the development of human life. Fear helps humans to act with caution when the situation dictates but also to respond with courage if need be.

Terror, on the other hand, is an emotion at a destructive extreme. When someone succumbs to terror it means that, at a fundamental level, they have lost all perception of self-control and strength of mind. On the battlefield no amount of imposed discipline can thwart its effects. In the chaotic and lethal world of war it can be fatal, both for the individual *and* for all around him. In the past, men who were seen to succumb to terror and were unable to assist in the battle were often shot by their own commanders for fear of the effect such a harmful emotion would have on the morale of his comrades around him. Letters home to loved ones in Australia from the dreadful battlefields of the Western Front in World War I described the descent of sane and strong men into madness at the relentless bombardment and death surrounding them. These letters showed that even the strongest man in the unit could succumb to terror given the right circumstances and time.

Under stress, all humans experience the chemical reactions in the body that produce 'fight or flight' responses, which are both physiological responses and behavioural responses. Normal physio-logical responses to stress include an increase in heart rate and blood pressure, faster and shallower breathing, and muscle tensing. Behav-iourally, people respond in one of two ways: take 'it' on, or withdraw from the situation. For the soldier in the midst of a bloody battle, however, things are quite different.

Armies – and the people who form them – respond in a variety of ways when confronted with extremely stressful situations. In some cases, the army or soldier triumphs by demonstrating outstanding courage in the face of action; in others, they succumb to their terrors and panic sets in. Rather than stand and fight, men as individuals or in armies flee, leaving the enemy with no resistance. To the soldier, the 'fight or flight' response can be a friend – or an enemy. However, the individual who performs a heroic action chooses to 'fight' as opposed to take 'flight' from the situation and this can often serve to bolster the morale and personal daring of those around him. Witnessing a comrade bravely take on an enemy position, with no apparent fear, must surely have a hugely positive effect on others around him. Even the simplest act of rallying the troops can inspire soldiers to intensify their courage at difficult moments in battle. Take, for instance, the story of a British battalion, the Royal Warwickshire Regiment, which was faltering during an action in Gallipoli in World War I. Sensing that all was about to come undone around them, a lowly private suddenly began shouting to those around him, 'Hold up your heads, Warwicks, and show them your cap-badges!' At this defiant call, the men of the Warwickshire Regiment seemed to rally and the fight continued bravely to success. On the battlefield, there is a significant difference between being frightened and getting on with the job and being frightened and not getting on with the job. Perhaps that's what makes the difference between heroes and others.

The reality is that people universally love to read or hear stories of success on the battlefield. We want to be regaled with stories of bravery, courage and gallantry perhaps to remind ourselves that, even in the most extreme situations, fear can be triumphed over. And where this does not actually exist, throughout history embellishments on the truth have no doubt been interwoven into stories, often without question. But perhaps this is not such a bad thing.

Today, stories of military courage continue to be told and reported, although it could be argued that we are not as enraptured by tales of military prowess and courage as previous generations used to be. For example, Private Johnson Beharry is a British soldier who was awarded a Victoria Cross, the highest military award for valour in the British or Commonwealth forces, in March 2005 for his actions on two separate occasions in Iraq in May and June 2004. This incredible occasion passed with little fanfare in Australia, apart from small articles in newspapers and a 'good news' story on the evening news. Private Beharry from 1st Battalion, the Princess of Wales' Royal Regiment, is the first person to receive the Victoria Cross since 1982 and the first living recipient since 1965. It's astonishing to believe that extraordinary feats of military courage like Private Beharry's can pass us by with such little consequence. By way of comparison, when news reached Australia that Albert Jacka, a 22-year-old acting Lance Corporal, was to be awarded Australia's first Victoria Cross in the Great War, the nation rejoiced in the exploits of this home-grown hero. His likeness was even used on recruitment posters. Less than a month after the ANZAC landing on the Gallipoli Peninsula, the Turks had launched large-scale frontal assaults against the Australian positions; one assault captured a small section of the Australian trench at Courtney's Post. Several attempts to counter-attack the newly-assumed Turkish position failed, until Jacka leapt in to the position, killing most of the occupants. He was later awarded the Military Cross in 1916 in Pozières and a Bar to his Military Cross in 1917 for further courageous actions in Bullecourt.

Most of the actions described in this book did not occur on the traditional battlefield such as those so celebrated in our past. Rather, the people who tell their stories here performed acts where their own lives were indeed under threat but not always in the face of the enemy. However, they all had to make a conscious choice, often in a split second, to behave in a way that would later be considered exceptionally brave, courageous or gallant. Perhaps most importantly, all who share their stories in this book genuinely felt fear at some point (whether they admit it here in this book or not), and were able to shield it from those around them so that, in each case, they appeared fearless. This, indeed, makes them courageous. The stories in this book also took place in circumstances far beyond the imagination; and these ordinary Australian men and women, who happened to be wearing the uniform of the Australian Defence Force, performed actions that changed the lives of many other grateful people forever. However, as you will find when you read their stories, written in their own words, they are reluctant heroes.

Who are Australia's past military heroes?

Before I introduce these exceptional stories of modern military heroism, I think it's important to understand who Australia's past military heroes are in order to see the kind of company these contemporary award winners now keep. Very few countries throughout the world today are without some kind of system in place that bestows honours and awards upon its citizens, and its military personnel in particular, for excellence, achievement, or for meritorious service. Australia, in both the past and the present, has not tended to overly endow its military personnel with awards for gallantry, bravery and courage. In fact the highest honour that can be bestowed upon an individual – the Victoria Cross – has only been awarded to Australian servicemen 97 times since its inception.

From Federation, Australia used the British (Imperial) system of honours. The Victoria Cross was introduced in 1856 by Queen Victoria, by a Royal Warrant made retrospective to 1854 to cover the period in which the Crimean War was fought. Clause Five of this Warrant decrees that 'The Cross would only be awarded to those

Officers and Men who have served Us in the presence of the enemy and shall then have performed some signal act of Valour or Devotion to their country.' What is so unique about the Victoria Cross is that it was made available to *all* ranks, a phenomenon that was most unusual for British awards. Clause Six of the Warrant further establishes 'that neither rank nor long service nor wounds nor any other circumstances or condition whatsoever save the merit of conspicuous bravery shall be held to establish a sufficient claim for the honour'.

Additionally, the Victoria Cross has been granted to people of non-Commonwealth origin. In many cases, these people were born in a non-Commonwealth country, such as Denmark, Ukraine, Germany or Switzerland, but enlisted and served in a Commonwealth country's force; therefore it is often 'claimed' by both the birth nation and the nation for which the person fought.

The first presentation of the Victoria Cross was made in Hyde Park on 26 June 1857 when Queen Victoria herself decorated 62 officers and men for their actions during the Crimean War. Queen Victoria elected to stay on horseback throughout the ceremony of awarding each recipient with the Cross. According to legend, while leaning forward from the saddle to pin the Victoria Cross on the uniform of the first of the recipients, Commander Henry James Raby, Queen Victoria inadvertently stabbed him through his tunic into his chest with the pin fastener. Apparently, the commander stood unflinching while his Queen fastened the pin through his flesh. The other 61 men were said to have come through the occasion unscathed, but this kind of legend certainly serves to point out the style of such a man who is to be considered eligible for this esteemed award!

The first Victoria Cross awarded to an Australian was done so under quite unusual circumstances. Although born in Sydney in 1843, Lieutenant Mark Sever Bell was serving with a British unit, the Corps of Engineers, during the First Ashanti Expedition. His citation reads:

On 4 February 1874 at the Battle of Ordashu, Ashanti [now Ghana], Lieutenant Bell was always in front, urging and exhorting an unarmed working party of Fantee labourers who were exposed not only to the fire of the enemy, but to the wild and irregular fire of the native troops to the rear. He encouraged these men to work under fire without a covering party, and this contributed very materially to the success of the day.

The first Australian (although British-born) to be decorated with the Victoria Cross while serving with an Australian unit was Captain (later Sir) Neville Howse for his gallant actions while serving as an officer in the New South Wales Army Medical Corps during the Boer War (1899–1902). His citation records his actions leading to his decoration:

On 24 July 1900 during the action at Vredefort, South Africa, Captain Howse saw a trumpeter fall and went through very heavy cross-fire to rescue the man. His horse was soon shot from under him and the captain continued on foot still under intense enemy fire and when he reached the casualty, he dressed the worst of his wounds. He then carried the man to safety, still under heavy fire all the while.

Even to this day, Captain Howse remains the only Australian serviceman from the medical services to be awarded a Victoria Cross.

The youngest Australian to win the Victoria Cross is Private J.W.A. Jackson. He was only 18 years old when he received his award in 1916. Private Jackson volunteered to act as a scout for a raiding party consisting of 40 officers and men on the night of 25 June near Armentières. The party located the forward trenches of the 231st Prussian Reserve Infantry Regiment and within five minutes, engineers with the party had successfully blown up two bomb stores while the remainder of the party attacked the enemy trenches.

Private Jackson got back safely through the 400-metre no-man's-land, handing over an enemy prisoner he captured during his dash through the trenches. When he learned that some of the raiding party had been hit by enemy bombardment, he immediately went back into no-man's-land, again under very heavy fire, and helped to bring in a wounded Australian soldier. On this third return, he and a sergeant found another wounded Australian and proceeded to bring him back to the trenches when they were hit by shrapnel from a nearby exploding shell. Jackson's right arm was blown off below the elbow and the sergeant was rendered unconscious by the explosion. Private Jackson then returned for assistance for himself and the two wounded men.

With a tourniquet on his wounded and useless right arm, he went out for a fourth time to look for more of his injured comrades for a further 30 minutes, ignoring the orders of the medical staff to return to the trenches for additional treatment. Jackson was awarded the Victoria Cross for 'his great coolness and most conspicuous bravery while rescuing his wounded comrades while under heavy enemy fire following the raid that took place near Armentières.' His Victoria Cross was also the first of many that were won by Australians on the Western Front.

Captain James Earnest Newland has the honour of being the oldest Australian recipient of the Victoria Cross. At the grand old age of 35, Captain Newland was awarded the Victoria Cross for 'most conspicuous bravery and devotion to duty in the face of heavy odds, on three separate occasions' between 7 and 9 April at Bapaume-Cambrai Road and again on 15 April 1917 at Lagnicourt, France. Captain Newland organised and led a bombing attack on an important objective rallying his heavily depleted company, which had suffered heavy casualties in bombing raids. The next evening, under the cover of darkness, the enemy launched an attack on the Australians, however Captain Newland and his men were able to diffuse the attack and regain their lost position. Later on 15 April, he organised his company to launch a counter attack on the enemy that had overpowered an Australian company to his left and were able to restore the Australian defensive line again. Captain Newland was wounded three times before returning to Australia in 1918 where he continued to serve as an officer in the Permanent Forces before retiring in August 1941, holding the rank of Lieutenant Colonel.

In modern times, it has been written in many post-operation reports submitted after battles that there was a particular moment that turned the tide of the conflict – it might have been an artillery round that took out an enemy position or a successful charge on foot carried out against an enemy position. A fine example of such a moment was recognised in the awarding of a posthumous Victoria Cross to Private Bruce Kingsbury of the 2nd/14th AIF Battalion for his valour on the Kokoda Trail in Papua New Guinea in August 1942. Private Kingsbury's Victoria Cross was the first to be won on Australian territory and the first awarded in the South-West Pacific area. The Australians of the 2nd/14th Battalion were facing an enemy whose strength was estimated to outweigh them at a ratio of six to one. In late August 1942, the large Japanese forces had broken through the Australians' stretched defence near the village of Isurava along the Kokoda Trail.

On the morning of 28 August, the Japanese began a huge and at times overwhelming attack in which wave upon wave of enemy soldiers assaulted the grossly undermanned Australians of the 2nd/14th. Reinforcements were too far away to provide any assistance and the Australians knew that they had to hold the area at all costs. When the enemy managed to break through the perimeter of the defensive line and directly threatened to overrun battalion headquarters, the Australians began hand-to-hand combat and Private Kingsbury volunteered to join a small party that would attempt to plug a hole in the defensive line.

Just as the enemy were massing to make a final assault on the area around the battalion headquarters, Kingsbury saw his chance. Armed with a bren gun, he charged directly at the Japanese firing his weapon from his hip, mowing down the attackers as he moved towards them. Witnesses to the charge said that he seemed totally fearless, inspiring them to feel equally as fearless. Accounting for at least 30 enemy soldiers himself, Kingsbury and his mates continued on the attack, forcing the enemy to retreat from their position. Just as everything fell quiet, Kingsbury was felled by an enemy sniper with a bullet to the chest. He died from his injuries shortly after.

It was not until some time later that the Australian headquarters came to see that this one defiant and gallant act by Private Kingsbury changed the course of the war in the Pacific. It was believed that if Kingsbury had not stopped the attack on the battalion headquarters that day, the enemy would have won the entire battle because allied reinforcements were simply too far away to provide any assistance. The Japanese would have assumed control of Papua New Guinea and therefore followed on to take control of Australia itself.

The last Victoria Cross awarded to an Australian was awarded in 1969 to Warrant Officer Keith Payne of The Australian Army Training Team–Vietnam (AATTV) a little less than two weeks after another Australian Warrant Officer and colleague had also been awarded the Victoria Cross in Vietnam. On 24 May 1969, Warrant Officer Payne was commanding the 212th Company of the 1st Mobile Strike Force Battalion when the battalion was attacked by a North Vietnamese force of superior strength.

The enemy isolated the two leading companies, one of which was Warrant Officer Payne's, and with heavy mortar, machine gun and rocket support, assaulted their position from three directions simultaneously. Under this heavy attack the Montagnard, indigenous Vietnamese soldiers assisting the Australians, began to fall back, break ranks and flee the area. Directly exposing himself to the enemy's fire, Warrant Officer Payne temporarily held off the assaults by alternately firing his weapon and running from position to position collecting grenades and throwing them at the assaulting enemy. In doing so he was wounded in the hands, arms and hip by rocket and mortar shrapnel that landed nearby. Despite Payne's demonstration of boldness in the face of the enemy, the Battalion Commander, together with several advisors and a few soldiers from the Headquarters element, withdrew.

Paying no attention to his own wounds and under extremely heavy enemy fire, Warrant Officer Payne covered their withdrawal by continuing to throw grenades and fire his own weapon at the enemy who were attempting to advance upon their position. Still under fire, he ran across exposed ground to head off his own troops who were withdrawing chaotically. He was able to stop them and organised the remnants of his and the second company into a temporary defensive perimeter by nightfall.

At significant risk to his own safety, Warrant Officer Payne moved from the perimeter into the darkness unaccompanied in an attempt to find the wounded members of his unit and other indigenous soldiers left behind during the withdrawal. He crawled on his stomach over to one group of displaced soldiers by tracking their glowing footprints in the rotting undergrowth on the ground, beginning a traverse of the area covering almost one kilometre during his search. Even though the enemy were moving around and firing the whole time, with complete disregard for his own life, Payne was able to locate 40 men, some of whom were wounded so severely that Payne was forced to drag them out personally, despite his own wounds. He also organised others who were unwounded to crawl out on their stomachs with wounded comrades on their backs.

Three hours later, Payne returned with his group to the temporary defensive perimeter he had left, only to discover that the remainder of the battalion had moved even further back in his absence. Undeterred by this setback and personally assisting the seriously wounded American advisor, he led the group through the enemy troops to the safety of his battalion base.

Payne's sustained and heroic personal efforts in this action were outstanding and undoubtedly saved the lives of a large number of his soldiers and several of his fellow advisors. Payne was presented with his Victoria Cross aboard the Royal Yacht *Britannia* in April

1970 by Queen Elizabeth II. He was also awarded the Distinguished Service Cross and the Silver Star from the United States, while the Republic of Vietnam awarded him the Cross of Gallantry with the Bronze Star. He retired from the Australian Army in 1975 but saw additional action as a Captain with the Army of the Sultan of Oman in the Dhofar War. His story, like the others before him, is simply astounding.

The Victoria Cross is the highest award that can be given to Australian military personnel, and as the last Victoria Cross awarded to an Australian was in 1969, it is obviously not bestowed lightly. Awarded to individuals who have performed an act of extreme gallantry or daring, or unsurpassed acts of courage, valour and self-sacrifice in the presence of enemy, it is generally accepted that the recipient faces an extremely high likelihood of being killed while carrying out the action.

The Australian War Memorial in Canberra houses the largest publicly held collection of Victoria Crosses in the world. The 59 Victoria Crosses, donated or loaned to the Memorial, are displayed together in the War Memorial's Hall of Valour so that the nation has the privilege of viewing them. You can easily spend hours in the Hall of Valour reading the citations of each of these men and simply admiring their blatant courage. Included in this collection is the first Victoria Cross awarded to an Australian, eight of the nine Crosses awarded for actions at Gallipoli, the first awarded to an Australian in World War II, and three of the four awarded to an Australian in the Vietnam War. It is an awe-inspiring room to immerse yourself in.

Last century saw the introduction of a wide range of lesser awards (in terms of the Victoria Cross) for meritorious service. Under the old Imperial system, officers could be awarded the Distinguished Service Order (DSO) and Military Cross (MC) and non-commissioned officers and other ranks could be awarded the Distinguished Conduct Medal (DCM) and the Military Medal (MM). However, due to the changing face of military service, soldiers, sailors and airmen are no longer in situations where feats of extreme personal bravery are required, and in line with this change, new Australian decorations were developed.

Australian awards for gallantry, bravery and courage

Australia did not have its own system of honours and awards until 1975. Along with other Commonwealth nations, Australia observed the British (Imperial) system to honour citizens for achievement or outstanding service. The way the Australian honours and awards system is set up now allows for both military personnel and private citizens to be acknowledged and rewarded appropriately. On 14 February 1975, the Australian system of honours and awards was instituted by Letters Patent, which comprised the Order of Australia; the Bravery Awards, which included the Cross of Valour, the Star of Courage, the Bravery Medal and the Commendation for Brave Conduct; and the National Medal.

Since then, an additional 27 honours and awards have been instituted, bringing the total number of awards and honours available to the entire Australian community, both military and civilian, up to 33. Within this new system, the awards for acts of bravery, courage and gallantry are divided into two streams: the bravery decorations, and the gallantry decorations.

The bravery decorations can be awarded to both civilian and military personnel where their actions occurred in a non–warlike situation and are available to Australian citizens, or citizens of other nations, with a stipulation that the act served to benefit Australia or her people. These decorations are not recognised by the Imperial system, which means that they are purely Australian awards. The order of precedence in which the bravery decorations are presented is the Cross of Valour, the Star of Courage, the Bravery Medal, the Commendation for Brave Conduct, and the Group Bravery Citation.

The Cross of Valour (CV) is awarded to individuals for acts displaying the most conspicuous courage in circumstances deemed to have put the individual in extreme peril, and the recipient of the Cross is entitled to use the postnominals 'CV' after their name. At the time of writing, this award has only been awarded on five occasions.

The Star of Courage (SC) is awarded to individuals for acts of immense heroism or conspicuous gallantry in action (for military personnel), or in circumstances of great peril (for both civilian and military personnel), and the recipient of the Star is entitled to use the postnominal 'SC' after their name. At the time of writing, it has been awarded 125 times since its inception.

The Bravery Medal (BM) is awarded for acts of bravery in hazardous circumstances, and the recipient is entitled to use the postnominal 'BM' after their name. At the time of writing, it has been awarded 800 times.

The Commendation for Brave Conduct is awarded to an individual for acts of bravery that are considered worthy of recognition; it is the most commonly awarded Bravery decoration. Unlike the previous awards, there are no postnominal entitlements with this award. At the time of writing, it has been awarded 1223 times.

As the name suggests, the **Group Bravery Citation** is awarded for a collective act of bravery by a group of people in extraordinary circumstances that is considered worthy of public recognition. Each member in the group being awarded is issued with a Warrant which describes the collective act. There are no postnominals and there is no ranking in the Order of Precedence of Honours and Awards.

The second stream is the gallantry decorations. This group of decorations was established in January 1991 and they are awarded for acts of gallantry to members of the Australian Defence Force in the presence of the enemy or under fire or in action. Based to some degree on the British system, the Australian gallantry decorations are honours that recognise service personnel for their actions of gallantry; however, unlike the British system, the Australian gallantry awards don't differentiate between the nominee's rank or their branch of service (Australian Army, Royal Australian Navy, or Royal Australian Air Force). Instead, they are awarded according to the degree of gallantry displayed. The order of precedence in which the gallantry decorations are presented is the Star of Gallantry, the Medal for Gallantry, and the Commendation for Gallantry.

The Star of Gallantry (SG), the premier gallantry decoration, is awarded for acts of great heroism or conspicuous gallantry in action in circumstances of great peril and the recipient of the Star is entitled to use the postnominal 'SG' after their name. At the time of writing, it has yet to be awarded.

The Medal for Gallantry (MG) is awarded for acts of gallantry in action in hazardous circumstances and, at the time of writing, has been awarded 24 times since its inception. The recipient of the Medal is entitled to use the postnominal 'MG' after their name.

The Commendation for Gallantry is awarded to individuals for other acts of gallantry which are considered worthy of recognition, and has only been awarded six times at the time of writing. There are no postnominal entitlements for this commendation.

As you will find, 12 of the 13 military heroes whose stories are told in this book have been awarded Australian honours for their inspiring acts of bravery and courage such as the Medal for Gallantry, the Star of Courage or the Bravery Medal. The final story tells of an Australian Army officer's action as a pilot in a British Lynx helicopter over Iraq in 2004, and this officer was awarded the **Distinguished Flying Cross** (DFC), the third-highest decoration in the modern British gallantry awards system. The DFC is awarded for acts of valour, courage or devotion to duty while flying during active operation against the enemy. The last DFC awarded to an Australian was in 1972; and recipients are entitled to use the post-nominals 'DFC' after their name.

Our modern military heroes

Most of us will live our whole lives without the challenge of doing anything outwardly courageous or brave. For sure, day-to-day acts of bravery are everywhere – the hidden bravery of a single mother forced to raise her children on a small wage is never acknowledged by society; the teenager surrounded by violence and despair who is able to lift himself above all that threatens to bring him down rarely rates a second thought when we think of courage. But what about those moments, those precious few moments when someone has the opportunity to save the life of another person, more often than not a stranger? Most people would say that they would do it without hesitation, but, in reality, less than a handful of people actually would.

The people whose stories feature in this book are among that small handful of people who have risked their own life to save the life of another. For whatever reason, the life of that other person became a higher priority than their own. After meeting them and hearing their stories first-hand, I truly believe that these people acted completely unselfishly. They were not thinking of how their action might serve their career better in the future. They were not imagining being a recipient of an award for their actions. They were thinking only about what they could do to save the life of another human being.

Those of us who have never been called upon to perform such things can only hope that, should we find ourselves in a similar predicament, we would act in much the same way. Throughout its brief history, past and present members of the Australian Defence Force have acquired international recognition because of their tireless enthusiasm, professionalism and willingness to get the job done regardless of the circumstances or context. Often, this happens in the face of extremely demanding and sometimes dangerous conditions. At an uncomplicated level, those in this book were simply doing the job that the Australian Defence Force had trained them to do, and they were in the right place at the right time – or indeed the wrong place at the right time. But on a more complex level, they then made the choice to go on. And it is for that reason they are real heroes.

More and more Australians are attending Anzac Day dawn

services and marches throughout the nation. Young Australians are making the pilgrimage to the Turkish Peninsula of Gallipoli in greater numbers each year to stand upon the shores that were once bloodied with our countrymen to pay homage to those Australians who went before them. Treks along the Kokoda Trail are highly sought after by young adventure seekers looking to discover more about the war that came so close to our own land. Australian back-packers are taking a detour during their European adventures to places like Ypres in Belgium, where the Last Post is still played every evening. The growing popularity of Anzac Day is a reassuring gauge of our growing strength as a nation, and this interest in our military heritage sets us apart from so many other nations because it is usually the older members of the community who take an interest in their history, not the young.

Young Australians, though, are using these opportunities to understand the spirit of the Australian soldier, sailor and airman – the Digger of days gone by – and in doing so, are gaining a better understanding of what it means to be Australian. That is why now, more than any other time in our recent history, stories of Australian Defence Force personnel who have performed feats of extraordi-nary courage, bravery and gallantry need to be told. Perhaps this book is just a stepping stone for Australians to embrace their own true heroes and continue to educate the younger members of our nation on the nature of true heroism. Perhaps Australians will recognise that while it is important for a nation to celebrate its past heroes, it is equally as important to celebrate the true heroes who live among us.

HELICOPTER CRASH

THE MILITARY BATTLEFIELD, BOTH ON THE GROUND AND IN the air, is an inherently dangerous place. Even on exercise, where realism is stretched to test those on the ground, in the air and at sea, 'pretend' warfare can be a dangerous thing. While all efforts are made to protect the lives of the men and women who wear a military uniform, nothing is infallible and, unfortunately, accidents happen. Often it is the unexpected that has the most significant impact upon the lives of Defence Force personnel. The Vietnam War introduced the helicopter as a swift and efficient means of moving soldiers around on operation and since then, man and machine have been pushed to the limit and the battlefield has become a more dangerous and complex place. Yet even a routine flight in a military helicopter can end suddenly in tragedy, just as the following story reveals.

In 1981, Captain Wayne Bowen was a passenger on board an Iroquois helicopter on a routine flight as part of a training demonstration. A few minutes into the flight, the helicopter clipped the tree tops and flipped over in mid-air, landing on its roof and becoming quickly engulfed in flames. Captain Bowen, along with the two pilots, was the first recipient of the newly established Bravery decorations. This is his story.

'HARD IS RELATIVE'

Captain Wayne Thomas Bowen SC AM

CITATION
STAR OF COURAGE

On 30 October 1981 Captain Bowen, then holding the rank of Lieutenant, was one of six passengers aboard a helicopter which crashed in thickly timbered country in Shoalwater Bay Training Area during Exercise Kangaroo 81. Captain Bowen, although dazed by the impact, immediately went to the assistance of a crewman who was trapped in the wreckage of the cabin of the aircraft and whose clothing was on fire. With the assistance of a crew member the fire on the man's clothing was partly extinguished and he was brought to safety notwithstanding the fierce fire then burning in the aircraft. Captain Bowen then proceeded to another part of the aircraft and attempted to free another passenger until smoke, flames and heat drove him clear. After obtaining a fire extinguisher he then attempted to put out the fire in the aircraft but was unsuccessful. During all his endeavours Captain Bowen accepted the substantial risk of the aircraft exploding. By his actions Captain Bowen displayed conspicuous courage and placed himself in great peril in effecting a rescue in such circumstances.

I GREW UP, ONE OF FOUR CHILDREN, ON A PROPERTY IN ROMA, Queensland in the 1950s and 1960s. The way you are shaped in your early years has a huge part to play in what you do throughout the rest of your life. As farmers, my parents were battlers and they brought up their children to be fairly tough and resilient and to bounce back quickly from any setbacks. You didn't get much sympathy for a bruise or a cut because you were out on the farm and you needed to just get on with things. Having said that, my parents were extremely loving towards us.

My grandfather was a huge influence in my formative years. It was his suggestion that I try for the Royal Military College (RMC), Duntroon. My grandfather was a member of the 2nd/12th Field Company Engineers. Taken prisoner after the fall of Singapore on 15 February 1942 he was interned in Changi before being sent on to Tovoy to build an aerodrome for the Japanese. He was a member of the first party to start work on the Burma railway and among the last to leave. He suffered spinal injuries when he was bashed by guards for having refused to bury an Australian soldier who was almost dead from cholera.

After the war he was a totally and permanently incapacitated pensioner and cattle farmer. Working beside him as a boy and a young man was an inspiration. I remember him saying to me after I had complained how hard and tough the job was, 'Your problem is that you have nothing to compare this with. Hard is relative. Just stick around this world for a while. You'll see worse.' After a brief pause, he added, 'And you'll see better.' 'Hard is relative' has stuck with me ever since.

In 1975, I joined RMC. I left home at 18 and have been in the Army ever since. Once I got to RMC, I realised it was everything I expected it to be. I loved my training and the five years I spent there was yet another experience that shaped me into who I was to ecome in my later life.

We had exceptional instructors at RMC, the majority of whom were seasoned, battle experienced officers and Senior Non-Commissioned Officers (SNCOs). Many of them were highly decorated with Military Crosses and Military Medals and other decorations for their military prowess on the battlefield. They always insisted that if you were going to be a leader, you had to look at it as not just a job or a position but rather as an attitude and an act. You had to lead from the front, you had to be decisive, and you had to be firm, fair, and friendly.

The instructors set a high standard and for that, I think they were great leaders. They demanded of you a knowledge of how to operate by means of brief, concise oral orders, based on the ground you can see, or on maps with little detail. They insisted on a high degree of battle cunning, constant tactical readiness, speed of thought, speed of decision and speed of action. This was drilled into me and I was very thankful for it once I was in command of my own men. They often related the training back to their own experiences so that we understood what they meant – it was put into a real context. They had been hardened in Korea, Borneo, Malaya or Vietnam, so they were great role models to all of us cadets. I'm pretty sure that's why they were posted to RMC. It was a very positive experience to be trained by these exceptional soldiers and officers.

As far as I was concerned, I was suited to Infantry and I couldn't think of anything better than leading men and being a member of the Infantry clan. I asked to be allocated to that corps and when I got it, I was delighted. I graduated from RMC in 1979 and went straight to the 2nd/4th Battalion, Royal Australian Regiment (2/4 RAR), in Townsville. To be posted there as a platoon commander was a great privilege.

The battalion was in the early stages of forming the Operational Deployment Force (ODF) when I arrived. It was a key time in Townsville where we were creating these two big battalions, the First Battalion, Royal Australian Regiment (1RAR) and 2/4 RAR, of the 3rd Brigade. We had our full complement of man power, with four full rifle companies in each battalion. I arrived there as a young platoon commander in charge of 33 soldiers. We were training very hard and we did a lot of field time to consolidate everything.

I had a really good time in the battalion. I was nurtured by a couple of really good Warrant Officers and Sergeants who kept an eye on all of us young Lieutenants and steered us through those first few years. I found that if we were prepared to listen to them, they would take the time to really mould us into good junior officers. One in particular who I thought was fabulous in shaping me was Bernie LeSeur, the Regimental Sergeant Major (RSM). He was the most senior soldier in the battalion and had been awarded a Military Medal for his actions as a corporal in Vietnam. He would often coach young officers, nurturing them and talking to them about what it takes to train and lead soldiers effectively.

Throughout my four years in Townsville, I'm pretty sure we spent more time in the bush than Tarzan ever did, but the Kangaroo exercise in October 1981 was the biggest exercise I had been on up to that point. The company second-in-command was going to be away for the length of the exercise so I was put up into his position even though I still wore the rank of a Lieutenant. For the purpose of the exercise, we were the enemy force for another battalion and we carried out a series of delaying operations, ambushing, and defence positions.

Towards the end of the exercise, it had been decided that we would put on a bit of an aircraft deployment display for visiting VIPs to show them the ODF at its finest. We would come into a landing zone on Iroquois helicopters, which back then were still owned and operated by the RAAF, and put on a fire and movement demonstration on the ground. We had done a few rehearsals of lifting and marshalling and coming in on wave after wave of helicopters, bounding out of them and rallying to show the VIPs what we were all about. It was going to be great.

On the day of the accident, I was sitting inside the helicopter towards the front on one side. I had headphones on so I was able to hear the pilots talking. We took off towards the landing zone and it was all normal flying. We were being buffeted by the winds as we were coming over the ranges, but that's normal. As we approached the landing zone, without any warning we had a tail rotor malfunction. The best way to describe what happened next is to say we heard a sound like a piece of metal snapping and the helicopter instantly began to auto-rotate, which means the helicopter began spinning violently under its main rotor. As soon as the pilots felt the tail rotor snap, they went into their drills and began calling in their mayday distress calls. As soon as I heard the pilots calling out 'Mayday, mayday, mayday, we're going down!', I knew then that we were going to crash.

I was hanging on with all my strength because we were in a crazy spin and the doors were open on both sides of the helicopter, and I was sitting on the seat nearest the outside. The pilots were fighting hard and with great skill to get some sort of control over the landing. Normally, if this occurred in an area where there are no trees, the aircraft would come down upright and under control, albeit with an almighty thud. Unfortunately for us though, we were in an extremely heavily wooded area of the Shoalwater Bay training area, north of Rockhampton. On our way down, the rotor blades and the skids hit tall trees, which caused the helicopter to flip, landing on its roof. The landing ruptured the fuel lines and within seconds, the helicopter was on fire.

I was quite dazed when we first landed because we hit so hard. We were upside down and I was dangling down, held in by my seat belt. The cabin of the aircraft was quite compressed. I released my seat belt and crashed down on to the roof. Despite the situation, I still grabbed my rifle and my pack before I rolled out. I was the first one out of the wreck. After dumping my gear, I crawled back into the wreckage and began yelling at the others who were on board to get out quickly because I could see that the fire was taking hold. At that time, I also noticed that two of the helicopter crew who had been sitting at the back of the chopper were already on fire.

The two pilots were having a bit of trouble getting out because they were tangled among harnesses and broken instruments. I noticed that the two Forward Observer Assistants, both of whom were big men, were in a tangle with all their equipment. For a while, they just seemed to hang there dangling from their seat belts, probably in shock. When I yelled at them, 'Fire!' and 'Go!', it seemed to rouse them and they exploded into action, untangling themselves from their equipment and each other, and they got out.

I grabbed a fire extinguisher and moved towards one of the helicopter crewmen who was burning quite badly. Unfortunately for him, a fuel line had ruptured on him and he was well and truly alight, but he was also stuck under a lot of the mangled fuselage. With the assistance of one of the pilots, I was able to pull him out eventually and put the fire out on him as best I could.

My mate, Craig Stevens, who had been the Artillery Forward Observer for the Company, was on the other side and I hadn't seen him since we crashed. I went around to the other side of the wreckage and could immediately see that he was in a bad way. When we landed, his rifle barrel had gone up through his face and taken out most of his lip and cheek. He was bleeding badly. We learned later that he also had broken his back.

When I got to him, he was partially hanging out so I released him from his seatbelt and he crashed to the ground, screaming. Then I grabbed him and dragged him free. He screamed every time I touched him so I knew he was seriously hurt but I had to get him away from the cabin because it was now well and truly on fire. I managed to drag him well away from the crash site – I can't think what distance it would have been – but I felt that if the helicopter exploded he was far enough away to avoid being hit by the debris. He was in such pain that I don't think he was fully conscious. Obviously I didn't know at the time that he had a broken back, but I knew he was in agony. I remember propping him up against a tree and I went back again to see if I could get one of the other guys, Private Paul Rooke, who was still in the crushed cabin.

I crawled in again and checked him. The cabin was full of smoke and the heat was very intense. Paul was badly tangled in the wreckage and I simply couldn't get him out. I ran around to the other side and by this stage, the two pilots had managed to get themselves out and were trying to free the other crewman who was trapped and on fire. A helicopter hovering overhead had dropped us another fire extinguisher at this stage so I used that to try to get Paul out but the heat and smoke drove me back. Private Rooke had only just arrived in the battalion not long before the exercise. He was only a young soldier and this was his first posting. He was learning to be a signaller and was with us on the company headquarters. He was such a young man and his death was a real tragedy.

I had to move Craig Stevens again as it wasn't just the helicopter that was burning madly – the dry Shoalwater Bay grassland was also now on fire. It seemed that no sooner had we got the guys into a safe place away from the fuselage, the grass fire caught up to them and we had to move them away again.

The two RAAF crewmen received some very serious burns and broken bones, but they survived the crash. My mate Craig Stevens had quite serious injuries as well. The two pilots escaped with bad bruising and one had a broken collar bone. I got away pretty much okay. I found out later that I had a couple of cracked ribs and I had torn some of the cartilage from my ribs and torn my stomach muscles, but at the time of the accident, I didn't think I was hurt at all. The adrenaline pumped in and I felt no pain at all.

In the minutes after the accident, there were far too many things happening for the reality of what had just happened to sink in. There was so much to do that I don't think I allowed myself any time to reflect on what I was doing. My adrenaline button had been pushed and I was moving fast. I was told later on that I had torn off bits of the aircraft fuselage with my bare hands trying to get to people inside. They said that there was no way I could have done it without the huge surge of adrenaline that comes in events like this. Mind you, I was at the peak of my physical fitness at that time, so that probably contributed to that kind of action as well. Essentially, though, I was in charge. These blokes on board, the Army soldiers, were my men so I was responsible for them. When the accident happened and I came through it unscathed, it became my job to get everyone else out and into a safe place.

It started to get really confusing once others arrived on the scene. It didn't take long after the crash for another helicopter to arrive and help out with the injured blokes. It did seem like an eternity at the time. When the bulk of help arrived, I was sitting with my men and that was pretty much when I knew my job as a rescuer was done and I let the newcomers take over. I think I sat for a minute, took a deep breath and then I got on a radio to report back to my headquarters what had happened. In training you are taught that you have to be able to remove yourself emotionally from events and simply report the facts. You can't worry about what has happened. Because Private Rooke was from my headquarters, I felt responsible for him so I knew I was the one who had to report his death back to my headquarters and let them do what they had to do. Fortunately, everyone else was accounted for.

It wasn't until I was put on another Iroquois to fly me to the field hospital that it sunk in what I had just been through. The more seriously wounded had already been evacuated by other means by then. Being put on another helicopter immediately after crashing in one was a pretty hairy experience initially. When it first took off, it seemed to give a sudden bump as the pilot was really racing it to get me out of there. I grabbed on with both hands and held tightly, and thought, 'Oh God, here we go again!'

I wasn't too well by the time I got to the hospital. I suppose the shock had set in and I was now feeling pain from my ribs. I didn't know at that point that I had hurt myself but I walked in and sat down in the hospital and thought, 'I don't feel so good.' Up until then I had been focused on looking out for other people or doing something. Once I had the time to just sit, I guess it all sunk in.

I was in hospital for around five days. I wasn't seriously hurt to warrant such a long admission but I suppose they kept me in for that time for observation. I had drips in my arms and a most unpleasant catheter inserted into a place I would rather not think about! I felt okay and I was more worried about others who hadn't come out as well as me. I had visits from the accident investigation team while I was in the hospital, and of course the battalion did a great job of coming over to see that I was being looked after, which of course I was.

My fiancée, who is now my wife, was informed of my accident through the normal channels. She was frantic when she heard the news, so she arranged for her girlfriend from Rockhampton to drive in to Shoalwater Bay to check on me. I never figured out how she managed to get in because it's a big military training area and civilians can't just come driving in, in the middle of training exercises. She must have done some great talking to get in but she managed to drive all the way to the training area in her little sports car; then she found the field hospital and simply walked in to visit me! Maryann, my fiancée, had told her to see that I was really okay and then to call her back and let her know everything! Happily, Maryann and I were married in December of that year.

In those days, we didn't have stress or trauma counselling. This was just after the Vietnam War era where there was a strong sense of 'You are fine. You are alive. Just get on with it'. That was my attitude as well and I didn't have any real problems. I am delighted to say that the trauma counselling, incident response and compensation process is much better today. It needed to be! After those five days in the field hospital, I was transferred to 4 Camp Hospital in Townsville, and that was only to check me before they discharged me back to work. I went back to my room, got my uniform ready and was back at work the very next day. That was the way the Army was then, but I had been bred to be tough and resilient, so that suited me fine.

On 5 November 1982, I was awarded a Chief of Army Commendation from General Sir Phillip Bennett. While the Commander of 1 Division, General David Drabsch, presented me with the Commendation, he indicated that I should expect something additional. In 1983, I was a newly promoted Captain when I received a letter to say that I had been awarded the Star of Courage and that took me by complete surprise. In March 1983

I found myself at an investiture at Government House in Canberra being awarded the Star of Courage. It was a wonderful day. My wife and parents were there for the ceremony and we were treated very, very well. The investiture was one of those really special occasions, and meeting the Governor-General, Sir Ninian Stephen, was a nice moment too.

I was the first person in the Army to have been awarded this medal, so that was quite humbling. As you can imagine, there was quite a fuss made about that at the time. I am a fairly unassuming person anyway, and I didn't much go for the ruckus being made. As I have said, at RMC I was surrounded by men with Military Crosses and Military Medals for their actions in battle. When I received my medal, I remember thinking that it wasn't the same. It wasn't like I was awarded it for doing something in battle. I had just done what anyone else would do in that situation.

Once it became known that I was being awarded the Star of Courage, I began to receive a lot of correspondence from all kinds of people, from my peers from my time in 2/4 RAR right up to the Chief of Army and the Prime Minister of Australia. They all said how great it was that I was being awarded the decoration and how much it meant to them. I guess that was when I became the most proud of being awarded it. It was clear that it was seen as being good for the Army to be producing young leaders who were able to do such things.

After that I just got on with my life and my career. I didn't really dwell on the accident, although the death of Private Rooke was deeply saddening. There have been times when I am reminded of the crash. On the 21st anniversary of the crash, I was the Task Force Commander of Sector West in East Timor. I was over there for nine months and as part of my job, I spent a lot of time in helicopters, and there were still occasions when I felt really uncomfortable. I love flying though, so it really didn't bother me too much. I was in a helicopter between three and five days every week, so there were a lot of those uncomfortable occasions!

On 30 October 2002 – the exact day of the crash but 21 years later – I had to go on a flight in an Iroquois with a New Zealand crew. Flying in East Timor is really tricky at the best of times. It has really high mountain ranges, tricky weather and we had underpowered helicopters. The Kiwis picked me up and while the helicopter had been playing up a bit, the pilots were quite happy to fly. We had just finished visiting a New Zealand company and the pilot struggled to take off. He tried to take off a second time but he still wasn't happy so he thumped it back down. I was starting to get a tad uncomfortable. I was thinking, 'Do I tell him what today is?' Eventually we got up and made it to where we were going safely, which was a bit of a relief!

Just as we were coming in to land on our way home, I said to them through the intercom, 'Hey guys, I just wanted to let you know that today is my anniversary.' They asked, 'Your wedding anniversary?' and I said, 'No, it is the 21st anniversary of when I went down in an Iroquois, flown by a Kiwi pilot!' They went quiet and looked at each other and didn't say a word. Pilots are quite superstitious people actually! Eventually one of them said to me, 'If we had have known that, we wouldn't have taken you up today.' We had a bit of a laugh.

I don't think being involved in that accident or being awarded the Star of Courage has changed me in any negative way. I think it gave me a lot of self-confidence that I had been tested and came through. I figured that since I got through that horrible event, there wouldn't be too much else that could faze me. For a young commander, having such self-confidence was really important. I didn't need to question my abilities as a leader. I knew that from then on through my career, I could face up to the tests that would be thrown my way as a leader. My grandfather's advice would flash back: Hard is relative. You'll see worse. Maintain a sense of perspective.

The whole concept of bravery is really interesting. Personally, I believe most people do things on instinct. I know that in my case, I reacted on instinct based on excellent training without any thought of the consequences. I knew that the helicopter was burning and I expected that it was going to explode at some point not long after impact because there was so much fuel leaking out and the fire was throughout the fuselage in minutes. Fire has a real effect on some people. Some people see fire and they can't react or they panic. I wasn't put off by the fire or that the chopper might explode. I was a leader and it was my job to do what I had to do. I guess what really went through my mind was something along the lines of: 'You're okay, they're not; get out and do something.' It was a split second reaction and I know that a lot of people would have done exactly the same if they were in placed in similar circumstances. For me a lot of this goes back to what the instructors at the RMC had drilled into me.

You hear stories of incredible Australians who, in the face of extreme adversity or danger, can do incredible things. But as for me, I was influenced, shaped, and nurtured by some tremendously talented people and I was in the right place at the right time. I don't think I am braver than anyone else. I was just lucky. We have a plethora of incredibly brave and courageous people in the Australian Defence Force, some of whom have been recognised, and I am humbled to be among them.

With over 30 years' service, Wayne Bowen, now a Brigadier, has continued to serve in the Army with numerous command, staff and regimental postings in Australia and overseas in countries like Germany, Canada, Malaya and East Timor. Brigadier Bowen was appointed a Member of the Order of Australia in 1999 and he received a Force Commander's Commendation for his performance as Commander Sector West in East Timor in 2003. His current appointment is as the Commandant, Australian Command and Staff College in Canberra, where he lives with his wife, Maryann, and two children, Nicole and Harry.

THE KIBEHO MASSACRE, RWANDA

THE TINY REPUBLIC OF RWANDA, LOCATED IN THE EASTERN centre of Africa, was plunged deep into a civil war in 1992 before protracted negotiations between the two warring factions – the Government forces and the 'rebel forces' – led to the involvement of the United Nations. In April 1995, an escalation of hostilities resulted in the event that is now known as the Kibeho massacre, in which over 2000 Hutus were killed. Four Australian Army officers were decorated for their actions at Kibeho, three of whose stories are included in this section.

Three ethnic groups make up the population of Rwanda: the Hutu, the Tutsi and the Twa. In 1959, violence erupted throughout Rwanda, continuing until 1961 when a Republic was established. The country was granted independence from Belgium in 1962, with Gregoire Kayibanda, a Hutu, named as Rwanda's new President. A rebel army of exiled Tutsis formed, returning to Rwanda in an attempt to overthrow the government in 1963. This takeover failed terribly, leading to a large-scale massacre of Tutsi people all over the country.

In 1973, the defence minister, General Juvenal Habyarimana – also a Hutu – led a bloodless coup that ousted Kayibanda. The self-appointed President Habyarimana was established in office without opposition until 1990. In 1990, a heavily armed force of 10,000 Ugandan-based exiled Tutsi who formed the Rwandan Patriotic Front (RPF) invaded Rwanda in yet another attempt to topple the Habyarimana government. At the request of the government,

Belgian, French and Zairean troops assisted the Rwandan Government Forces (RGF) to repel the RPF.

In mid-1993, President Habyarimana and Colonel Alex Kanyarengwe of the RPF signed a peace accord. This accord included a timetable for democratic elections to be held in 1995. Both sides called upon the United Nations to provide a peacekeeping force to monitor the cease-fire and in October 1993 the United Nations Assistance Mission in Rwanda (UNAMIR) was formed.

In this volatile climate, President Habyarimana and the president of neighbouring country Burundi were killed in a plane crash at Kigali airport in somewhat suspicious circumstances, leading to yet another widespread massacre of Tutsi and any perceived enemies of the Hutu, beginning with the murder of the Prime Minister and her family as well as 10 Belgian members of UNAMIR by members of the Hutu Presidential Guard. Within months, at least half a million Tutsi were killed, and hundreds of thousands of others fled to neighbouring Tanzania and Burundi.

After the murder of the Belgian soldiers, the size of the UN mission was scaled down significantly. However, with the escalating violence and humanitarian crisis of hundreds of thousands of displaced people fleeing the violence throughout Rwanda, the UN authorised the formation of UNAMIR II in 1994. In June 1994, the UN approached Australia with a request to send Australian troops. Initially, the Australian government baulked at the request but as international outrage over the genocide in Rwanda gathered pace Australian troops were included as part of the UNAMIR II contingent of 5,500 personnel, recruited mainly from African nations, such as Zambia.

The Australian contingent consisted of 330 personnel from the three branches of the Australian Defence Force and its primary mission was to provide medical support to UNAMIR II. It also had a smaller role to assist in the provision of the humanitarian relief effort. The advance party arrived in Kigali on 7 August 1994 while the main body of the Australian contingent arrived over several days from 21 August 1994. In February 1995, the second rotation of the Australian contingent began arriving to take over from the first contingent. By the end of August 1995, all Australian personnel were withdrawn from Rwanda.

As members of the Australian Treatment Section Group (AS TSG), all four Australian soldiers who were awarded the Medal for Gallantry were deployed to work in the internally displaced persons (IDP) camp in Kibeho, approximately 100 kilometres south-west of Kigali. The AS TSG consisted of medical, nursing, dental, preventative medicine, infantry, transport, SASR patrol medics and intelligence personnel. The AS TSG was accommodated at the university medical students' accommodation block beside the University Hospital in close-by Butare. The group was broken up into 'packets', smaller groups who would travel out to the various humanitarian aid sites each day. Each packet would usually contain a medical and nursing officer, a handful of medical assistants, an evacuation crew and up to a section of infantry riflemen for protection. Preventative medicine and dental personnel would go with one packet each day. A resuscitation team would always stay on stand-by at Butare, 15 minutes' drive away. The AS TSG conducted daily visits to the IDP camp in Kibeho, which housed approximately 150,000 displaced people at the time of the massacre.

The infantry riflemen who travelled with each packet were to provide much-needed security for the personnel, equipment and facilities of the Australian contingent. Security at a deployed medical clinic was essential because the desperate internally displaced persons (IDP) would rush at the support teams as soon as they arrived. This meant that the infantry had to enforce strict crowd control measures, such as the setting up of barbed wire fences, to ensure the safety of the medical personnel trying to do their job.

For several months leading up to the Kibeho massacre, the Rwandan Government and the newly renamed Rwandan Patriotic Army (RPA, formerly known as RPF) were becoming increasingly frustrated with the lengthy process of repatriation of the IDP and refugees. The Rwandan government wanted the camps closed and the people within them moved on. People within the camps, with Kibeho being the prime example, were said to be using the camps as shelters for members of the forces of the former Rwandan government and as bases from which raids were being mounted against the RPA.

Paranoia and aggression towards the IDP within the Kibeho camp became the adopted approach by the RPA and in April 1995 these tensions escalated devastatingly. The RPA became increasingly ferocious in their attempts to close the IDP camp, beating anyone in the frightened crowd who resisted the clearance procedures. RPA at the checkpoints searched the IDP for evidence of identity that indicated their involvement in previous atrocities against the Tutsi under the Hutu rule and anyone thought to have been involved was taken away from the camp and presumably killed. The IDP tried to stay close to the wire near where the AS TSG had their casualty clearing station, fearful of the retribution of the RPA.

As early as 18 April tensions in the Kibeho camp were high. Inhabitants were cordoned off by the RPA and eight people were known to be killed and many more injured. On 19 April, the AS TSG set up a casualty clearing post (CCP) to treat the injured inhabitants. The following day, widespread random executions began when some from the crowd of displaced people began throwing stones at the RPA. They retaliated with rifle and machine-gun fire into the massing and panicking crowds. Women, children and men were gunned down or hacked to death by machetes throughout the camp. The UN and non-government organisation observers could only watch on in horror, powerless to stop the RPA. However, this was only a prelude to what they were to observe two days later.

The Kibeho Massacre

On 22 April 1995, a small Australian team of medical and infantry personnel, along with a larger force of Zambian peacekeepers, were witness to the massacre of over 2000 people by the RPA. This figure is believed by many to be grossly underestimated as the AS TSG and other UN observers were not permitted to stay in the camp once evening fell, so the RPA were able to lighten the count by removing bodies overnight.

Many in the crowd had been without food and water for almost five days and were becoming agitated and restless. Throughout the morning sporadic gunfire sounded across the camp. As midday approached, the mood of the camp became increasingly uncomfortable and tense. As a tropical storm doused all with thick drops of rain, the RPA began firing into the terrified mass. Those who tried to flee the RPA's bullets were attacked by machete-wielding hardliners from within their own camp. Either way, the inhabitants of the Kibeho camp suffered greatly. For close to one hour, people within the camp were indiscriminately shot or attacked with machetes, as well as fired upon by mortars and rocket-propelled grenades. Soon the red dirt was littered with coloured clothing and the blood of the dead and dying.

Fully conscious that they were restricted by the UN Mandate and the Rules of Engagement, the Australian infantry soldiers and the medical team could only look on in horror at what was unfolding in front of them. Using every ounce of self-discipline, the Australians did not fire upon the RPA, even when they deliberately tried to pressure the Australians and other UN soldiers to react by executing women and elderly people directly in front of them. Under fire and often under personal threat from the RPA, the Australians managed to set up a casualty evacuation station and conduct triage and treatment for wounded Hutus.

There were many mothers killed with their babies still strapped to their backs. The Australian infantrymen and SASR troopers freed dozens of such babies throughout the day. Everywhere they stepped they feared standing on children who had been crushed or shot as they struggled for life under the piles of debris and rubbish. By the end of the following day, the Australians and Zambians had a confirmed count of over 4000 bodies.

Very few people will ever know the true magnitude of the atrocity that occurred in the Kibeho camp. Four of those who were present to witness it were awarded the Medal for Gallantry for their actions, and three of those people's stories are included here. These decorations were the first gallantry awards to be awarded since the Vietnam War and the first to be awarded since the inception of the gallantry decorations. One of those to be awarded the Medal for Gallantry was Major Carol Vaughan-Evans, a doctor in the Royal Australian Army Medical Corps. She is the only Australian woman to be awarded a gallantry decoration. Lieutenant Steve Tilbrook was the platoon commander of the infantry group providing security on the day of the massacre. His cool head under highly charged circumstances saw him receive the Medal for Gallantry. Corporal Andrew Miller was a section 2IC (second in command) in Lieutenant Tilbrook's platoon. His courage and calm manner led to him also being awarded the Medal for Gallantry. Andrew is unique in that he was the first of the gallantry award winners and is therefore the first Australian to be awarded a gallantry decoration since the Vietnam War.

'Heroes in baby blue helmets'

Corporal Andrew Colin Miller MG

CITATION
MEDAL FOR GALLANTRY

Corporal Andrew Colin Miller is cited for the Medal for Gallantry for his exceptional courage and leadership in hazardous circumstances during the extraction of wounded throughout the massacre of civilian refugees at the Kibeho Displaced Persons Camp in April 1995. Corporal Miller was a section second-in-command [2IC] who was tasked with the protection of Australian Medical Support Force members as they sought to extract, treat and evacuate the wounded displaced persons from the Kibeho Camp. Throughout the period of the massacre, the Australian Medical Support Force and the Infantry Protection Unit were placed under intense pressure and immediate physical danger. Corporal Miller displayed exceptional judgement, gallantry and leadership as he performed his duties throughout the action. Corporal Miller organised stretcher parties into the Kibeho Camp to extract wounded displaced persons for treatment. During these tasks Corporal Miller displayed sound judgement and courageously led Australian stretcher teams, with their wounded, to positions of safety through direct small arms fire from snipers.

The leadership and gallantry displayed by Corporal Miller ensured the safe conduct of the extraction of wounded displaced persons while avoiding loss of life or injury to his fellow soldiers. Corporal Miller's personal courage and the disregard for his personal safety whilst in action ensured that many civilian lives were saved where they may other-wise have been left to die. Corporal Miller's extraordinary courage, judgement and leadership ensured that Australian Medical Support Force members could successfully save the lives of many wounded displaced persons throughout the period of the massacre. His courage, commitment and dedication to duty were in the finest traditions of the Royal Australian Infantry Corps.

I WAS BORN IN SEPTEMBER 1969, THE YOUNGEST OF FOUR BOYS. My parents moved to Australia from the United Kingdom in the 1970s. My father served in the Royal Navy in the United Kingdom and both my grandfathers served in the British Army as well, and as I was the only one of my brothers to join the Army, I suppose I picked up the military gene in the family. Joining the Army was something that I always wanted to do, even when I was a little kid.

When we arrived in Australia, we settled in Kwinana in Western Australia. While I was at school, I joined the school's Army cadets and developed a really strong interest in all things Army. Around that time I knew that when I left school, I would join up. I applied when I was 17, but Recruiting told me to go away and work for a year and that if I was still serious about joining after that, I should come back. I got a job working in a supermarket, which wasn't really all that appealing, so as soon as I turned 18 I went back to Recruiting and said I still wanted to enlist. I was very serious about joining; there was no doubt about that. While my friends would be going down to the pool or to the beach on the weekend, I would put my pack on and go hiking up in the hills. I wanted to go to the Infantry Corps because I figured that if you were going to join the Army, then you join to do what infantry soldiers do.

I enlisted on 3 May 1988 and went through my basic training at Kapooka in New South Wales and then on to infantry training at the School of Infantry in Singleton. After completing both of those courses, I marched into the 2nd/4th Battalion, Royal Australian Regiment (2/4 RAR), in Townsville in January 1989. I was posted to Charlie Company as a private soldier.

In my time in Townsville, I met my wife Kelly and we got married. Just prior to going on one of the specialty courses that are available in Infantry, our first son, Jeremy, was born, and then our second, Travis, was born the following year. I went to the Mortar Platoon in 1991 and spent just over two years there before I went to Bravo Company. I was probably one of the most senior privates in the unit at the time because I had over five years in the unit as a Digger.

After a couple of overseas trips, I was part of the rotation of soldiers who went up to Tully in North Queensland to be the enemy section for the Battle Training School. That was really interesting because over the years I had always been on the 'other' side, trying to 'kill' the enemy. Now I was getting the chance to play the enemy and be the 'hunted' instead of the 'hunter'. It was great fun. While we were in Tully, we were warned that we would probably be going on the second rotation to Rwanda to take over from Alpha Company which was currently there. We saw it as an opportunity for getting paid to do for real what we are trained to do. Later that same year, I did my course for promotion to Corporal. At the end of that year the whole company went on leave, knowing that when we came back we would be heading over to Rwanda.

As soon as we came back to work after Christmas, we started our pre-deployment training in Townsville. Six weeks before I left for Rwanda, my third child – a daughter, Rhiannon – was born. It was pretty tough having to leave her; it certainly made the trip difficult knowing that I was leaving her as a tiny baby. I knew that when I came back she would be nearly eight months old and I would have missed so much. That took away any excitement that I had about going on operation.

I believe that being on the second rotation put our company at an advantage. A couple of my friends were in the first push with Alpha Company and I had a few letters from them while they were over there. They outlined the things they were doing and told us not to expect to do any 'war-ry' stuff like patrolling or fighting or the kinds of things that Infantry soldiers do. They said that all we would be doing was security work like guarding check-points and people.

When we did our pre-deployment brief, they talked about things like the threat of mines and the genocide that started the whole problem in the country. Because we were going there under the auspices of the United Nations as peacekeepers, we also covered the Laws of Armed Conflict and other issues with the legal officer. We had an American talk to us about the situation regarding mines in Rwanda and he told us that if we saw anything that he didn't cover in his presentation to let him know. That was a bit of a worry! I think we were well prepared, and certainly better prepared than the first rotation were, but on the other hand there are some things that you can't prepare for. For example, when the Kibeho massacre occurred, there was nothing we could have been taught or told that would have prepared us for that experience. Nothing.

Our arrival in Rwanda was amazing. We touched down at the Kigali airport at around seven at night, so it was already dark by this time, but we could still feel the immense heat. Getting off the plane was quite a weird experience because the airport was surrounded by extremely bright lights. What struck me was that although it was trying hard to run like a normal airport, it was anything but. The building itself was riddled with bullet holes, part of the roof had been blown off, and there was broken glass everywhere. It was so confronting.

There weren't enough seats on the vehicles they had brought to take us to the compound, so they left a section of us behind, standing alone in the airport car park. We were thinking, 'This is just great! Welcome to the country, fellas!' Not long after that, the power went off in the airport, so we were a little alarmed to say the least by this stage. I think it was a little awe-inspiring to realise that we were not the most popular people around and here we were, unarmed, standing in the car park. That didn't do much for morale for any of us! Eventually the vehicles came back to take us to the compound to join everyone else. I remember driving through the dark streets on the way to the compound looking really hard into the houses and surrounds, just trying to get a greater sense of the environment. I know I felt excited, and more than a little curious.

The next day, my section picked up their first guard duty. Later that day, we were tasked with driving some of the local people, who were employed in our compound as cooks, to their homes. That gave us a chance to have a better look around the local area. In the beginning, Rwanda looked like a war-torn country, but it wasn't long before we became so used to it that it didn't seem that bad anymore. It began to seem normal.

During our deployment to Rwanda, the three platoons from Bravo Company took turns to cover three different weekly rotations. One week would see the platoon take on the security guard-tasking for the front gate of the compound. The next week we would rotate to undertake the area security task, which involved roving picquets [security detail] during the night and providing security escorts for anyone going outside the compound. For example, if the 'blowflies' (environmental health personnel) wanted to go out to fog an orphanage for mosquitoes, we would send a section of infantrymen with them as security. Some days we could all be tasked, and other days none of us went anywhere.

The third week was at the hospital where we would do front and rear gate security as well as assisting in the resuscitation bay as casualties came in. When we were on the hospital rotation, we would allocate soldiers from the section to work on stand-by as stretcher-bearers as well as provide an additional man to do the job of pack storeman. The pack storeman was not a really popular job among our guys – the job involved assisting in the resuscitation bay like lifting the casualty, cutting their clothes off, tagging all their clothing and putting them in a bag, and putting a tag on the casualty. It seemed that every time I did the job, something horrendous came in, so I loathed having to work in the role.

There were only a couple of us in the section who could do the pack storeman job. Some of the others couldn't stomach it. To be honest, I don't know if being a pack storeman became harder or easier after seeing the massacre at Kibeho. I really hated it when children came through. I think it was because I had my own children at home. I tried to remain focused on the job at hand, regardless of the casualty's wounds. As a section 2IC, you have to be able to do this so perhaps it came naturally.

If you were on guard duty, it was always interesting but rarely exciting. Little Rwandan kids would hang around outside the front gate of the compound and ask us for cigarettes, and biscuits, things like that. I reckon they did it because they knew it was annoying and they got some kind of pleasure out of pissing us off! There was one young kid we dubbed George 'Melon-head'. George was a very intelligent young man. He was quite trustworthy. We could give him some money, tell him to go to the shops and buy us a soft drink, and he would come back with the drink *and* any change.

He was a good kid but we knew he stretched the truth a bit as kids tend to do. We would ask him why he wasn't at school and he always had an answer: 'There was a bomb' or 'It is closed today' or 'The teachers said not to come back until next week'. One of our guys asked him where his parents were and he always said they were dead. Then, one day, his mum came walking up the street and gave us an earful because her son was hanging around with us when he was supposed to be at school. He scampered off pretty quickly and we didn't see him again for about a week after that! We liked him though. We spent time talking to him about Australia and we taught him how to kick a footy. Most of the kids were ratbags, but George was different. He respected what we were doing as guards and he knew not to take stuff from the front gate, like our torches or notebooks or pens. The other kids would do that to annoy us, but not George. I often wonder what happened to him. I try not to think about what he and some of the other kids are up to too often. The reality isn't too nice.

We tried to have good relationships with the Rwandan people.

We believed that as infantrymen we were the interface between our contingent and the Rwandan people, so we did try hard to be friendly, especially to the kids. The military hierarchy was concerned that we looked too mean because we shaved our heads – they felt the look was a bit too menacing. We thought that was a bit of a laugh. How mean can an Australian look wearing a baby blue-coloured helmet? I think we looked anything but menacing! We'd play soccer with the kids and teach them to speak English and that kind of thing. If we needed to be tough, we would, but most of the time, we were nice guys. They didn't seem to be too concerned by our shaved heads!

My section had their three days recreational leave in Kenya in mid-April and when we got back, we were all pretty tired to say the least. We were walking up the road with all our gear, feeling pretty sorry for ourselves, when the Company Sergeant Major came running up to tell us to get ourselves fully kitted up as we were going to Kibeho the following day. I thought, 'Here we go, where's Kibeho?' As it turned out, one of the infantry sections was down at the Kibeho camp with the legal officer and eight people had been killed, so the UN were getting a bit worried and wanted an extra section down there. All we wanted to do was go to bed, but instead we had to dump our gear and go back to get extra ammo. Every time we went anywhere, we always drew extra ammo, just in case the proverbial hit the fan.

The next morning we awoke at 0300 hours for the drive down to the Zambian Battalion (ZAMBATT) headquarters. Our section spent the next 24 hours at headquarters recovering from our leave while 5 Section went down to Kibeho. The following day, we rotated with 5 Section. I can remember driving along this empty road and it was such an eerie feeling. When we got to the top of the hill overlooking Kibeho, we could see millions of people; it was like looking at a crowd at a footy match. There were people everywhere. When they saw us coming along the road, they ran towards our vehicles. We had to send two of our guys up the road ahead of the vehicle to push people back just so we could get our vehicles through. We eventually arrived at a house that had been used the day before as an aid post, and we stopped there to wait for tasking while the medical team set up their aid post again.

We got a tasking to take a Canadian officer to the landing zone (LZ) located about a kilometre from our compound. This officer had been taking photos of the displaced people in the camp and had been caught by the Rwandan Patriotic Army (RPA) and asked to leave. With half my section and one of the intelligence officers in tow, we had to escort him up to the LZ. He was taking photos even as we were escorting him through the crowd, and that led to another confrontation with the RPA. There was a bit of a stand-off between the RPA and us for a while there. My view on the RPA was that they were just bullies and if you stood up to them, they would back down. So that is what we did. I was only a Lance Corporal but I told the RPA officer that he couldn't have the Canadian; he was coming with me to the LZ and he was flying out and there was nothing the RPA officer could do about it. I was completely right. There wasn't anything he could do about it, and he knew it. Thankfully he didn't want to start a fight so they eventually backed down and let us get rid of this guy. That was my first real experience at Kibeho.

The Kibeho camp really wasn't a nice place to be. We weren't allowed to stay there overnight, so every afternoon at around 1600 hours the aid post would be packed up and we would all leave, just to come back and do it all over again the following morning. The poor Zambian peace-keepers would stay there though. They would be up all night worrying for their lives with this grand final crowd all around them. When we arrived in the mornings, they would disappear to catch up on their sleep.

The RPA were complaining to the UN that the vetting of the people in the camp wasn't fast enough and as a result the tension was really high. The RPA believed that Kibeho was a training camp for the militia rather than just a displacement camp and they wanted it closed. Subsequently they were making all the people in the camp leave their little shanties and were trying to channel them through collection points. The problem was that the UN hadn't organised transport for those who had already been put through the vetting process and the RPA were getting really frustrated. Basically there was a crowd of people who had been cleared, sitting on the side of a hill with nothing, because the RPA made them dump their belongings and wouldn't let them take anything with them, and they couldn't go anywhere because there was no transport. Back inside the wire were all the other internally displaced persons (IDPs) who didn't really want to leave, or who did want to leave but were slowed by the process. They were getting angry and the RPA were getting angry. It degenerated into a very tense situation.

The day the massacre occurred, we arrived as normal at the small house where we always set up. At the front of the building was a bunker, which was really just a sandbagged wall. On the other side of that wall was the body of a man who had been shot by the Zambians during the night. He had apparently come hurtling out of the crowd waving a machete and running at the Zambians, so they shot and killed him. That was how we started our day – looking over the wall and thinking, 'Crikey! That's a dead body there.' It was the first real, fresh, dead body that most of us had ever seen and we started then to really become aware of the tension that was in the air.

It was a funny kind of day. It started off overcast, then it went hot, then overcast again. We got on with our normal tasks of providing security along the wire fence that was set up to keep the displaced people from amassing on our aid post. A crowd of the RPA came along the road and looked at us, cocking their weapons. By now we knew that there wasn't much we could do if they did want to have a go at us because there were apparently two battalions of RPA and there was only one section of us; and even that was pretty thin on the ground because guys from the platoon were all over the area on tasks. Under the circumstances, the gestures made by the RPA towards us were quite intimidating.

As the morning progressed, things started to heat up between the RPA and the displaced people in the camp. It began to rain and then the shooting began. My understanding of the day is that the RPA opened fire in the first place and said that they did so in self-defence because the crowd surged towards them. The RPA later said that the people in the camp surged forward because of the rain, and they thought they were going to be attacked so they began shooting into the crowd. I never bought into that theory, though. I always thought they opened fire on someone in the crowd they didn't like, which caused the crowd to surge; or that people within the crowd behind them started to attack others with machetes, which caused them to surge away from the attackers towards the RPA. The fact that it was raining is irrelevant.

Unfortunately for us, the aid post had been set up right in the middle of it all. Prior to the RPA opening fire, the tension in the air was really unlike anything I had felt before. I said to colleague Brad Collins, 'Go find the boss [Lieutenant Steve Tilbrook]'. I could tell something was going to happen. The Lieutenant couldn't be found; as it turned out he was on the other side of the compound. So here I was, just a young Lance Corporal on my own with only five of my section, among this palpable tension. The Section Commander was on a task away from the rest of us, so instead of nine from my section, there were now only six of us on the ground. 'Here we go,' I thought.

The initial surge started at around 1000 hours. We knew something didn't feel right and we were trying to get the crowds back from the fence. The crowd knew something was going to happen, too. I remember that just before the start of the shooting, the crowd was very panicky. Clearly something was going on among them. Some young kids who were at the front of the crowd were getting crushed into the barbed wire fence we had set up. We were pulling the kids off the wire and putting them back while trying to get the crowd to calm down, yelling, 'Move back, you're being stupid.

People are being crushed.' They moved back a little but when the firing started, they all moved up against the wire again. There is a photo of me that I saw in a magazine with my hands up trying desperately to get the crowds to move back off the wire. It was crazy.

As the shooting continued, the crowd figured that the safest place to be was with us on the other side of the wire so they just surged over the top of the wire and came in among us. That's how we got involved. People were being crushed; old people, mothers, babies, children. They just swarmed on our location. I told the two scouts who were with me to move back to the rise behind us so that we were in a safer and higher position away from the crowd. But once the crowds surged we lost contact with each other.

During the commotion, a guy came racing towards me from out of the crowd with a stick and he started hitting me with it. I was thinking, 'Mate, I'm wearing a flak jacket and a helmet! You're not doing too much damage.' I also had my own 'get back' stick that we all used to push people back off the wire with. He and I had a flogging match with our sticks, but he was wearing just a shirt and a pair of trousers, so it wasn't a fair fight. It was sheer madness. After a while, our sticks broke into nothing. Another colleague, Billy Ochman, was on higher ground above me and could see the fight. He could also see that the crowd moved in on me once my stick broke.

Another guy approached and threw a rock at me. Because I didn't have my stick any more, I grabbed my weapon, which we had to have slung at all times, and I cocked it. The rock didn't do any damage given my body armour but I started to get a bit concerned that the situation was going to escalate because the crowd were just running around crazily by this stage and people were getting shot. The rock thrower disappeared. My guys, who were able to see what was happening, thought I was going to open fire because it was madness all around me, but I wouldn't have because I knew that it would be the last thing I probably ever did. I was able to push my way through the crowd to get to the rest of my guys. Once I got there, I told them to fix their bayonets on their weapons just in case.

All this time, the RPA were shooting at people around us. Not long after we had fixed our bayonets, things started to quieten down a bit. We felt safe enough to start bringing in bodies and to kick the crowd out of our compound. We weren't allowed to have them hiding among us as that went against our agreement with the RPA. We found people hiding underneath our vehicles. Some were even hiding in the wheel arches.

Virtually all the deliberate killing started around 1400 hours and that was when it really went crazy. The RPA would see someone, chase him down and kill him, and then target someone else, like it was a sport. By this stage, we were pretty flat out in our little world trying to get people out of our compound and going out to retrieve the casualties near us. We would see people go down and we would run out with a stretcher and bring them back in to the medical team. Lots of them died, though. The medical people were working on hundreds and hundreds of people, but so many died.

At one stage, a whole crowd of people were running down the hill and the RPA were firing after them. The entire hillside was littered with the different colours of the people's clothes as they lay dead on the ground. The RPA stood at the top of the hill and just picked people off as they ran away. It was pretty full-on to watch that. I remember one of my guys saying offhandedly, 'We're going to die here today,' and I thought, 'Oh God, shut up. Don't say that out loud.'

I can't tell you how long the big push took because it was sheer bedlam. When it quietened down, there was indiscriminate firing around us for at least an hour. We were supposed to leave at 1600 hours, but there was no way we would have been able to get out of the compound with this going on around us. We would have been attacked for sure. It was decided that we were probably safer where we were behind the walls and sandbags.

Gradually things quietened down. When it was time to leave, our convoy of six vehicles had grown to around 19 vehicles because all

the non-government organisations (NGOs), who were also providing assistance in the Kibeho camp, didn't want to stay there
anymore either. When we left that night at about 1800 hours, it was
getting on dark. Our convoy was driving up the road when we
were stopped by the RPA at the checkpoint. Now, all the NGO
vehicles had wounded people in them and we knew that. We didn't
have anyone in our vehicles because there wasn't any room with all
our stores and equipment, but as we were driving out, the RPA
stopped us at the first checkpoint and kept us there for about
10 minutes trying to intimidate and hinder us.

Eventually they let us through and then they stopped us again
further up the road. As we pulled to a halt, one of my boys said,
'You know, we are the only people who know what happened.
They might have sent a battalion up the road to get us.' At this
checkpoint, colleague Jason Saint and I had to get out of the vehicle
– Jason had the night vision sights and I had a 14 millimetre illumination round. Of course, it had also begun to rain at this point so we
were less than pleased to be outside in it! Our section commander
wanted us to walk up the length of the convoy to let the NGOs
know that we were still with them. We tapped on the windows of
each of the vehicles just to let them know that it was okay.

We ended up spending the night at the ZAMBATT building,
and we were a pretty shocked lot that night. My memory is that we
all sat around feeling stunned and not really saying too much. We
were in our own worlds with our own private thoughts. Then,
instinctively, we fell back to doing what we knew, like checking and
cleaning our weapons and trying to keep warm. Most of us were
still wet from the rain and didn't have dry clothes. A lot of detail
about that day and night is forgotten now.

Our section had a wide range of guys. Some had been in the
battalion a good couple of years while others had only been in a
short while, and as in any group of people, there were some mixed
personalities. Each man responded to the events of that day differently. During the worst of the shooting, I sent some of the men

back to have a break to get away from what was going on. At one stage, I decided that I should have a break away from it, too. I pulled back from the wall and made myself a brew. I could see that the medical people were working flat chat with all the wounded people we'd been bringing in and there was no way they would be taking a break, so I took my brew over to the medics and offered it to them. That was the last I saw of it because between them it disappeared. They were just so busy that none of them had time or the thought to make a brew for themselves.

As a 2IC, my responsibility was to my Diggers: to watch what they were doing and make sure that I rotated them through to take a break. I'm not sure if doing so meant I missed witnessing a lot of stuff or whether I unconsciously forgot a lot it, but much of that afternoon is hazy in my memory. I don't know what we were thinking when it was all going on. I remember that when Jason Saint and I went down to the sandbagged wall near the wire, there were a few rounds coming in around us and I thought, 'No, I don't think I want to be here.'

I don't know what was going on in our minds when it was all happening. I am not sure if it was self-preservation or if our infantry drills took over. I think all we did was look for casualties, get out to them and bring them back when we could. When the massacre started, we didn't go out too far at all because we didn't have to; the bodies were right there in front of us. But as it started to quieten down near us, we went further out into the area where thousands of the displaced people had been living. In that area we found hundreds of casualties and bodies. It was horrible out there.

Leading up to the massacre, the RPA had been trying to get the IDP to leave the camp so they turned off the water supply and stopped them from getting access to their latrines, not that they were much good though. There was human excrement everywhere through the compound; they were living among it. It was terrible.

Inside the compound, where the displaced people had been shot and wounded with machetes, there was a RPA sniper up on the veranda. Whenever we entered the compound, he would parade around with his rifle and occasionally fire at us, but then disappear before we could see where he went. We had pinpointed him as being on the veranda but would never see exactly where he was laying up. We cautiously entered the compound armed with our rifles in one hand and blankets in the other to use to carry the casualties out and bring them back to the medics.

On one occasion, as we were walking in there, I was pointing out which casualties to bring in when a group of RPA opened fire. Instantly, all the displaced people inside this area dropped to the ground. So here we were, us nine dickheads, standing in the middle of a shooting gallery wearing our pretty baby blue helmets thinking, 'Excellent!' I think it was around that time when we decided that we didn't want to be in there anymore, so we went back to the compound where the aid post was. When it was safe for us to do so, we went out to grab casualties and bring them in again. How safe it was I don't really know, but I know there were shots ringing out all around us. The compound housing the displaced people certainly wasn't safe.

We were the only section present when the massacre happened and we were also the last section there when they closed the Kibeho camp down. What annoyed us the most was that we left on the eve of Anzac Day and we just wanted to have some time to adjust to what we had seen at Kibeho. But we were informed, 'Okay lads, dawn service at 0300 hours,' and we had to go. I was furious, but not with having to do the Anzac Day thing. Anzac Day should have been a wonderful experience given the fact that we were on operations, and they had a Ghurkha playing the bugle and they had made a cenotaph – but then the RPA came in to the compound for the ceremony and laid a wreath. This really riled me up. I was thinking, 'Hang on a second, these are the jokers who are killing thousands of people down south and here they are laying a wreath as though nothing has happened.' I knew it was all very political but I didn't care about that. I just felt they shouldn't have been there.

Before we left Rwanda, there were rumours getting around that five people had been nominated for medals. At the time we thought it was for a Conspicuous Service Medal or another similar kind of medal. We never contemplated it was a Medal for Gallantry (MG) because it's a war medal. When we got back to Australia, I was posted to Reconaissance platoon at 2/4 RAR and I was instructing on a course when the section commander got a commendation. We thought that was it – a 'Great stuff, well done! Now let's get on with it' kind of thing.

In October 1996, I was in Louisiana as part of a trip we had to the US. I phoned home to say hi to Kelly and the kids. The first thing she said to me was, 'Next time you go overseas and get a medal, make sure you're at home to sort it all out!' I had absolutely no idea what she was talking about. As it turned out, the letter announcing that I had been awarded the MG turned up while I was overseas. Kelly opened it because she needs to attend to things in my absence – that's what our wives have to do – but when she read the letter, she didn't know what it meant, so she called a friend of mine and asked him what it meant. He came straight over and said that it was great and took the letter to the Commanding Officer. Obviously they were delighted but Kelly reminded them that they weren't supposed to tell anyone.

Back in Hawaii, the Officer Commanding (OC) of Delta Company came in to wake me up at about 0300 hours the day we were due to fly back to Australia and started congratulating me about being awarded the Medal for Gallantry. I told him that I already knew about it, but it was supposed to be a secret. Obviously he'd been told about it so that he could tell me before I arrived home. When I arrived at Townsville Airport the battalion duty officer was standing there with a handful of minutes and other notices to give to me before we got back to the battalion, and they were all essentially messages of congratulations from various people in the Army. As it happened, the day I returned to Australia coincided with the day I was allowed to tell people, so when we got off the bus back at the barracks, I told the guys from my section at the time and they all thought it was great. One of the guys who was with me in Rwanda said that one of the points on the stars was his, and if you look at the medal the star is a seven-pointed star, a point for each of the guys in the section. I think that is great. When I wear it, I wear it for all of them.

The investiture was an interesting experience. My parents came across from Perth and Kelly came down to Canberra with me from Townsville. It was nice to have them there. Finding service dress to wear for the ceremony proved difficult because no one I knew had anything in my size and I certainly didn't have my own set. Apart from that small problem, the whole event went smoothly. At the investiture itself, I had my medal presented first because I was the lowest rank of those getting the MG, so mine was the first of its kind presented since the Vietnam War. That was a pretty big honour in itself. It was also the first of the new gallantry awards presented since its inception.

I have been told that what I did was brave, but I don't believe I did anything more extraordinary than anyone else who was there. My job as the section 2IC is to look after the men in my section. That is just what I did, nothing more. If you think about the things that I saw in Rwanda and compare it to what a Digger in World War II saw and did, my experience was nothing. I used to think that I didn't deserve this medal at all. Think about what the Victoria Cross winners did in World War II – they stormed enemy machine-gun posts single-handedly, killing 30 enemy with only their rifle butt and bare hands. I have asked myself many times, 'Does my decoration belittle their medals?' I know the circumstances are different. I understand that. I know I received a MG because someone who saw what I did thought I deserved it.

Over the years I have stopped feeling embarrassed about it. But in my own mind, I still don't feel I did anything different to anyone else. To me, someone who is brave stands up for what is right and does exactly what needs to be done when it needs to be done regardless of the outcome. Charging a machine-gun post is madness, but it is still brave. It was something that needed to be done, so the soldier did it, despite the fact that it could kill him in the process. A true soldier is someone who does everything a soldier needs to do without question or hesitation. If you don't do it, you aren't a soldier. I guess that is all I did. I did what I needed to do, but I was one of nine guys. If I didn't have those nine guys there, would the outcome have been the same? I believe you are only as good as those around you.

Warrant Officer Class 2 Andrew Miller is now serving in an Army Reserve unit in his home state of Western Australia as a Training WO2. Since returning from Rwanda in 1995 he saw overseas service in East Timor in 2002. He is nearing the end of his 17-year career in the Army and is looking forward to his future. He and his wife Kelly have four children – Jeremy, Travis, Rhiannon and Chase.

'THERE WAS NO CAVALRY COMING TO HELP US'

Lieutenant Thomas Steven Tilbrook MG

CITATION
MEDAL FOR GALLANTRY

Lieutenant Thomas Steven Tilbrook is cited for the Medal for Gallantry for his acts of gallantry while commanding the Infantry Protection Force at Kibeho, Rwanda during the massacre of civilian refugees in April 1995. As the Infantry Protection Commander, Lieutenant Tilbrook was responsible for the security and protection of the Australian Medical Support Force at Kibeho. This responsibility included the disposition, deployment and coordination of the infantry force, the coordination and tasking of support for the medical team, and liaison and negotiation with the Rwandan Patriotic Army Forces.

The fighting that erupted on 22 April placed the Australian Medical Support Force under intense pressure and immediate physical danger. The camp population made two attempts to escape from Kibeho. The first attempt occurred at 1100 hours and resulted in the death of approximately 130 people. The second attempted escape occurred at 1710 hours and resulted in the deaths of thousands of people and an overwhelming number of casualties.

Throughout the entire crisis, Lieutenant Tilbrook displayed outstanding leadership and personal courage. His decisive leadership, clear orders, consistently accurate assessment of the situation and personal example maintained the security of the medical team, allowed the evacuation of humanitarian workers and more than five hundred casualties, and ensured that the medical team could continue to operate throughout the entire period of the crisis. On a number of occasions on 22 April, Lieutenant Tilbrook led his men into the camp to evacuate the wounded, often while small arms fire was impacting around them. When advised that three humanitarian workers were separated and alone in one of the camp buildings, Lieutenant Tilbrook immediately led a small team to rescue them, again while firing was continuing. On the morning of 23 April, Rwandan Patriotic Army troops began a sweep of the hospital in the camp with the intent of clearing the hospital. Lieutenant Tilbrook was able to negotiate successfully the evacuation from the hospital of non-walking casualties, who, otherwise, would have been forced from the hospital, regardless of their wounds.

Lieutenant Tilbrook's acts of gallantry and leadership were crucial to the success of the Australian Medical Support Force's operation at Kibeho. That success has reinforced and enhanced the reputation of the Australian Medical Support Force, the Australian Defence Force and his country. His personal courage, leadership and dedication to duty were in the finest traditions of the Royal Australian Infantry Corps.

I WAS BORN IN NOVEMBER 1972 IN INVERELL IN COUNTRY NEW South Wales, the middle child of three siblings. The eldest is Sue-Ellen who is married with three kids and the youngest is Anginette who is also married with one child. My father was a New South Wales police officer. Just after I was born, we moved to the Blue Mountains where Dad was working as the Detective Sergeant at Katoomba and I did most of my primary school years there. Then, in 1987, Dad was forced to retire from the police service through an injury he sustained while working – he broke his back while involved in quelling the bikie riots in Bathurst during the races held every Easter. Once Dad was out of the police service, we moved to Lowood, a little town located between Ipswich and Toowoomba in Queensland.

Growing up, I was always going to join the police service like my dad, or the Army, like my grandfather who was an Army officer in World War II. I don't recall that there was a particular time when I made a conscious decision, though. Obviously, with Dad being a police officer, that profession appealed to me. However, I remember that as a little boy I used to play 'army' with the other neighbourhood kids and as I grew older I enjoyed reading books about military history and looking at military artefacts, so I think that was where my interest really did lie. I joined the Army School Cadets when I was 12 and stayed in cadets until I finished high school. My father had talked me out of becoming a police officer so the only other option I liked was joining the Army.

When I was in Year 11, I applied for a scholarship to go to the Australian Defence Force Academy (ADFA) and was successful. Once I saw that all my mates were going to go to university in Brisbane, I began to have second thoughts and I figured that if I was at ADFA in Canberra, I might be missing out on something! Instead of committing myself to go to ADFA, I took the money offered by the scholarship and went to university with my mates. I soon realised that my heart wasn't in doing studies at a civilian university and that I should have gone to ADFA in Canberra instead.

In 1992, I applied for the Royal Military College, Duntroon (RMC), and was successful. I started at RMC in July 1992 at the age of 19. I was fortunate as my family were very supportive of my eventual decision to join the Army. My mum, like most mothers, was a bit concerned about it but my dad was extremely supportive and proud of me. Because his father had served in the Army, Dad knew a bit about what I would be doing and I suppose part of him wished that it was something that he had done, too. Although he had a very successful police career, deep down I think joining the Army was something that he would have really liked to have done, as he has always been interested in military history, too.

I absolutely loved RMC and it was everything that I imagined it would be. I certainly didn't over-achieve, though! In fact, I was probably in more than my share of strife when I was down there.

It wasn't ever for vindictive or malicious stuff; it was more for larrikin kinds of things. I was actually very fortunate to graduate. Despite that, I had a great time at RMC. I was really interested in military history, military tactics; that kind of thing. The sporting aspect of military life appealed to me, too, and the camaraderie and the mateship that developed made my experience at RMC just fantastic.

After finishing at RMC in December 1993, I was allocated to Infantry Corps and sent straight on to do my Infantry Regimental Officer's Basic Course in Singleton. After completing that course, I was posted as a platoon commander of 4 Platoon, Bravo Company, 2nd/4th Battalion, Royal Australian Regiment (2/4 RAR) in Townsville in February 1994. My first 12 months as a platoon commander was fantastic. I really enjoyed my time before my deployment to Rwanda, but the learning curve was very steep. I was a bit younger than many of the other officers, so I relied on some of the more senior guys who had been in the battalion like Tom Biedermann, Mark Jennings and Dave Smith to provide some guidance. Just as I did at RMC, I had my fair share of scrapes but I loved being in the battalion. The lifestyle was great, I enjoyed the work, I enjoyed the Mess, and I enjoyed being around the soldiers.

In early 1994, we went to New Zealand for a three-week exercise. I really got to know my soldiers quite well in that time as I was working very closely with them and spending a lot of time with them. In those 12 months, we did all the other normal exercises that you do in an infantry battalion like a rotation to Tully, live fire exercises and other training exercises. They were great because it gave me time to get to know the men in the platoon quite well and work on the standard operating procedures that we had in place. When I took over the platoon, their standard was quite high. I don't believe my arrival added to the platoon in any way. They were a good bunch of lads who were well trained in their individual skills.

The bonus that I had, as opposed to what is happening more and more now, was that my junior non-commissioned officers were extremely experienced. They had all done at least 10 years in the Army and were mature, experienced individuals who were very competent and capable at doing their job. My platoon sergeant was also an experienced soldier. He had done 15 years in the Army, knew his stuff, and knew what needed to be done. He was a good sounding board for me and he was a good balance to my youthful exuberance and enthusiasm.

The first contingent to go to Rwanda, which included Alpha Company from 2/4 RAR, left in August 1994. In around November, headquarters gave the warning order that Bravo Company would be on the second rotation, so this gave us a bit of notice. By the time our company left as part of the second contingent, I had been with my platoon for 12 months. As the company prepared for the deployment, there was an overwhelming sense of excitement and anticipation.

Back in the early 1990s overseas deployments were very rare. It had been a long time since we had been anywhere. In 1993, 1 RAR had done their thing in Somalia and a couple of the lads from Delta Company 2/4 RAR went to Cambodia that year too, but overall, the Royal Australian Regiment hadn't done much overseas work since the Vietnam War. Consequently, there was an incredible sense of enthusiasm and jubilation to be going on an overseas deployment. I believed that I was very fortunate to be in the right place at the right time to go. It wasn't based on selection or merit; our company was simply picked as the company to go. Knowing that we were going in the new year put a real bustle in the company and everyone became more focused. We knew we had something specific to train for and it increased the enthusiasm immensely.

Having said that, I do remember some private occasions where I reflected inwardly on my abilities as an officer to go on this operation: Was I going to be good enough? Was I going to be able to stand up to it? I did speak to the guys I lived with at the time –

Andrew Hocking, Andrew Lowe, and Lachlan McDonald – about my concerns, as they were fellow platoon commanders and great sounding boards. I certainly remember questioning myself more profoundly in the immediate stage before departure. During the lead up time, we were all very focused, but as it got closer to our deployment date I remember spending a lot of time reflecting on whether I had crossed all the t's and dotted all the i's, so to speak.

Looking back, keeping those questions to myself was normal, I suppose, particularly in the Army with the personalities in the Officer Corps, and among the soldiers as well. Essentially, nothing less than perfection is what we are after and in your normal day-to-day functioning you can't allow yourself to question out loud whether you are good enough. You just have to do it. I would assume it is a natural thing, but I can't say that I spoke with any of the other guys who went over with me about it. But you'd probably be a bit of a robot if you didn't think about those kinds of things.

Landing in Kigali was a bit of an anti-climax because it didn't match the picture that I had developed in my mind as I prepared for the deployment. I was struck initially by how green and lush the countryside was. I was also struck by how business-like the Alpha Company boys were when they met us at the airport. I hadn't had the opportunity of talking to any of them before I arrived, which was quite unfortunate. Some information had been filtering back from them during their six-month stint, but our Officer Commanding (OC), Steve McCrohan, went over seven days before we arrived so he was able to send a lot of information back to us which was really helpful in that final preparation phase.

I remember the drive from the airport to the compound as being a little unbelievable. I know we were all taking in as much as we could because we were very excited. I can remember the sights and the smells quite vividly, even today, and the fact that it all looked pretty routine. There were many people on the streets, riding their bikes or walking, and even the odd handful pushing wheelbarrows along. There were markets operating. I've never forgotten the smells.

The drive into the compound itself was something that struck me powerfully because, like the country itself, nothing matched what I had imagined it to be. When we arrived in the compound, the three platoon commanders, Dave Little, Steve Brain and Mark Jennings from Alpha Company, were there waiting. The catch-up with them was good, but the handover period was very quick. We got in pretty late, said g'day, had a quick chat and then organised a time for early the next morning to get together for a handover so that we could all get our heads down for a sleep. We only had 12 or 18 hours to walk around with the other platoon commanders before we were into it on our own.

Our platoon took over the security job of the compound from Mark's platoon. Chris Smith and Tom White were the other two platoon commanders from Bravo Company. One of them took their platoon over to the hospital to take over the security job there and the other took his platoon to the outside tasks and made up the contingent's Quick Response Force (QRF). They took us around and told us of their experience for the past six months and we were trying to take it all in. Obviously, our OC had been over there a little longer and had done his own appreciation of his job and he had a number of things that he wanted to change immediately, particularly surrounding the routine and security of the location we were working out of.

As the platoon commander, my job was to liaise with whomever we were responsible for providing the security force to, ensuring that we understood what their needs were or whether there was anything additional we needed to know. It was also important to consider the well-being and motivation of the soldiers in my platoon and to check that the routine we put in place was being adhered to. It was much more complex than that, of course. I had a lot more freedom to step outside the mundane routine than the soldiers did because they were locked into section tasks that required them to be sitting behind a sandbag wall in a bunker watching a machine gun or doing a patrol. I tried to join in with these kinds of things, not to become an essential member of the task, but to see that the internal control issues were being maintained and also just to have a chat with them to see how they were doing.

We had been in country for two months before our first visit to Kibeho. The OC and a couple of other members of the headquarters had been down there for a reconnaissance and I had flown over it in a helicopter, but I hadn't been on the ground there. Alpha Company had done quite a bit of work there during their deployment with the French and some of the other contributing nations who were involved in the UN mission to try to disarm a lot of the militia who were in the camp. For us, it was a bit of a 'no go' zone in the first part of our deployment.

We knew things were beginning to deteriorate in the Kibeho camp around 18 April. I was due to go on leave. I had made sure all the guys in my platoon had taken their short leave, and the two other platoon commanders and I had organised to take our first short leave together in Nairobi in Kenya. It was going to be our big hit out. The boss encouraged us to do this because we'd been locked down and working hard for eight weeks and hadn't had a beer the whole time. It was going to be a bit of a blast for the three of us!

We were due to leave the next morning when the OC came up to me in the afternoon and said, 'Mate, I need to speak to you. I am quite happy for your platoon sergeant to take charge of the boys while you go on leave, but I thought you should know that there is a job on in Kibeho. We are going back into Kibeho, we have been tasked to provide a security force for a casualty clearing post (CCP) there, and it looks like things are going to blow up a bit down there. The RPA are trying to clear the camp.' He went on to explain what he knew about what the RPA were doing and I said straight away that I was going with my platoon and that I was fine about not going on leave. There was no way that I would have missed it.

Up until this stage, things had become very mundane and I had only been out of Kigali a couple of times on visits to the north, and we always knew that the south side of the country was very volatile. I was very keen to be part of the mission.

The guys from the Intelligence cell briefed us and then we received orders from the Operations cell. We were told that we were to provide a security force for a CCP that was being set up under the command of one of our doctors, Carol Vaughan-Evans. The medical team was only a very small group. Their task was to provide assistance to the Zambians who were in location and any additional abilities that they were able to provide to the humanitarian effort that was already in place in the camp. At that time, I already had a section in place down there as they had escorted the legal officer to the camp. One of my sections was still on short leave and my other section, Brian Buskill's, was available and came with me. We also took a section from Tom White's platoon down with us to augment ours to almost full strength. In addition to the infantrymen, I also had a couple of signallers, a couple of drivers and the medics and doctor who were providing the medical support.

We packed up and headed down to Kibeho with the sole task to marry up with the Zambians and then get on with it. That was all we knew. None of us had ever been there and we didn't really know the situation on the ground. We knew that the RPA were trying to close the camps and there had been some issues associated with that but nothing more than that. We knew that there was an immensely large amount of displaced people in the camp at Kibeho but in our minds we weren't able to fully fathom just how many there were. We only had a vague picture of what we were heading into.

Navigating our way in was difficult in itself as the only maps we had were very sketchy and from a variety of sources. To actually locate Kibeho on the map and then find it on the ground was tricky, but eventually we got there. As we drove in to the camp, I can remember saying to the driver, 'We're too late mate, it's all over' because as we came over the hill, the camp was empty. It was a sprawling area and there were thousands of make-shift shelters made of UNHCR tarps and branches which were all abandoned. There were personal effects scattered everywhere, many of the shacks were burning; there was general chaos. We could see cooking fires still burning so we knew that whatever happened here had not happened that long ago. It was obvious that we had only narrowly missed it. We figured everyone had been rounded up and taken somewhere. Later we found out that was exactly what had happened.

As we approached the top of the hill where the church and mission were located, we saw the people. They were massed into a small area along a ridgeline. One of the lads described it as cattle in a feedlot. There was literally hundreds of thousands of people crammed in to this small area. It was a bit of a shock to see. And their expectations of us were quite high – as soon as they identified that the new arrivals were white soldiers, a huge cheer went up; they were screaming out 'Muzungu, Muzungu, Muzungu', which means 'white man'. Their expectation of us was that we were there to fix their situation for them.

The crowd surged towards our vehicles, which was a real shock. We hadn't anticipated they would do that so we hadn't planned for it. They were obviously quite panicked and spooked at that stage. There were a lot of RPA soldiers around the outer cordon who were holding the people in this small area. We had to actually push through the crowd so that we could get our vehicles through. That in itself took quite a while. It was probably only 300 to 400 metres along the ridgeline from the area where the internally displaced persons (IDPs) were to where the Zambians were located but it took well over 30 minutes to get there because the people were packed so tightly around our vehicles. In order to move our vehicles, people had to be pushed out of the way. That was quite an eerie experience. It was all unknown. We didn't know the mindset of the people in the crowd. We didn't know how they felt about us being there. We didn't know if they would try to pull guys off the back of the vehicles. We didn't know if they had weapons or would take equipment out of our vehicles as we went by.

I was sitting in the front passenger seat of the vehicle and I wound my window up when they surged towards us. There were literally thousands of faces staring at me through the glass, which was quite confronting. It was frightening to wonder what they were thinking about me.

We finally moved in and touched base with the Zambians who were stationed there. They didn't seem to be expecting us and they weren't sure how we could fit in. They stuck us on a post outside their secured location and we occupied an abandoned house and set up security around it. Carol and her team tried to set up their medical facility there and get started on providing medical assistance to the displaced people in the camp. Unfortunately, the RPA didn't allow our medical people to provide any medical care to the people who had already passed through the checkpoint, so they were very limited as to who they could actually treat.

From our position we could see across the ridgeline back to where the RPA were and we were able to see what they were doing with all these IDPs. There was one checkpoint at the far end of the mass of people, which we had passed through when we first drove in to the area. There they were checking the identification of the IDPs and then packing them up on to the backs of trucks and driving them back to their villages. From what we understood, the RPA wanted these camps closed with everyone back in their home villages so that things would go back to normal.

What they were also doing at the checkpoint was acting as the police, judge, jury and executioner. The families of those who were killed during the genocide were literally lining the sides of the road and as the IDPs passed through the checkpoint, they would point or grab at some of them and a discussion would ensue between them and the RPA. Those people who were identified in this way were then taken over the hill and presumably killed. There was a lot of tension in the air. Well over 100,000 people were concerned, quite rightly, about their personal security; and there were over 1000 RPA holding them there with rifles. There were also the Interahamwe [ex-military Hutu hardliners] within the mass of people, so everyone was tense and on edge.

The Zambians were completely over-extended and over-run in their compound. Their compound had also been breached so they had no security. Then there was us, a small group of Australians who had just plonked themselves down in the midst of it all. We set up our position and as the people were trickling through on their way to the trucks, Carol and her team were trying to identify people with injuries or wounds that needed treatment, of which there were a number. There were a lot of old injuries and some newer injuries and she was able to treat a couple of people in that location, but the RPA didn't want us involved. In fact, they made it quite clear that they didn't want us involved at all. They were very aggressive with their weapons and as the medical people began to treat someone, they would appear with their weapons, shake their heads, grab the patient off us and push them away. There were a few RPA officers who spoke English and they approached us to tell us to stop treating the IDPs. The discussions were quite tense.

The OC was down there with us at this time, so he was doing the negotiations and trying to work out what we were there to do, but it was very stressful. We needed to work out what we were allowed to do and avoid any major incidents with the RPA because theoretically, they weren't our enemy. They were the recognised government, so if you boil it down, we were there to support *them*. The UN had recognised that the new government was in power and therefore the RPA were the Army that belonged to that government. We wanted to avoid an incident at all costs because we were a long way from home and in very small numbers.

My job as the infantry commander was to ensure the safety of the medical personnel there, not to get into a stoush with the RPA. If it meant we had to negotiate, barter or compromise, then I was perfectly prepared to do that. It was their country and it was their operation. They had a fairly strong sense that the UN had already had a couple of cracks at it and hadn't been successful, so we, as part of the UN, weren't thought of particularly highly. Before we got there, the UN had tried to repatriate these displaced people back to their home villages, but it hadn't worked and the RPA were fed up. They decided that they would do it themselves. The last thing I wanted to do was to cause an incident because it wouldn't be in line with what my task was, which was to secure the medical team. If I had become aggressive towards the RPA then I would have been putting the medical team at risk.

Throughout the day, an odd shot went off every now and again. We would hear a burst of machine-gun fire or firing from an AK-47 going off on semi-automatic around the camp, and there were certainly disturbances in the crowd. At one stage, we observed that 12 or 13 people had been trampled to death. There was also an indication of machete violence happening from within the group of IDPs, as we began to see a lot of fresh machete wounds as well as wounds from blunt instruments.

We could see that things were becoming increasingly unsettled further around the ridgeline, about 200 to 300 metres from us. There were waves of people moving away from something happening in their midst. Then the sounds of gunfire would ring out and the crowd would swarm in another direction. It was clear to us that there was a lot of tension but we just didn't know how deep it went.

When I look back at it all, I don't think I was ever frightened by what was going on. I think I was more concerned about what could happen; and because my task was to secure the medical team – to maintain our security perimetre – I think I was concerned more for them than I was for the lads or myself. Obviously, to see that sort of thing happening for the first time directly in front of you is quite shocking and confronting. But I think we were far away enough from the situation to feel as though we weren't going to become directly involved.

That afternoon, my superior officer Steve McCrohan was due to go back up to Kigali and as he was leaving, he took me aside and said, 'Mate, there is not a good feeling here, something is going to happen, so use your judgement. Stay calm. Make decisions as you see it but I know you will do the right thing. The fact that my boss had enough faith in me to make the right decision settled me. Once he left, though, it was a bit lonely because I knew that I had lost the support you get by having a superior around to make ultimate decisions. The decisions were now solely mine to make. I had to get it right, otherwise things could go really badly. My platoon sergeant wasn't there either and that was a double blow because it meant I didn't have anyone there to bounce ideas off or run an idea past before I made a decision. The boys were extremely focused, though; they displayed no outward fear or concern about the task or the situation. In hindsight, however, there should have been at least a company of men on the ground. We were quite prepared to do what we had been tasked to do but the situation really required greater support. But no one had any idea about what was going to happen and hindsight is a remarkable thing!

Each day, the tension in the camp increased profoundly. We could feel it every time we re-entered the compound to set up the CCP. After only a couple of days on our own, we shifted closer to the Zambian compound on the other side of the ridgeline because I was concerned about being caught out in an isolated position. The Zambian compound was far more secure – it was surrounded by razor wire, and there were bunkers established around it. We then assisted them in securing their perimeter. It was better for Carol Vaughan-Evans and her medical team to set up their CCP in there as well. Médecins Sans Frontières (MSF) had a hospital nearby so Carol was now able to liaise more closely with them and provide some assistance.

Tensions continued to escalate. The IDPs were not being allowed food or water. On a number of occasions we tried to get water to them but the RPA forced us away. The IDPs had started to collect rainwater off filthy tarps in an attempt to fill their bottles. It was terrible. We saw mothers picking through their own faeces to pull out pieces of corn and bits of grain or anything else that they might be able to re-boil to feed to their children. They were desperate. By that stage, they had seen that we weren't there to make it all go away or that we couldn't make it all go away, so they were disappointed, and there was a palpable sense of desperation among them.

As the lack of water and food became an issue, there was an increased amount of fighting among the IDPs for physical space because the area in which they were confined was so small; also personal possessions had been long lost. Isolated acts of violence among themselves were escalating, and as I've mentioned already, Carol and her medical team were now seeing more and more wounds caused by blunt instruments or machetes.

Also, the number of people going through the checkpoint had slowed down to a trickle because I think word had gotten around that if the people on the other side of the checkpoint singled you out once you got through, you would be taken away and killed. The IDP were very frightened about what would become of them and they didn't want to move on into the unknown. Life wasn't great for them inside the camp, but they probably figured it was better than facing potential death on the other side of the checkpoint. The tensions flowed on to the RPA because they could sense that the crowd was extremely desperate, and all their tension then flowed on to the Zambians and us, because we were sitting back helplessly observing it all.

The RPA suggested that the catalyst for the massacre was when the crowd surged towards them as a large rainstorm came over, but I think the massacre would have happened anyway. Prior to this surge there were a number of smaller incidents that, in retrospect, were signposts for what was to come.

There was one incident to the south of the camp, about 400 metres from where we were, where a group of around 500 IDPs broke through the RPA's cordon and tried to run across the valley in the direction of the neighbouring country, Burundi. The group made it through the inner cordon but were picked up before they reached the outer cordon and were shot. The RPA soldiers from the inner cordon turned outwards and began shooting and the soldiers from the outer cordon swept in, picked them up in the valley, and hunted them down. It was all so systematic that we just watched in shock. We could see blokes running, trying to get away, and the RPA firing on them until eventually they were hit by a round. Then the RPA would walk up to where they lay wounded and 'bang' – they'd finish them off. I guess this heavy-handed act demonstrated to the crowd what would happen to them if they tried to run, too.

There was so much happening at this time for us in the compound. I am sure this is why specific memories of that day are a little faded now. We had a large number of Priority 1 casualty evacuations going out on helicopters back to the hospital in Kigali. As a result, I had almost half my platoon under Corporal Buskill up at the helicopter landing pad securing that quite exposed area and the other half, which was only a section, under Lance Corporal Miller on the ground with me in the compound.

Whatever triggered the massacre is still unknown to me. Certainly a huge rain storm came through, but I think things had already begun before then. The whole crowd of RPA seemed to mass to the north and at the same time, our compound was breached by thousands of IDPs looking for security. At the time I had a section of my lads up on the heli-pad, I had half a section being over-run by thousands of people who had surged over razor wire to get into the safety of our compound, and then the RPA initiated wholesale shooting because of it. Things became very busy.

We managed to get the guys back from the heli-pad and secure the compound as best we could. We also realised that [Lance Corporal] Andy Miller had been knocked over in the rush into the compound and he was out on his own on the perimeter among thousands of IDPs. We didn't know where he was. I ordered the lads around me to fix their bayonets and we tried to get the IDPs to move out of the compound. Around this time, we noticed that some of the IDPs were carrying weapons. One of our lads confiscated a grenade.

We were quite worried. I didn't have any communications with Lance Corporal Miller because when he was knocked over, he lost his Motorola. We didn't know whether he was safe. We eventually got back to the perimeter and located him with his big stick trying to keep people away from him. We managed to circle around him and clear the IDPs from him. Then we established the cordon, managed to get people back over what was left of the razor wire fence, and hastily re-built it.

While all this was going on around us, there was a lot of gunfire, but in all truth we weren't conscious of it. Getting the IDPs out of the compound and back into the area where the shooting was occurring took some effort. Some of the IDPs had climbed up under the wheel hubs of our vehicles to hide, while others had climbed into the Zambians' shit pits – that was how desperate they were; I'll never forget that.

The RPA formed up at the top of the camp near the church and then came down in force, firing deliberately into the crowd. There was so much shooting going on that the helicopters had stopped flying in to evacuate casualties. It also meant that no one else was going to be able to come in to give us a hand. Once the IDPs saw how aggressive the RPA's response was, they panicked even more and attempted to run for their lives. In most cases they got killed in doing so – as the panic level rose, so too did the number of killings.

My main concern throughout all this was with the Australians. Anyone in an Australian uniform got my full attention in the first instance. It didn't even cross my mind that we weren't going to succeed in regards to that. I was still taking in all the killing around me but I had to force it to the back of my mind and stay focused on my task. Our communications with the headquarters back in Kigali was very scratchy; when we could get through, I could barely hear them and they could barely hear us. On a number of occasions, headquarters asked me to provide a summary of what was going on – the idea was to get us out of there if they could. However, I didn't see that there was any way we could be removed from the situation safely. I was positive that if we left the compound, we would become trapped somewhere along the line and not make it out.

At this point I really concentrated on staying focused. Once I had that control, I found I was able to look at the situation calmly. I really believed that we were going to be able to take care of ourselves, even though we only had a section on the ground; however there were still some Zambians around at this point.

In my communications with headquarters back in Kigali, I was speaking initially to the Duty Officer and then as the situation heightened, I was speaking with the Operations Officer. By the end of it, I was speaking to the Commander of the Australian Medical group, Lieutenant Colonel Roche. I can remember quite clearly his conversation with me at one stage when things were looking pretty hairy. I had explained the situation and it had obviously shocked everyone back at Kigali.

Although they had been receiving an increasing number of Priority 1 and 2 casualties from the camp by helicopter, I am not sure headquarters fully understood the complexity of the situation in the beginning. I was relaying what was going on via the radio and they quite rightly felt helpless sitting a couple of hundred kilometres away. They couldn't get anyone down to us to extract us or to provide extra troops on the ground. Lieutenant Colonel Roche said something like, 'You are the commander on the ground, you are the only man in a position to make a decision, and I trust your judgement, good luck.' That was the bottom line and it was at that stage that I realised that there was no cavalry coming to help us out of this and that we just had to get stuck into it as things arose.

Effectively, the way the Australian soldiers responded to watching around 10,000 people being attacked in front of them was superb under the circumstances. Their restraint probably went on to save maybe 50–60,000 more lives. Had any of them responded by firing their weapon at the RPA to stop the massacre, I don't think anyone would have really learned what happened in Kibeho because none of us would be here to tell the story. I know that for a fact. We were a platoon minus of infantry soldiers and the RPA had at least a battalion's strength of soldiers there at the camp. We were significantly outnumbered and had no opportunity of reinforcements. We didn't like what was happening, but we knew that we couldn't do anything to stop it. What we could do, though, was help as many of the wounded as we could. We put ourselves between the RPA and the wounded whenever we could and through bluff – which was all we had – we were able to save lives and influence situations that were in our control. I tried to emphasise this to the lads afterwards. Sure, the massacre was terrible but we saved a lot more people from a similar sort of fate. They did well. They did the right thing.

Never again should Australians be put in that situation. While I am still around, I will do whatever I can to ensure that they aren't. We were under Chapter 6 of the UN Charter, which meant that we could only use our weapons in self-defence. The RPA fired upon us on numerous occasions so, theoretically, we could have used our weapons. But I ordered the boys not to because of the greater impact on the situation. We should never send Australian soldiers in to similar situations again. We should go in with robust, open rules of engagement and with enough force to provide adequate protection for ourselves. I think that lesson has been learned as subsequent deployments have gone under Chapter 7 of the charter, and certainly, force protection has taken a higher precedence.

At RMC, a lot of time was devoted to the theoretical components of the military arts. At the time, I found it interesting but didn't always see the link to the contemporary officer and the job we would be doing. At Kibeho, though, I know that the leadership lessons, historical analysis of commanders in desperate situations and all those other elements of officer training helped me, as did my intimate knowledge and faith in my soldiers in their abilities and training. I trusted them to do what I was asking them to do. I think

I was lucky that I was able to 'crisis manage'; I was able to make many decisions in a short space of time, without being too overwhelmed by the situation. I didn't feel as though I was rushed. Even though things around us were happening extremely quickly, I felt like I had plenty of time to make decisions. If something cropped up, it felt like everything around me slowed so that I could react to it.

One such decision was made when we received word that there were some Médecins Sans Frontières (MSF) doctors trapped by the massacre in their hospital. The MSF hospital was a flimsy excuse for a building located 50 or 60 metres further around the ridgeline. When the breakout came, the bulk of the IDP went in that direction so there was a lot of firing impacting into the northern side of our perimeter as well as into the MSF hospital. The building offered the MSF no protection from any small arms fire, so I made the decision to take two of the lads with me to try to retrieve the doctors trapped in the hospital with a view to bringing them back into our compound to give them some protection, and also to perhaps help Carol Vaughan-Evans do what she was doing in our compound.

By now, we were getting an overwhelming number of casualties coming through, so any help she could get would have been welcome. I grabbed two of my lads and we took off towards the hospital. We had to go across an open space where there was a huge amount of firing criss-crossing the area. The Interahamwe were firing from inside the compound at the RPA, who were firing from the other side back towards them and the other fleeing IDPs. Unfortunately, the area was obstructed by a large metal gate that we had to scale while all this firing was going on around us. It was very hairy.

When we got to the hospital it was a complete mess of dead and injured people everywhere. One of the lads found the doctors huddled up in a back room in the hospital. They were French, and most of them didn't speak any English. I was concerned whether we had everyone because I didn't want to have to make this journey again – I figured I might be pushing my luck running across that open area under fire again. As it was, we knew we had to go back across it now to get back to the compound, which wasn't a nice thought, especially having the doctors with us. I explained to them how I wanted them to move back with us across the open area and showed them how to move to try to move in small bounds to avoid exposing themselves to fire. They did it very well. As it had been raining, the ground was very slippery and we all slipped a lot on our way back but eventually we got everyone back up to the compound in one piece.

Once we got them inside the compound we took them over to see Carol at the CCP, which had been set up behind a stone building to offer them some protection. I then told them to stay put because I didn't have the time or resources to send people out with them so that they could retrieve the wounded, which they didn't like and complained bitterly about. Nevertheless, that was my assessment at this stage. I don't understand why I made the decision to look after the MSF people; they weren't even part of our organisation. But as they were members of another aid agency who were there to help out, I suppose I felt obliged to be concerned for their welfare on top of everyone else's.

Not long after we got into the compound, one of the MSF doctors came up to me in hysterics, saying that there was someone left behind in the hospital. I was furious because they had assured me at the time that we had everyone and that no one was being left there. I didn't want to go back there but they confirmed that there definitely was someone missing. They believed she was still alive because she'd been seen not long before we arrived to rescue them. I reluctantly made the decision to go back. I chose not to ask the same two guys to come with me because they had already pushed their luck once. I grabbed another two guys and, using the same methodology that I used earlier, we got back to the hospital unscathed.

It took us a little while longer to find her because she was actually hiding in a cupboard. We got her out, moved her back up to the compound, and again, somehow, got through it unscathed. It was even more scary the second time because I knew what to expect. Additionally, the RPA and Interahamwe had seen us come through before and knew where we had been so I figured we could become a genuine target this time.

Overall, the role we played at Kibeho was very stressful and there were many engagements with the RPA that could have gone belly up. Our medical people would find someone who needed treatment and the RPA would come along and point their weapons at us and say that we couldn't treat them. On a number of occasions we had our weapons up and pointed at them in response to the way they were behaving towards us. They were very aggressive. Whenever we did this, they would just laugh and go back to firing back into the crowd.

Once the heavier firing had started to settle, we knew that there were many injured people around, so we started sending stretcher teams out. Half the call sign remained behind to continue providing security and the other half went out to collect the wounded. The boys located wounded where they could – initially they didn't have to go far as there were hundreds of bodies literally in front of the wire of our compound. As they located patients, Carol's medics were triaging on the run, saying, 'Yep, take that one in, we can do something about that' or 'No, leave that one, we can't help him'. This was happening right up until we departed that night and continued almost non-stop over the following two days.

We didn't get away that first night until well after dark, when there was a lull the shooting. I didn't want to stay there that night at all. Under the current situation, the camp was certainly one place I didn't want to spend the night, but we were still unsure about what was going on around the roads in the area. I secured an agreement with the local RPA commander that my convoy was going to move out on the main road and that we would be allowed to travel all the way through. However, the RPA didn't have any communications so we were stopped at each roadblock along the road. At the first roadblock there was a particularly tense situation with the RPA soldiers because they weren't convinced that we had been given the clearance.

On the way out, we could see what appeared to be thousands of bodies in every direction. It was so surreal. Eventually we stopped at a village just north of the Kibeho camp where a number of Australians had been flown in that day to marry up with us. We got back to our firm base location at around midnight and then we made preparations to get back in to the camp at first light. By 0400 hours the next morning we were on our way back in with a larger number of troops and a second medical team.

Even though we got there very early, we could clearly see that most of the bodies we identified the night before had been cleared away. The Zambians said that there had been more incidents of shooting overnight and that there had also been incidents involving grenades, so there was more wounded. Our lads brought back all the wounded they could and with the extra medical team (and the experience from the day before), the combined CCP staff were able to look after the casualties more effectively.

Throughout the day, sporadic gunfire continued. Someone also began taking pot shots at our guys as they entered the IDPs' compound to retrieve bodies. By this time, the number of IDPs in the camp had dropped off from hundreds of thousands to around 5000; the rest had either gotten out or had been shot and killed. The whole place was scattered with abandoned personal effects and ID cards. You couldn't step anywhere without stepping on a body. Underneath nearly every single tarp we checked was another couple of bodies. We were literally picking our way through this rubbish tip of disaster and death.

When I look back, I wonder how I was able to deal with this mass destruction, and the only suggestion I have is that perhaps because they weren't our own Australian soldiers, I was able to distance myself from it. That sounds dreadful, but that is what we had to do to not become affected by stepping on bodies everywhere you walked. It was still shocking to see dead babies, children, and women, but I think that because it wasn't one of my guys, or someone wearing an Australian uniform, I was able to separate myself from it.

During the massacre, I was forced to do things that I wouldn't ordinarily want to do, nor ever imagine myself doing. On one occasion, a RPA soldier was shooting into the crowd and I stepped in front of the barrel to try to stop him from killing anyone else. We had a huge stand-off – I figured that if he was going to fire his weapon, then he was going to have to shoot me first. That bluff worked and he backed down, letting us take the wounded away to treat them and get the others to move on.

There were other occasions when I needed to move injured people but the RPA wouldn't allow it, so there would be yet another stand-off with weapons pointing at each other until the RPA stood back and let us do what we needed to do. By the end, I was just walking past them and pushing their barrels away, telling them to fuck off and get out of the way, because I was sick of them. I had become numb to them.

I was reaching my limit because my emotions were starting to affect my ability to make sound judgement and sound decisions. No sane person does those kinds of things. Stepping in front of a recoilless rifle to stop it shooting is clearly a sign that my ability to make sound decisions was compromised. I remember that when Tom White's platoon came down to relieve us on 24 April, I gave him a handover and came back up to our area to sit down and have a smoke. I really had to think hard about how to get back up again. One of the boys had made me a brew and I started to shake. I realised then that it was no longer my responsibility and my body could relax a bit more. It wasn't until I'd handed over to Tom that I knew that I had reached my emotional limit and needed to be rotated away to have a break. The sheer magnitude of what had just occurred, coupled with physical and mental exhaustion, had caught up with me.

When we got back to Kigali, there was a lot of excitement and a real buzz around the camp with everyone wanting to hear about it. Obviously those back in the compound in Kigali had been involved in receiving and treating all the casualties that we were sending back. It had been overwhelming for them and they knew what we had witnessed must have been even more overwhelming. The OC did something that I think was fantastic – Anzac Day was the next day, and he wanted us to be involved in the dawn service. It was great for all of us.

Then he decided that the front bunker in front of the accommodation area needed rebuilding and he tasked the platoon to do this job straight away. As soon as we were back we were tasked with completing this big engineering job. The boys transitioned into doing something physically difficult but something productive, something tangible. It was like a soft pat on the back for what they had done down at Kibeho, but reminded them that the world was still turning and to get on with their job. It was good. The blokes used that time to chat about things that they saw a little bit.

We had a nursing officer, Major Mary Brandy, who was absolutely fantastic; she assumed a bit of a maternal role towards us guys. She used a soft, feminine approach to helping the guys sort out what they were feeling. I know all the boys responded to it. Infantry lads don't mix with women much as part of their jobs, so Major Brandy's approach was ideal for getting them to open up a bit. She and the padre set up a debriefing session where we sat in a circle and she facilitated the discussion among the boys, which was something that we had never done before. It would have been more normal to give them a kick up the arse and tell them to just get on with things!

Things did go back to some degree of normality after Kibeho. There were still a couple of incidents that happened after Kibeho but the boys responded appropriately. The thing that I struggled with the most was convincing the boys that the RPA were the 'good guys', or that they had come through this genocide and were now liberated. The boys in the platoon saw them only as animals for what they had done in Kibeho. My main concern was that if anything happened like that again they would respond out of anger or hatred in the wrong way and shoot someone. I didn't trust myself to respond appropriately either, because I had a decent hatred for what they had done as an Army and as humans as well. I wasn't confident to guarantee that my response was going to be appropriate, so that was a bit concerning.

Over there the soldiers were magnificent in every aspect. They were typical Australian soldiers – they were larrikins; they got in the shit when they had been drinking; they said the wrong thing to the wrong people; they caused administrative problems and they complained about everything. Yet when the job was on, they were brilliant. They never questioned an order, they never shunned their responsibility, and they never took a backward step. They never displayed any fear, they were all courageous, and they were compassionate. All of them deserve a medal for what they did. It was very satisfying for me to see men respond to an order that they obviously believed in and respond to it in a way that suggested they weren't concerned for their own safety. They knew they were there for a reason and they just cracked on with it. They behaved like that for the rest of the tour and I was immensely proud of them.

At the end of 1996, I was sitting at my desk in my new posting at Kapooka in Wagga Wagga. A letter arrived on my desk via the Commandant and the Adjutant informing me that I had been invested with the Medal for Gallantry for acts of bravery in Rwanda. That was the first I had heard of it. It had been 18 months since I had returned from Rwanda and nearly two years since the incident. Receiving the letter was a huge shock for me; I had never had any inkling that it was going to happen. I wanted to know who else had been decorated, too.

The investiture was amazing. It was fantastic to catch up with people from the contingent. They organised for my parents to come down and attend the ceremony at Government House. It was all a bit of a fairy-tale, I suppose. To go into Government House and meet the Governor-General and the other generals was great; a really interesting experience. It was such a proud moment, but very humbling too.

I don't think getting a Medal for Gallantry (MG) has changed me as a person, but I think that going to Rwanda has. I try to keep a fairly level approach to things, so having a MG is not something I let people know about, really. Mind you, some people might argue that having the MG has actually allowed me to get away with a few things that I probably wouldn't have without it! Ultimately, I wear it on behalf of the boys who were there. While the medal theoretically highlights a couple of individual acts, it wouldn't be possible to single out one person and praise them when all the boys from my platoon did so well, too. It is a decoration that I wear in recognition of what they did. I am also glad that I have tested myself and know now that I can respond well under certain conditions. It has given me a lot of confidence as an Infantry officer, knowing that when push comes to shove, I am capable of making a decision; and that while it may not be the most brilliant decision, it is a decision that is sound and logical and will result in a good outcome.

In Kibeho, I was doing nothing more than my job and what I am trained to do. I wasn't doing anything extraordinary or brave. To me, the people who were living in that terrible existence in the camp were brave. For them, the situation was so hopeless and yet they continued on trying to make the best of it. There were also so many actions of individual soldiers that were brave. They were isolated and did things to keep themselves alive and in control of the situation, even though it got completely out of hand. Nothing that happened in the camp was something that any of us had ever been prepared for — how do you prepare soldiers for witnessing innocent people being massacred and not being able to do anything about it? You just can't.

I was simply an officer leading Australian soldiers. I was responsible for their welfare and responsible for commanding them in a capable manner. My actions were all a means to an end as opposed to being a conscious act to show the lads that I was brave. I'd like to think that any one of my peers, my fellow Infantry officers, would have responded in the same way, and I am absolutely sure that 95 per cent of them would have.

Now holding the rank of Major, Steve Tilbrook is currently a student at Command and Staff College. He is married to Angela. He maintains contact with many of the members of Bravo Company and was instrumental in organising the reunion of the 10th anniversary of the deployment of Australians to Rwanda in 2005. Since his time in Rwanda, he has served overseas in the Middle East (Israel, Syria and Lebanon) and the Solomon Islands.

'THERE WAS NOTHING I COULD DO TO STOP IT'

Major Carol Louise Vaughan-Evans MG

CITATION
MEDAL FOR GALLANTRY

Major Carol Louise Vaughan-Evans is cited for the Medal for Gallantry for her inspirational leadership, personal courage and exceptional performance of duty as the Medical Officer in Command of the Casualty Clearing Post at Kibeho, Rwanda during the massacre of civilian refugees in April 1995. As the Medical Officer in Command, Major Vaughan-Evans was responsible for the operation of the Casualty Clearing Post which included the collection, assessment, and evacuation of over five hundred severely wounded casualties.

Immediately on arrival at the camp on 22 April the Casualty Clearing Post was established and Major Vaughan-Evans and her team moved into the camp to assess and collect casualties. As the day progressed and more casualties were sustained, Major Vaughan-Evans' calm, clear directions and medical expertise ensured that the team at the Casualty Clearing Post continued to operate at maximum capacity and with exceptional efficiency. In the afternoon the security situation deteriorated and intense firing erupted around them. Nevertheless, Major Vaughan-Evans continued to treat casualties despite the risk of personal injury. On numerous occasions Major Vaughan-Evans accompanied casualties to the helicopter landing zone whilst firing was still occurring in and around the camp. Throughout the entire crisis, Major Vaughan-Evans displayed acts of gallantry, inspirational leadership and exceptional performance of duty. Despite being fatigued from treating casualties and administering medical support, Major Vaughan-Evans was undaunted by the hostile rifle fire and the mass casualty situation which confronted her.

By her gallant performance of duty, distinguished leadership and tireless and selfless efforts, often under fire and always under appalling conditions, Major Vaghan-Evans was directly responsible for saving the lives of many Rwandan people. Her calmness in the life threatening situation and her ability to make clear and accurate medical assessments under pressure were of the highest order. In addition, her compassion and dedication to those she was treating, ability to improvise when supplies ran low, and outstanding medical expertise were in the finest traditions of the Royal Australian Army Medical Corps. Her acts of gallantry and leadership whilst under fire were an inspiration to all members of the Australian Medical Support Force Team at Kibeho.

I WAS BORN IN JOHANNESBURG IN 1967. I GREW UP IN SOUTH Africa but most of my family holidays were spent at our family property in Zimbabwe, or Rhodesia, as it was called then. We emigrated to Australia from South Africa as a family group in December 1982. I was 15 at the time. My first year was spent in the Hunter Valley in New South Wales, then our family moved to Tasmania where I did my final two years of high school and proceeded on to university with a scholarship from the Army. I failed my first year of medicine and repeated first year after going through an appeals process. After that close call, I never looked back – I finished my degree in Tasmania and then moved to Sydney where I did my internship for only one year.

I always wanted to do medicine, and after being in a terrorist attack when I was about 11 or 12 in Rhodesia, I decided I wanted to be an Army doctor. My family didn't quite like the idea of my going into the Army, as their exposure to military doctors was limited to those they saw in South Africa – they were seen to be the second-rate doctors of society. My parents' expectations were that I would be excellent at whatever I did, so joining the Army really worried them.

When I first joined up, I expected that I would be going away, doing things with them immediately, even though I wasn't yet a qualified doctor. I felt that even though I had joined as an under-graduate, I should still be living the experience of an Army doctor! When I moved into military accommodation in Tasmania, it was wonderful. Two Army doctors, Ray Simpson and Rob Walters, took me under their wings. They encouraged me to join the Field Ambulance, which I did, and I really gained a lot from that experi-ence. When I moved to Sydney to do my internship, I again moved into military accommodation. Unlike Tasmania, living in the Mess while doing my internship was surprisingly difficult to do. The hours that I worked were very long and it was easy to feel isolated. Most of the people I shared the Mess with at Randwick didn't understand why I was being unsociable – there would be days where they wouldn't see me; but I was either working or sleeping. Having said that, they did all they could to make me feel welcome. I really liked living in the Mess.

Once I had completed my internship, my first posting was to Duntroon Medical Centre in Canberra in 1994. It was a horren-dous experience for someone like me who hadn't been through any kind of military training because it is the premier training establish-ment. The cadets march everywhere; not just along the pathways outside but even to the toilet. I have a vivid recollection of my first day, going to work. I was staying at a place called Nimmo House, which was 500 metres from the Medical Centre. I left my room at something like five in the morning so I wouldn't have to salute anyone! I was absolutely petrified. I felt a little more confident the next day, so I left at a more civil hour and, of course, a cadet saluted me and I walked directly into a tree! From thereafter, though, things improved and I never walked into a tree again.

I was only at Duntroon for 12 months before I was posted to 1 Field Hospital in Sydney. That posting coincided with an expectation that I would go to Rwanda with UNAMIR. At a ceremonial dinner in 1994, Brigadier Buckley asked me how I felt about going to Africa. Having grown up there, the offer was like a golden carrot dangling in front of me. I loved the idea of going back and after I saw a peer who was on the Direct Entry Officer's course with me go over, I was terrified that the mission would be finished before I got to go. Even in January 1995, when we were in Townsville on the pre-deployment training, I remember thinking that they were going to call it off and we would be sent home.

Until Brigadier Buckley spoke to me in late 1994, I didn't know that there would be a second contingent to Rwanda, and I was very fortunate to be considered for it. Our total commitment was for 12 months, and since I knew something of the country, I didn't think I would have much trouble adjusting. Even though I had seen some images of the atrocities that the first contingent had encountered, I was very excited and I think that enthusiasm seemed to wash away the reality of what I was seeing in these images. I was delighted to be given the opportunity of making a difference there.

The pre-deployment training was very comprehensive; I thought it was fantastic. They covered a lot of medical components as well as some of the more frightening aspects of the deployment. I remember one lecture was how to dig yourself out of a minefield with your bayonet! At the time I thought that if I had to dig myself out, I was in big trouble. I could see myself shoving the bayonet right into the middle of the mine and causing it to explode. The funny thing was I didn't even have a bayonet in Rwanda. Was someone going to throw one to me? With my luck, it would land on a mine . . . it was quite hilarious, really.

But it was very exciting for us women coming from a field hospital to be surrounded by the infantry soldiers who were deploying with us. They were just everywhere, and the *esprit de corps* developed very quickly. Being surrounded by so many women was a new experience for the guys, too, so it made for some interesting times in the early days.

As a doctor, I think I was very fortunate because I completed all of my courses in my first year. I felt that I was very well prepared. I did the Regimental Medical Officer's (RMOs) course and my Direct Entry Officer's (DEOs) course straight away and then went off to do the Regimental Officer's Basic Course (ROBC). At the ROBC, one of the other students had just returned from Somalia and I remember being really envious of him and his experiences. I had also done the Early Management of Severe Trauma (EMST) course, which I found extremely useful. As a doctor, I believed that I would be fine clinically, but knowing what I know now, I probably should have thought more about it. My basics were very strong so that probably made a difference, but there were still so many holes in my knowledge.

I was the only Captain RMO on my deployment. My boss, Major Peter Wheatley, was the Commanding Officer. We also had three RAAF doctors deploy with us for our six months; we had a good team. Throughout the deployment, Reservist doctors from all three services would come over for short deployments of six weeks; they were often specialists like intensivists, anaesthetists, orthopods and surgeons and each one bolstered our numbers and energy as they arrived.

I was still extremely negative about whether the mission would go ahead, even up to the day we got on the plane. We had a terrible time with the plane, so I was sitting in the Townsville airport saying, 'See, I told you we won't be going!' But when we finally got on the plane, I became very excited. I felt like I was finally going home to Africa. I couldn't sleep because I was so excited. The plane ride itself was dreadful but I didn't care.

When we landed in Kenya, I was beside myself with excitement. I knew what to expect. Everyone else was tired and overwhelmed – it was a country with a different language, different people, and it smelled a bit. But I was walking around sniffing, thinking, 'Yes, this is Africa.' Although I was extremely tired, I was ecstatic to be back in the country.

Looking around the airport, I remember thinking that although there was a lot of damage, there was also a bit more infrastructure than I'd expected. It was dawn when we arrived so everything had been larger than life: the smells were more pungent, the desolation seemed more pronounced. Driving through the streets of Kigali was everything I had expected – the city was full of contrasts. Arriving at the compound was interesting because at first glance the buildings appeared normal, but closer inspection revealed bullet holes all the way up the walls, huge holes in the roof and no glass in the windows. The women in the contingent were accommodated in the top floor of a three-storey building and bullet holes tracked all the way up. The room I was staying in still displayed evidence of a massive shoot-out. There was a stain on the floor and I wondered whether it was mud or blood. Part of me didn't really want to know. I was so tired that it was immaterial.

I didn't know a great number of people from the first contingent and because we had been delayed leaving Townsville, we didn't have as much time with them for a handover as was initially planned. We were told to get some rest for a few hours and then we could catch up for the handover, but I had a fitful sleep, being woken on numerous occasions by an odd sound or an odd smell.

Then I went straight down to the hospital to have a look around. That was quite eye opening. I knew I would be working in the Casualty Clearing Post (CCP) as the RMO. Even though I had done my ROBC, I wasn't entirely sure what it all meant. Frankly, I would have agreed to do anything over there. I would have agreed to be the car-park monitor so long as I was going to Rwanda! I paid little regard to being told that I was going to be running the CCP – I figured I would just wait and see what it meant when I got there. I had a general handover of the area from Michelle Barrett, with whom I had done my DEO course the previous year, and that was it. The first contingent left for home that evening and we were on our own.

From early on, the team in my CCP worked together to ensure we had everything we needed to achieve our mandate. At that stage, it was decided that we would have the capacity to provide a roving element to support the troops that went out from our compound, as well as the other nations there under the auspices of the UN. We also provided medical treatment to a local orphanage, run by the Sisters of Mother Teresa. We would go there at least once a week, sometimes twice a week, for the six months that we were in Rwanda.

My job at the orphanage was to provide a medical service to the people there. We took environmental health personnel, a dentist and even engineers, so that this little orphanage received a whole range of services. Some other work had already been done before we got there; jungle gyms were built for them, their buildings were repaired. The Sisters in the orphanage took in adults as well as orphans, so there were a whole range of diseases and injuries: tuberculosis, HIV, wounds. While the wounds didn't require the patients to be taken into the hospital, they did require a certain degree of care. There were always sick children. I would have these little children climbing all over me wanting a cuddle, and they had terrible, snotty noses, and lice or scabies! I would go home with snot trails completely covering my uniform. On a more serious note we were always really concerned for the kids because we thought the Rwandan Patriotic Army (RPA) might single them out for what we were doing there and punish them for receiving assistance from us. Fortunately, this never happened, but it did concern us. I know before I went I promised myself I wouldn't become attached to those little children but, after six months, leaving was one of the hardest thing I had to do. In that amount of time, you see changes in children, particularly the little ones. You see them grow up. That was hard.

I also worked in the United Nations hospital as part of the second resuscitation team. The first team would be called in for the first resuscitation of the day, and if any more came in and the first team hadn't finished theirs, the second team was called in to help out. There was always at least one resuscitation team called in to play every day. Once we heard a mine explode in the distance and about 45 minutes later the first casualty from that explosion arrived. Then shortly after the next casualty arrived. That hospital was an incredible place to see infectious diseases you would only ever read about in textbooks. I saw at least three cases of tetanus. It was certainly primitive. Even more primitive were the conditions in the local Rwandan hospital – the doctors working there were less -han adequately trained. I think the majority of the fully trained people had been killed during the genocide. We had to make some really difficult decisions in that hospital. You'd go in with your Australian background behind you – where you don't really have to regularly make difficult decisions about patients and their care – and you'd have to choose between two patients; which one you would treat. They only had limited facilities and I suppose their ability to feel the kind of compassion that I extend to my patients had liter-ally been worn out over time, so they couldn't care for every patient in the same way we would try to. That was one of the least pleasant experiences that I can recall.

My CCP team was a very tight knit group right from the begin-ning. That was wonderful. The only change I had was when my nursing officer changed. When I started with the team, the nursing officer was Lieutenant Susie Busch. Susie was rotated out to the ward and I got Lieutenant Robbie Lucas as her replacement. That change was fairly pivotal because they are two very different people. Susie is efficiency and fore-planning personified, whereas Robbie is more compassionate, and also a very capable fore-planner, but he offered a very human element. After the massacre Robbie really paid for the consequences of being so compassionate.

Working so closely with them, I got to know my people really well. Milan Nikolic, or Niko as he was called, was one of our corporal medics and a fantastic person. As an officer, there are occa-sions where your rank gets you some perks. Some time towards the end of the deployment, I was offered a trip down to Gikongoro but was told that I could send someone else if I didn't want to go. I didn't think they really needed me to go so I nominated Niko to go in my place. Unfortunately, Niko was involved in a terrible car accident where the driver of the vehicle went over the side of a mountain and Niko's rifle barrel went through his thigh and up into his pelvis. It was a very traumatic time for me and I really felt bad about that for a long time. You don't ever want to select someone to participate in something that ends up with an adverse outcome. I thought I was giving him a reward and yet he nearly died. It caused a tremendous amount of grief.

I remember the first time I got to go out on my very first field trip. I was so excited. We had been so heavily kitted up with ammunition for the trip that I felt I could have supplied another Army. The morning of our departure, I was sitting in the vehicle with my webbing on and it felt a lot lighter than it should have. I didn't know when my period was due and I had to be well prepared so I had sacrificed one of the pouches on my webbing for tampons. I realised that I had forgotten to put my ammunition back in after I had stocked up on tampons and that's why it felt so light. I thought, 'Here I am, going into battle, and all I have is my tampons!' I had to feign another reason to run back to my room and collect my magazines of ammunition, so I said, 'Hang on guys, I need to get my lipstick! I'll be back in a minute!' It was very embarrassing.

The deployment for Kibeho happened very quickly and with very little warning. We had heard increasing stories of killings in the internally displaced persons (IDP) camp but not in a way that was relevant to me as a doctor. Around this time, there was also a volcano that was expected to explode, so I had that to think about as well. As dreadful as it sounds now, a few executions of some IDPs in a camp that was a good couple of hundred kilometres away wasn't a major part of my working day. I know it sounds terrible but what was going on down there was all just lost in the noise.

Major Peter Wheatley called me one afternoon and said they were worried about the camp at Kibeho and that there ought to be a UN representation down there to help facilitate people leaving the camp. There was a huge amount of packing after this. We tried to envisage what we would need and we thought we would use the Trendelenburg tent, which in retrospect was the most ridiculous thought. We packed with a real sense of enthusiasm and urgency. We had some briefings up until around 2300 hours that night and we had to leave at 0400 hours, so we had little sleep. There wasn't really enough time to think about whether it was going to be frightening. My thoughts were really focused on what I would see: war-related injuries or medical conditions. In the end, I decided that we should take as much gear as we could. Most of the briefings I attended focused on military topics such as security issues and the situation down there, none of which meant much to me as the doctor.

We left on a Wednesday morning in the dark. The Casualty Clearing Post (CCP) fitted into one vehicle, which is incredible given the amount we had packed. There were also two patrol medics attached to us, Trooper Jon Church, who has since died in the Black Hawk crash, and Corporal Paul Jordan. They went down to Kibeho in an ambulance. In my CCP there was Sergeant Terry Pickard, Lieutenant Robbie Lucas, Corporal Tim Whyte and Niko. We all squashed in and off we went. Excited as we were to be heading out, we all soon nodded off.

As we got closer to the camp, I could see the landscape covered with abandoned makeshift shelters made out of bushes and scraps of plastic. We had a feeling that we were too late because we drove for kilometres, winding our way through this deserted camp, and there wasn't a soul in sight. We could see that the camp had been used recently because there were still some fires smoking.

Then we came around a corner and were confronted with a sea of people right in front of us. I remember feeling an overwhelming sense of awe when I saw the sheer number of people. I thought, 'Look at how many there are. They are so cramped.' They were waving at us and clearly very happy to see us.

Then it dawned on me that our group was just a drop in the ocean in terms of what we could do for them.

We immediately went to the Zambian position and made contact with them. They told us about the previous nights' events and explained what we would be allowed to do. There was a lot of discussion as to where we would be situated. I didn't really care whether we were north, south, east or west, frankly. By now, my mind was starting to work over the situation from a medical perspective. Eventually, the Zambians sent us to what I think was an old abandoned school on a hill some distance from them.

We weren't sure if we could fully set up there so we had a bit of a look around, wondering what we were there to do and how and where we would begin. Naturally, the best-laid plans always go astray and the Rwandan Patriotic Army (RPA) had their own ideas about what they wanted us to do. I remember that Steve Tilbrook had some very heated discussions with the RPA about what we could do. Eventually, through some very interesting negotiations, the RPA said we had to stay outside the camp perimeter and as the IDPs passed through the checkpoint, they could come to us for medical treatment. The RPA officer with whom Steve was having these negotiations had a walkie-talkie in one hand and a pistol in the other, and as he spoke, he was waving the pistol around, gesturing. The most frightening thing was that he had his finger on the trigger the whole time! We could clearly see his finger moving on the trigger, pulling it back as he tried to make his point. And instead of pointing at us with his finger, he was pointing at us with his pistol!

We all wised up pretty quickly to this and began to form a line behind each other. When the person at the front of the line realised that the gun was pointing at them, they would step back a bit, and the next person in the line would then have the pistol pointing at them, and so on. We all moved around a lot during the discussion. That RPA officer really had me worried.

Eventually we set the CCP up outside the checkpoint where the RPA agreed we could go. In accordance with the agreement made with the pistol-pointing RPA officer, there were certain guidelines we had to follow. We were not allowed to feed or clothe the IDP; we couldn't have them for more than five minutes because the RPA wanted the traffic to continue going forwards; we couldn't treat them on the roads – instead, they had to be taken down away from the road for treatment and then sent back up to continue on; and finally, we weren't allowed to keep anyone.

I sent the medics up to the roadside, just beyond the checkpoint and out of sight of the displaced people. I gave them some criteria to use in their observations; to look for the obvious things, like if they are limping or coughing, and then to bring them down. We would do what we could for them and send them back. That said, there were some people we did try to keep because they had terrible injuries or illnesses that needed more of our time. Throughout the day, the RPA would come down to check on what we were doing and we would say to them, 'Look, this person really needs to go by bus, they can't walk,' and they would nod, 'Yes, okay'. Then, later that afternoon, you would see them walking along the road with everyone else.

We also fed people if we could. A child would come down in rags and would go back up to the road in a t-shirt. We figured that as long as we didn't stop the flow, it would be okay, we would get away with it. Every so often the RPA would come by and give us a hard time for holding on to some people, but we did make a difference, I think.

We got some emergencies because every now and again people would be injured in a stampede or a crush. At the end of each day, we had to pull the CCP down and leave. We would head back to the Zambian position each night and head back the following morning to continue doing what we could. That was really a decision made for the safety of the group. The tensions were obviously very high within the camp and it wasn't safe for us to stay throughout the night. The RPA were being exceptionally cruel to these people. They had no water, no food, and they were crammed into a tiny space. I remember one incident where a RPA soldier had turned on the water at a water point and of course, the camp massed towards the water point to collect water. As they got closer, he turned it off and beat them. They played all kinds of games like that.

We all carried weapons, but my staff and I wore them slung while we were working. We weren't comfortable leaving them on the ground because the RPA were always coming through and would probably take them. Everything I needed, I kept on me. Anything I put down, I did so knowing that it might be pinched. I wore my helmet and flak jacket a lot, but on occasion I did put them down. There were very negative repercussions for losing your helmet or flak jacket, though, so we found it easier to wear them all the time, despite their obvious discomfort. At least then we wouldn't get into trouble for losing them!

We worked continuously, and while the patients didn't have huge things wrong with them – a broken leg or broken arm for example – it was more the compassionate care that meant we worked non-stop. We were just continually dishing out compassion because there often wasn't much more you could do. I don't recall eating or drinking during the day at the camp. I was mindful that I didn't want to be seen doing it in front of these people. I didn't know when they would next get water or food so to eat or drink in front of them would have been cruel. One day on the way out of the camp, I was in agony all over. I couldn't figure out why I felt so much pain.

Then I realised I hadn't passed urine all day. I guess I was just so focused on these people that I hadn't even given my own needs a thought. As it turned out, I was also hungry and sore from crouching all day. But as a woman, it wasn't easy for me to take toilet breaks because I couldn't go up against a tree like the men, and it wasn't safe to go wandering off for some privacy. It was simpler just not to go.

I always found it very disheartening to leave at the end of the day, as we would drive out past all the people who had been cleared from the camp who were now making the long slog on the roads to who knew where. There was one woman who was hobbling, using two sticks to walk with. Earlier that day I had begged the RPA to take her in a vehicle but there she was, walking along the road in terrible pain with her sticks. Also, often at the end of each day, mothers would try to give us their babies to take with us, or have others beg us to shoot them. It was terrible. On one occasion, there was a pile of belongings on the side of the road and we knew that the RPA had taken the owners of those belongings away and killed them. Earlier, they had come by our vehicle and said, 'Please help us, they are going to kill us.' But we weren't allowed to help them, and then later we saw that they *had* been taken off and killed. How do you prepare your mind for that?

I have never forgotten one incident because it fills me with pride for the compassion shown by the soldiers. One of them had found a little girl. We think her mother was killed so she was alone. She would have either been killed or who knows what else, and the soldier asked whether we could get her out of the camp. One of the medics started bandaging her up, covering her little limbs in bandages as though she had injuries. She was only tiny. The RPA came to check the vehicles on our way out, so we gave her some diazepam in some cookies. When they first checked us, she was still crying, probably more from terror or wanting her mum. But they saw her bandages and let us shut the door, and we moved out.

Although we felt relieved, we knew we had to get through the next road block, and the next group of RPA soldiers mightn't be as lenient. We didn't know if she was old enough to talk, and were petrified that she'd say something to them that would give it all away. We didn't understand much of their language so we wouldn't have known what she was saying either. Fortunately, the diazepam started to work and when she got sleepy, we were able to put her up in one of the storage bins on a bed of dressing packs! She snored the whole way back to an orphanage. We always remember that as a small victory. Despite all the RPA did to that mass of humanity, we got one little girl out of there alive.

Leading up to the massacre, the mood in the camp changed so much. It's funny, but it mimicked the climate. In Africa, there is an understanding that mood is related to the climate, particularly leading up to a storm. On the day of the massacre, there was an incredibly huge storm and it just pelted down on us. Tensions were very high and signs were definitely there that terrible things were going to happen.

Late in the day prior to the massacre, we went via the Zambian headquarters on our way back to our camp to say that we would be back tomorrow, 'business as usual'. Suddenly we heard a lot of shooting going on behind us towards the camp. A man was brought in to me and to this day I still don't know how the physics of it worked, but he had been shot in the top right of his chest and the bullet came out the other side of his chest near his shoulder. He quickly developed bilateral tension pneumothoraces, which means that air was getting into the cavity around his lungs on both sides, causing his lungs to collapse and affecting the functioning of his heart. I didn't have any chest drains and his wounds were so large they would have been redundant anyway.

I already had a patient in the vehicle that we were evacuating back to hospital and they plonked this new casualty in front of me. While it was probably the hardest resuscitation I have had to do – there were very little stores – it was commendable on the part of everyone involved and we got him through a five-hour road trip to a hospital where some CARE Australia nurses came to take him off our hands. I got Robbie to put his hands over both wounds intermittently to try to reduce the pneumothorax. Amazingly, he didn't die. He must have lost almost his entire blood volume but a couple of months later we were told he had survived. In all the despair, we could sit back and say that fellow, despite the odds, had made it through.

The day the shooting began, I was already so busy. We still had many patients from the previous night's events and that morning I arrived to find 70 people requiring treatment waiting at the Zambian position. We started on those people immediately because the RPA had indicated that they would kill anyone not capable of moving on. By the time the full-on massacre started, I had a lot on my plate. I saw the shooting but I just couldn't afford to stop treating people who had already sustained injuries. It was the only thing that gave me a focus; it was something that I could do something about. I knew I could do nothing to stop what was going on out there. The only time I recall stopping specifically because of the shooting was on the last occasion we took people to the helicopter landing zone. All hell had broken loose and we had to come back to our compound for safety. We huddled together in the back of the ambulance and as we came back through the position, we knew there was a lot of shooting going on in our direction. We moved from the back of the ambulance to the safety of some sandbags set up in our compound.

I felt very safe with the infantry around me. They had a terrible job; they were constantly exposing themselves to danger when they would enter the compound to find casualties to bring back to me. There were occasions where they were actually being shot at, yet they kept going back out there. Without them, I couldn't have done my job. I am so thankful for them. I am not sure if I ever thanked them afterwards.

One of the first casualties that was brought to me after the worst of the shooting was a little child. Jon Church carried in this little boy who looked like he was just riddled with shrapnel and bullets. It was actually very difficult to tell what his injuries were. It was a terrible sight. I knelt down on the ground to start looking at this kid and I remember saying, 'Why? Who could do this to a child?' He was the most gorgeous boy. About 30 metres away there were RPA soldiers, just watching and laughing. I started to stand and swing my rifle up, and someone told me, 'Remember you're the doctor, you can't do that'. I began to realise what I was about to do. At that point, watching these soldiers laughing at the distress of a child was something I couldn't deal with anymore. I've long since come to the conclusion that I don't think I could actually kill anyone, but right then, I believe I could have shot those soldiers. For them not to respect human life the way I did devastated me.

In a way, I am shocked that I nearly lost it. I reflect on it less and less now. To me, not trying to stop the killing was unacceptable and yet, it wasn't my decision to make. We knew that the RPA would have no qualms about shooting us – they had no qualms about us being in the general area where the shooting was going on, so for them to take aimed shots at us wasn't completely unfathomable.

There were two occasions when there was mass shooting. I worked through the first one but during the second bout, we really didn't do much or move very far because there were so many bullets coming our way, and it was getting dark. Leaving that night was a very hard thing to do. It is really hard to go when there are people who need you. When we went back, the day after the massacre, there were a large number of casualties already evident. Our manpower had been substantially increased with the arrival of another medical team overnight, and fortunately they brought a resupply of stores with them as we had just about run out the day before. At the beginning of that day, the people we were seeing were quite shocked, and so getting intravenous access was very difficult. We'd try a couple of times to get a cannula into a vein and then get a new cannula and try again. But by the end of the day, we didn't have the luxury of getting a new cannula, so we had to do whatever it took to get it into that patient.

We did run out of IV fluids, morphine, and things like that. However, these were incredibly stoic people. There is a photo taken of me kneeling next to a man who is lying almost in the crucifix position. He had been shot in the abdomen. I had asked him how he was and he replied he was okay. He died shortly after. My lesson from that was not to ask anyone how they were feeling. Instead, I would try to make them comfortable, give them comforting words, and treat them with as much compassion as I could. There was one person who had been shot int he thigh and the bullet had obviously taken out his femoral artery. He passed away very quickly after we got to him but I know there was nothing we could have done differently for him. Another man had been shot in the abdomen and he died very quickly too. I believe his aorta had been destroyed, so there was nothing we could have done to save him apart from make him as comfortable as possible under the circumstances.

We set the ambulance up as the intensive care unit. It could hold four patients and Robbie looked after that area. We could hang IV fluids from the ceiling. We set the UNIMOG (truck) up as our ward and the triage was on the ground near the UNIMOG. We didn't have many stores for the ward so we had to triage what we used there. As we began running low on morphine, for example, we would only give it to people who were really in a lot of pain.

The day after that we were sent back to our compound in Kigali. Again, I felt dreadful leaving Kibeho, but I know we were all terribly fatigued. As we were resting, we could still hear the sounds of the camp and all of us were profoundly disappointed to not be back there working. I think we were all still thinking through what we'd seen and were wondering what we could have done differently. To an Australian, people killing other people is murder on a grand scale. It was something beyond our comprehension. We spent a bit of time talking among ourselves about the experience. It was very surreal coming back. I don't think they knew what to do with us because we all looked a bit shell-shocked. I just remember all my friends giving me a cuddle and it felt so hollow. I wanted to draw something off these people but I didn't know what. They didn't know what to say. We had some debriefings with a critical incident team who were flown over especially for it, but I found more comfort in throwing myself back into work. I was sent on leave in Kenya but after working so hard for so long, a weeks's leave felt really strange and I didn't get anything out of it. It wasn't a particularly restful experience because I fell into a bit of a heap.

Everyone reacts differently and I remember feeling an incredible sense of loathing about myself because I hadn't done anything physically to stop what was happening. From a humanitarian aspect, I found my behaviour unacceptable. I don't try to think about that now. I am too disappointed in myself. But we had a lot of people come through us and I am happy with the medical side of things. I will always reflect on the decisions I asked other people to make. I asked the medics to make some very big decisions about who they would bring to me. We couldn't waste resources on people who probably weren't going to make it, so I asked these guys to make some tough decisions. I have probably condemned them to some horrible recriminating thoughts, much like the decisions I had to make back at the Rwandan hospital or the UN hospital in Kigali. That is what you have to do in triage, but I feel terrible for forcing that on other people.

I don't think any of us are too kind to ourselves. Robbie was forever changed by what he saw in Kibeho. I tried for a long time to be there for him and I feel dreadful about how he took it. I wish I had the maturity I have now to help everyone deal with it better. My focus was so much on treating the casualties, but perhaps some of my focus should have been on how my own people were coping. I should have been considering their needs too and not just focusing entirely on the patients.

I immersed myself into work for the rest of the deployment, and we returned home in August. The following year I was doing the underwater medicine course and I received a phone call from my commanding officer. He told me there was an official envelope from the Governor-General for me. I didn't have any idea what that meant so he suggested he open it for me. He read it out to me and my first thought was 'What is gallantry?' I didn't ask him what it meant but he said that I had to let them know whether I would accept it. I remember thinking that there must be some kind of mistake. I felt that you couldn't really give someone a medal if they didn't do everything they should have.

I called my parents and asked them what I should do. It was only after they said that being decorated would ensure that we would never forget what happened in Kibeho or the lives lost that I made up my mind to accept the award. The medal is a reflection of what really happened there. I'm disappointed that the group didn't get a citation. No one was sitting down having a break. We were all working hard. There were some incredible people there with me who should have received medals too.

The day of the investiture was simply a nightmare for me. I was petrified that I would trip over the carpet or do somehting equally as stupid. After all, doctors don't do drill! The ceremony was held in Government House in Canberra. It was an overwhelming yet special day, as we were surrounded by politicians and senior ranking officers. It was also a great day for my parents, who are really just typical parents. I'd told them plenty of things about Rwanda but they just didn't get it, even though their foresight had helped me decide to accept the award. But when my citation was read out, someone was sobbing behind me in the audience. It was my mother! She had absolutely no idea what I'd been through. For her to hear about what happened in this way was very hard for her, but to see their pride in me brought us closer together. Remember, for them, military doctors were mediocre, but according to my decoration, I hadn't been mediocre. It was a great day. I have some great photos and wonderful memories.

In the military, my gender has never been a factor in what I have done. I don't like the attention that I have received because of being a woman and receiving this decoration. I didn't do anything more than any caring doctor would have done; being a female isn't a factor. While I may be the only female to have been awarded a MG, I didn't get it *because* I am female. When someone makes a big deal about it, I get very uncomfortable. I do think my Medal for Gallantry (MG) has opened a few doors for me. I worked as the RMO at Special Air Service Regiment (SASR). Although I suspect they were very desperate for doctors at the time, I think my MG helped them feel a little more comfortable with their choice. Perhaps it demonstrated to them that I wasn't a piker. If the going gets tough, you will look around and see me right there working. If I am hurting, I am not going to let on. I am just going to keep doing my job. At the end, I might say, 'Phew, thank goodness that's over!' but at the time, no-one will know I am hurting!

I hope that this decoration has helped the Australian Defence Force (ADF) in recruitment and retention of personnel. I believe that it shows that the ADF do recognise people and their contribution: we have good people and their efforts don't go unnoticed. What I did was not brave. What we did and saw was terrible; I have no doubt about that. There were many things that happened that I just filed somewhere. We were busy so it was easy to do. However, when someone said, 'Didn't that get to you?' I'd cringe and say, 'Why bring that up now?' It triggered the memories and they'd all come flooding back. The emotions of watching someone in the distance getting beating up — and knowing that by the time you get there to help, it was all over — are really hard to deal with.

If I were truly brave, I would have gone a step further and put myself between the soldier and the person they were going to shoot. That's bravery to me. I didn't do that. All I did was my job. All I did was treat people who needed me to give them medication, tidy up their wounds, or get them to a hospital. The fact that they were shooting around us was irrelevant. These people were in the same circumstances too, but they were the ones being shot at. Every now and then, a bullet would go over my head and ricochet around me and I would think, 'That was a close one'. Nevertheless, what other choice did I have? I couldn't very well hide and not do what I needed to do. I did just what I had been trained to do.

A Captain at the time of the Kibeho massacre, Carol Vaughan-Evans was promoted to Major prior to the investiture ceremony. After returning from Rwanda, Carol saw more overseas service in East Timor with INTERFET and in the Middle East. Dr Vaughan-Evans has since discharged from the Regular Army and is now an anaesthetics registrar at a large tertiary hospital in Queensland. She continues an affiliation with the Australian Defence Force as a Reservist Specialist Officer, and in her spare time she works as a doctor for Careflight.

THE BLACK HAWK TRAINING
ACCIDENT

E VERY GENERATION HAS A PIVOTAL MOMENT; WHEN SOMETHING happens that is so significant that people can remember exactly what they were doing when they heard about it. As a serving officer at the time of the Black Hawk training accident, this is one such event for me. Indeed, the effect that this terrible accident had on the entire defence force was profound. Most people in the Army at that time knew someone who had been killed or injured, and memorial services held throughout Australian Army bases were heavy with emotional outpourings of grief.

Shortly after dusk on 12 June 1996, the largest peace-time disaster to strike Australia's armed forces since the *Voyager* collision in 1964 took place. Six Black Hawk helicopters were involved in a training exercise at the High Range Training Area near Townsville in Queensland. On board the helicopters for the 60 kilometre journey from RAAF Base Townsville to the training area were 24 aircrew from the 5th Aviation Regiment and 43 soldiers from the Special Air Service Regiment (SASR).

The SASR members, the Regiment's current counter-terrorism squadron, were poised for action in harness gear, night-vision goggles, and carrying large amounts of ammunition and explosives. Their mission was to descend in darkness by ropes from the helicopters to take out their targets in a live-fire assault. The men on board knew that the profession of arms carries the ultimate danger. They were not fearless or immune to fear, but they were accepting of the risks involved in their training. During times of peace, the sensible and correct preparation for operations – particularly in the very risky area of counter-terrorism – requires vigorous and realistic training. To achieve real life conditions, members of the SASR and the pilots and crew from the 5th Aviation Regiment are often exposed to a wide variety of elements in training. This training scenario was as authentic as it could possibly be, but was still the kind of operation that the military describes as 'routine'.

As the Black Hawks approached the target area, the SAS men on board all four trooping helicopters were positioning themselves to drop to the ground from the right sides of the aircraft, with weapons and harnesses at the ready. Seconds from their drop zone and 50 metres off the ground, a Black Hawk on the left-hand side of a three-aircraft formation lurched inexplicably to the right, its main rotor hitting the tail of the middle Black Hawk. It crashed to the ground, landing upside down and was consumed almost immediately by fire, killing 13 of the 14 soldiers and crew on board.

The second Black Hawk, also with 10 troopers and four aircrew on board, entered a flat spin after the collision before its pilot crash-landed it in an upright position. Amazingly, 10 men were hauled to safety before it, too, was destroyed by fire. All told, 18 Australian servicemen – 15 from the SASR and three from the 5th Aviation Regiment – perished in the crash and a further 12 were injured, some critically. The fact that they survived is a miracle.

What was to immediately follow could not be planned or prepared for. In the face of this terrible accident, heroic acts were carried out on the ground. The reaction of those alive at the crash scene was cool-headed, courageous, and swift. Despite the confusion that comes with such a collision and the subsequent crashes, along with the danger of flames and exploding ammunition, those at the scene on the ground and in the air acted quickly and decisively to evacuate the injured and save the lives of their colleagues. Their immediate instinct was to save their mates.

As a result of this dreadful accident, soldiers and officers were scarred for life; some physically, others mentally. Three of the survivors, Dominic Boyle, Sergeant Gregory Kirkham and Lieutenant Colonel Jim Ryan, share their stories. Dominic Boyle and Lieutenant Colonel Ryan were members of the SASR at the time of the accident, Dominic as a trooper and Jim as a troop commander. Greg Kirkham was an aircrewman with the 5th Aviation Regiment. For their actions on that evening, Dominic and Greg were awarded the Star of Courage, while Jim was the recipient of a Bravery Medal. Each man has a slightly different recollection of that terrible night.

'A MATTER OF SURVIVAL'

Corporal Dominic Boyle SC

CITATION
STAR OF COURAGE

On the evening of Wednesday 12 June 1996, two Army Black Hawk helicopters from 5 Aviation Regiment collided in mid-air and crashed at the High Range Training Area, south west of Townsville, Queensland, during a training exercise with the Special Air Service Regiment. Black Hawk 1, on crashing to the ground upside down, burst into flames and was quickly engulfed. The second helicopter, Black Hawk 2, crash landed and also rapidly exploded into flames. The situation was made even more hazardous due to live ammunition and explosives being on board the aircraft at the time. Corporal Boyle was aboard Black Hawk 2 when it crashed. Although he sustained a fractured left elbow in the crash, he placed the lives and welfare above his own safety. He made numerous attempts to save those trapped, to free the bodies of those killed in the wreck of the burning fuselage, and to quell the fire with extinguishers. With complete disregard to his own safety, he entered and re-entered the wreckage of Black Hawk 2, despite the added danger of exploding ammunition and devices. When ordered to, he left the wreckage to obtain treatment for his own arm and during the evacuation trip to hospital, performed cardiopulmonary resuscitation on another injured airman. By his actions, Corporal Boyle displayed conspicuous courage.

I WAS BORN IN ENGLAND IN APRIL 1966, AND MY FAMILY MIGRATED to Australia when I was about six months old. My mother's sister was already living in Sydney, so we lived there for a few years. When I was about six years old, my family moved to a small country town called Cygnet, which is south of Hobart in the Huon Valley, one of the largest apple and pear growing regions of Tasmania. I went to a small Catholic school called St James College. Back in those days, schooling for most children only went to Year 10; only the smarter boys went on to do Year 11 and Year 12. Because of our geographical isolation, the boys who wanted to do their senior years needed to go to the big city [Hobart], which was a two-hour bus trip each way, so not many boys went on to do their senior years, including me.

Growing up, when I wasn't at school, I spent all my time in the outdoors, exploring, shooting and hunting around our paddocks, splitting firewood and those kinds of hands-on things that you just have to do on a farm. I had quite a lot of freedom and I loved running around wild as a young lad. That was the norm for kids around where we lived. Our house was surrounded by paddocks on one side and a cliff looking out over the ocean on the other. I remember looking over those cliffs as a young fellow and being excited by the thrill it gave me.

I remember wanting to join the Army from as young as 10 years old. When I left school at 15, I got a job working in a bush timber mill and as a farm hand where I stayed for three years to fill in the time before I could join the Army. The day I turned 18 I went to the recruiting office and enlisted on the spot. I waited until I was 18 because I wanted to sign on the dotted line myself. If I'd been 17, my parents would have had to sign for me. I was always a bit independent, so I did it my way. One month later on 22 May 1984, after having my physical and aptitude tests, I was in the Army.

As far as I knew, all there was to the Army was soldiering; running around the bush with a gun. It wasn't until I arrived at Kapooka that I started to learn that there are other corps in the

Army, like Transport, Catering and Medical. Before then I had no real notion about what the Army really was. I just figured that everyone went to Infantry – although I didn't know what that was at the time. I loved the Army. I was very fit because I had come from the bush where we led a really physical lifestyle. I got the award for 'Top Recruit' for my recruit course because it all came quite naturally to me. I loved every aspect of Army life; running around in the bush, learning about guns, wearing greens. During my recruit course, they asked us which corps we wanted to go to and I said I wanted to go to Infantry.

After marching out of Kapooka, I went to the School of Infantry at Singleton for my Initial Employment Training (IET) course. Again, like my recruit course, I had a great time, learning more about weapons and infantry tactics. I was only 18 years old, and I lapped it up. As far as I was concerned – and this was a thought that wasn't actively discouraged – the only corps in the Army that mattered was Infantry. No other corps mattered at all; they were there to support the Infantry, or so I thought. It wasn't until I was older and wiser and I was in Special Air Service Regiment (SASR) that I realised that the jobs that the other corps do in the Army are equally important. But up until then, as far as I was concerned, anyone not in Infantry was a pogue and we weren't interested in them.

After completing my IET, again topping the course, I was posted to 2nd/4th Battalion, Royal Australian Regiment (2/4 RAR) in Townsville. I arrived in December 1984, just in time to start rear details. I think my first three days were spent dixie-bashing in the Mess, which is a nice way of saying I spent my whole time cleaning dirty plates, pots and pans in the kitchen. It was a great 'welcome to the Army' for all of us! The whole time I was thinking how much it sucked. I ended up staying in the battalion for just over three years until I left to do the selection course for SASR in March 1987. Once I had heard about SASR at Kapooka, I decided then and there that was where I would go. I didn't just want to be good,

I wanted to be the best, and I figured that if I got to SASR, I would be. I never found fitness a big challenge back in those days. I didn't play sport apart from the occasional game of football, but whenever my commanding officer wanted someone to do the cross-country or running or the obstacle course for the company or battalion, I always put up my hand. Physically, I didn't think I had any problems being ready for the selection course. In fact, my build-up training was a trip to New Zealand where I drank for six or seven weeks! Not the best way to prepare for an SAS selection course, but I was so fit and young I thought I would be fine. I had talked to others who had done the course before and they gave me an idea of what to expect.

When I arrived at Swanbourne in Western Australia for the selection course, it was everything I expected it would be. Tough. Hard. Challenging. I was 20 years old. There were a number of Vietnam veterans on staff and they brought a lot of history and character with them. That was something that inspired us all because they were good blokes who had high expectations and we rose to meet those expectations. I knew I would pass the selection course. I had every confidence in myself, but I still found it very challenging. I don't believe anyone who says afterwards that they

think it was challenging. I believe that confidence is 90 per cent of that course. I was physically fit and confident, so that worked in my favour. Yet anyone who came on the selection course who was physically fit but not confident would not pass.

I passed the selection course and was accepted into the Regiment. I went on to the Patrol course, which was interesting in its own way. Admittedly, I had quite an unusual beginning in the Regiment. I got kicked out of the Regiment after 18 months for mucking up and got sent back to the battalion for two years. I loathed being back in Townsville – I should have been in the Regiment. However, I paid my penance. Eventually, they agreed that I could come back after only one year, but I had to do the selection course again. I would have done whatever it took to go back to the Regiment so I did the selection course again in 1991. In a way, it was harder to do it again because, although I knew how to handle the mental side of the course, I also knew what was ahead on the physical side.

Also, they had moved the interrogation component from the Patrol course to the selection course, so I knew that it went for a set period of time and that it was going to be the hardest thing mentally and physically that I would have to do. I guess I was at a disadvantage because I knew just how much it sucked and how much it was going to hurt!

In about 1993, I was selected to go as a detachment with an Australian medical team on deployment in the Solomon Islands. By this stage, I was a Patrol Medic and I got to go with a team of Australian medical personnel to help out. This was part of a project that the Australian government had developed as a way to assist our neighbours in the Pacific. It was a really interesting part of my career. I got to do things as a medic that you would never do or see in an Australian hospital. Odd things, like working with dentists, made the experience really rich. We also worked on an immunisation program for a disease called yaws, which is an infectious, non-venereal disease similar to syphilis. It presents as ulcerative skin lesions, which are unlike anything you could possibly imagine. It occurs mainly in kids under the age of 15 and it is spread by direct contact. None of us had ever seen anything like it before. What made it really sobering is that the Solomon Islands is only a three or so hour flight from Brisbane and here they are with this terrible disease, so close to us.

The Solomon Islands is made up of numerous islands so a lot of our travel was on the Zodiac water craft. Because I had worked with these back in the Regiment, I was the safety and security advisor for those trips. It really was a great trip for me profession- ally. I also was deployed to Rwanda in 1995 and that was a very good trip for me professionally, too. To experience the disaster that had occurred in that country was incredible in itself, and the kinds of things I was seeing as a Medic meant that I faced a very steep learning curve.

Before the Black Hawk training accident, as a regiment we had never contemplated such a catastrophic event on such a scale. There were always stories of what we termed 'near misses'. For example, the year before the accident, a bloke got hurt falling off a rope. Despite all the safety precautions used during the exercises, sometimes accidents just happen. We were doing a dangerous job and we accepted those risks, but no one once thought that such an enormous and traumatic accident like the Black Hawks collision could ever happen.

On the first day of the exercise – which was a live fire exercise – we were working with the Black Hawks from the 5th Aviation Regiment; they were tasked to take us to the target area. We viewed the Black Hawks as taxis, getting us from point A to point B. We would get in, hook ourselves up, wait to be delivered to the target area, and then fast-rope down. We generally don't think about anything until we're told that we are minutes, then seconds, from the target area. That's when we start to go through a mental checklist: Do I have my gloves on? Do I have my strap ready? Is everything clear? Is anything tangled? Then we start to look around to make sure there's no gear caught up with anyone else's. We need to trust others, and in this case we trust the pilots to get us to where we are needed to go safely, so that we can then do our job. We know that they are good pilots because that is their job – they aren't foolish, nor do they take risks with the safety of their crew or their passengers. As their passengers, we are literally blind; we don't know what is going on around us and we trust them and their abilities without question.

On this particular occasion, after we had the two-minute call, we unhooked ourselves. At the 30-second call we checked all our gear, making sure nothing was caught up and that all our equipment was right to go. At approximately 20 seconds out from approaching the target, those of us on the floor of the helicopter were all up on our knees waiting to go. The ropes would have gone out next and we would have then gone down them. But then something happened. In retrospect I'm really glad we were unhooked, because if we were still hooked on when we went down, it would have been even more disastrous.

The first thing, I remember, was a loud noise. Then we veered to one side. At the time, I didn't have any idea that anything was actually wrong. I guess I just thought the pilot sneezed or something! There were six Black Hawks flying in formation, and I was in Black 2. In a normal flight on the way to a target area, it isn't that abnormal to have a look outside at the other helicopters to see what they are doing; but generally you are more interested in what you are doing yourself, and what your team is doing. I remember seeing Black 1 early on in the flight, but once we got going, I can't say that I remember noticing them again. At no stage did it look like any other helicopter was too close.

Next, someone on my left hand side began yelling, 'Oh fuck, oh fuck, oh fuck!' I immediately thought that someone from Alpha 2, our team, had fallen out of the door of the helicopter. Then I heard an almighty crash and a tearing noise. The helicopter seemed to tilt a little bit to the left and then it seemed to steady itself again. I was sitting on the floor at the front between where the two loadmasters are located. There were four guys sitting in a row along the back seat of the aircraft and there was another four or five of us on the floor. Then the aircraft started to fall into a gentle spin. In this time, I managed to go forward on the floor on my hands and knees and grab the leg of the loadmaster's chair. Within seconds the aircraft started to spin quite violently. Things happened very, very quickly from there on.

The helicopter began to do these awful fast spins, the kind of spins that people pay money for at the Show. Whether the helicopter was going around on its main rotor after it lost its rear rotor, I don't know, but the sensation of spinning was very powerful. It felt like my eyes were going to explode. Even at this stage, I couldn't say that we were aware that there was going to be an accident but I do remember that I was sitting on all fours ready to get out of the aircraft. I must have sensed that something was going to happen. I also remember saying to myself that no matter what happens, I will live, and I thought of my wife and kids. I don't remember feeling any fear, but that was because I wasn't really aware of what was going on. It was dark outside and I just figured the pilot was having a bad day. We hadn't upturned or hit the ground yet, so as far as I knew, we were okay.

Then, straight after those spins, we hit the ground with enormous force. The impact was tremendous. I didn't feel any injuries at the time. I had night vision goggles and my helmet on, both of which came down on my face when we hit the ground, and broke my nose badly. I also fractured my left arm and sustained a few little burns on my legs on impact, but I didn't feel that at the time. Even when we hit I didn't realise it was the catastrophe that it ended up being. The aircraft had crashed into the ground in an upright position and I could feel intense heat coming from the flames that had started within seconds of us hitting the ground.

I turned around to look at the rest of the guys who'd been sitting behind me at the back of the helicopter. They were completely crushed in half. I could see the lower parts of their torsos with their legs sitting there just like normal, but the rest of their bodies were gone, completely crushed. The rotor shaft, or the components holding the rotor shaft, had come right down and squashed them. I didn't really notice where the other guys were, who had been sitting on the floor with me. My thoughts were focused on just getting out. It was a matter of survival now.

As I've mentioned, I could feel the flames and heat almost immediately. I got out through the right-hand side door. Gary Proctor had also been on the floor like me, and I think he got out through the left-hand side door. We met up near the front of the wreckage and we noticed the pilot and co-pilot staggering away. Gary and I got a hold of them and we ran up to a big tree that was ahead of us. I don't know why but the big tree looked like a pretty good place to be right then. Then I looked back towards the helicopter and thought, 'Holy shit.' Even then, though, it still didn't seem to be as bad as it turned out. I knew that there were the four guys dead at the back of the aircraft, but I figured that was it for fatalities. Everyone else would have been able to get out and were going to be fine.

I'm not sure why, but I didn't even notice the other Black Hawk. I only ever noticed the remains of our helicopter. We asked our pilot, Dave Burke, if he thought it would be safe to go back to the aircraft but I can't remember his answer. Regardless, Gary and I ran back to the wreckage to see if there was anyone else who needed help getting out. Before leaving the tree, I took off all my gear – my helmet, night vision goggles, rifle, and gun belt.

A lot of people were beginning to mill around by now; obviously they were the safety observers and ground staff for the exercise. As we approached the wreckage of our helicopter we could see that the loadmaster was stuck, so we got him out. Then I went back to the right-hand door and Gary ran around to the other side. All I can remember seeing then was a pair of legs of another person who had been crushed inside the fuselage. I found out later that it was Michael Bird. I climbed back inside the helicopter and came across Glen Sutton, who was unconscious. I dragged him out, and he regained consciousness just as I was passing him to the other people who had come to help out, waiting at the door of the wreckage. Then I went back inside. I grabbed Russell French who was also unconscious, and passed him out too.

By now the flames were getting quite hot and I yelled out for a fire extinguisher because I wasn't able to see any more bodies that I could reach. Bob McCabe passed me one of those little extinguishers that you use in your car or boat. I climbed back inside and sprayed the back right-hand side of the wreckage. I used that one up pretty quickly and then called for another. While I was spraying I remember ammo going off everywhere, but I didn't think that I was in danger. After a while I think I just got used to it and stopped hearing it, but I know now that there were many explosions the whole time. I certainly wasn't thinking about whether they were going to hurt me, though.

By the time I emptied the second extinguisher the flames were out of control throughout the wreckage and they didn't look as though they were going to settle down. I know I tried to grab Michael again because I wanted to get him out before the flames took hold. I knew he was dead; he had to have been because he was completely crushed from his upper torso upwards and only his legs were sticking out. I tried to grab him with my one good arm and other guys from the squadron were behind me outside the aircraft, pulling on me like a daisy chain as we tried to use our weight to pull his body out. But he was totally pinned.

I think there were two other bodies that were trapped too, but I could tell they were dead. That was six fatalities that I knew of. It was really horrible, but we still tried to get them out because you wanted to know that you did everything you could. I didn't want them left inside to burn.

However, people started to pull me out because it was getting really hot and we knew we weren't going to get anyone else out. Since the accident I've been asked many times about the guys we couldn't get out. We did the best we could and even now there is no doubt in my mind that there was no one left alive inside before we pulled back. The entire rescue took no more than two or three minutes in total. Due to the intense heat and the increasing amount of exploding ammunition, I had to get out of the wreckage, too.

After we had pulled back, I looked around to see what I could do next. I saw George Taulelei doing cardiopulmonary resuscitation on one of the guys from Black 1. That was when I realised that another helicopter had been involved as well. George told me that Black 1 went down too and there were only a couple of survivors. That was when I first started to appreciate the seriousness of what had happened. I realised that it had all turned out quite badly.

I helped George work on him for a while and then I treated another one or two others who were nearby. Then three other guys came over and took over doing the cardiopulmonary resuscitation [on the soldier from Black 1] while I held the torch for them. But all attempts to establish an airway were futile – it turned out that his airway had been torn from his lungs in the crash. He just wasn't getting any oxygen. We thought we had the artificial airway in incorrectly, so we were constantly reinserting it to try to get it in right. We tried really hard on him. We soon ran out of oxygen so I ran to the ambulance because I knew they had two of the large oxygen cylinders on board. I tried to get one out but I couldn't because my left arm was now almost useless. I ran over to Pete Green and told him that the guys needed some more oxygen for the Black 1 soldier they were treating. He said he would take care of it, and that I would be on the next chopper out.

The whole time I was on the ground, everyone was so professional and dedicated, either working on the dead or wounded or organising stretcher parties, or evacuation flights. No one was giving up on anybody. I didn't see Gary Proctor again until we were on the helicopter together, being evacuated. When we got on board there was another body in there and he looked dead; he was blue and cold. Gavin Bone, a squadron medic, was working on someone else on board so Gary and I started doing CPR on the guy who looked dead. He appeared to have a tension pneumothorax, so I started putting in a thoracic needle in the hope that it would reverse the problem in his lungs, and then kept going with the CPR. Eventually, I began to realise that my arm was broken and said to Gary that I had to stop because I couldn't put any pressure on it anymore. That was a really difficult thing to say.

We landed on a huge oval near the Townsville General Hospital and the thing that struck me immediately was the amount of media waiting for us to arrive. They'd obviously heard about the accident and were taking photos of the bodies on stretchers and shoving microphones under our noses asking us all kinds of ridiculous questions about the crash. What really ticked me off about it is that we hadn't even had a chance to call our wives at home to say that we were still alive. I can't imagine how a wife of one of the dead or injured would have felt about not being told before the media knew. I certainly didn't want my wife Carolyn to find out that way. I hated the idea that they were going to broadcast scenes from the accident on television when I didn't even know the full extent of it. I was involved in the bloody thing. I said, 'What the hell are they doing here? Can't we get rid of them?' All the families at home would know from the reports is that two Black Hawks crashed and that people were killed. They weren't going to know which Black Hawk their loved one was on, and they would be frantic until they heard from them. It just wasn't right. All those family members would be waiting for phone calls from their husband or boyfriend. And for most, the phone calls they were going to get weren't going to be the kind they wanted.

When I was finally able to call Carolyn, I just said, 'Don't panic, I'm alive. You're going to hear something but I am okay.' She just thought I was drunk or something! Then, a little while later, a padre pulled up at her house and that really confused her. Wives always know that if a padre turns up at your front door, something terrible has happened, and although Carolyn had heard me say I was fine, she didn't know what was going on. I hadn't told her anything else over the phone so she was completely in the dark. The padre told Carolyn what had happened and she was on the next plane to Townsville along with the commanding officer of SASR and another wife, Tracey Bampton. Tracey was yet to find out whether her husband, Gerry Bampton, was going to live or die because he was one of the more seriously injured men we rescued from Black 1.

It wasn't until we got to the hospital that I learned more about Black 1 and that they had only dragged out one guy alive. That was when we all started to realise that we had lost a lot of good blokes that night. When we hit the ground, the impact was so hard that many guys on board died of major injuries to their internal organs. From the outside they looked fine, as though nothing was wrong with them, but later in surgery or in autopsies it showed that they had been killed by massive internal damage. In many cases, they had probably already died despite anything that anyone did for them, either up at High Range or in hospital. There was just nothing that we could have done for them.

Then we started to piece together who had made it and who hadn't. That was pretty tough. The staff in the hospital were amazing, though. They had never had anything of this magnitude come in before, but they looked after us so well. They even looked after the wives as they arrived. Carolyn didn't even need to leave the ward. If she wanted a coffee or something to eat, someone would go across the street to the shop for her, or the coffee shop owner would bring things over. I don't think we can ever really thank the staff or the people of Townsville enough for their support.

The whole night seemed so surreal, so unrealistic. It felt like we were doing things in slow motion. But everything went in perfect clockwork: there was no yelling or screaming out and, even more importantly, there was no panicking. Everyone seemed to instinctively know what they needed to do and worked together. Some went inside the burning wreckage, others carried bodies away from the site, others treated the wounded, while others set up and coordinated the landing zone for the evacuation helicopters. The atmosphere was sombre and dark, but everything came together, which no doubt resulted in saving the lives of several of the urvivors that night.

I have no idea who nominated me for the Star of Courage. It may have been as a result of a culmination of everyone's statements of the event. One of the first things we were asked to do after the accident was write a statement of what had happened. Carolyn made sure I wrote my own personal account. I guess they looked at everyone's statements to work out who would get awards. But I feel that everyone should have been awarded something because everyone played an important role. Maybe the squadron should have been given an award. They may not have been going inside the burning wreckage, but they were doing something equally as important, like organising the evacuation flights and coordinating the treatment of the wounded and the dead. No one did anything more significant than anyone else. The investiture was pretty good, though – it was great to see everyone because I hadn't been back to work at that stage because of my injuries. It was a very sombre occasion.

I certainly don't think that what I did was out of the ordinary or brave. Anyone would have done what I did if they were in my position. I would do it again tomorrow, too, in the same circumstances. When I ran back into the helicopter, I didn't think my life was in danger. I do remember asking Gary, 'Wait, is that going to blow?' and we asked the pilots (who we took to the tree) and they thought that it might. But we still went back down there because our blokes were in there. They were trapped and someone needed to get them out whether they were alive or dead. I was simply using my soldierly instinct, I guess; you are taught to act on instinct and that was all I was doing. That's why I say that anyone else in my position – any other soldier – would have done the same thing.

To me, when you look at World War I veterans going 'over the wall' knowing full well that they were going to be killed, that is brave. They weren't doing it for any particular reason, they weren't getting any more pay, they weren't protecting their family. As soon as they got the whistle, up they went to face an almost certain death, or at least be seriously wounded with no chance of recovery. That's bravery. There wasn't a major catastrophe or drama; they just woke up one morning and knew that was the day they were probably going to die. But they still did it. I think it takes far more balls to run over a wall knowing that you are going to die.

In our incident, it happened; we were there; and we had to do something. I think the blokes who watched the accident happen and then ran in to help are brave. But someone like me, who was involved in it, and really didn't have any idea about the true circumstances, shouldn't consider themselves brave. Perhaps if I had known the true dangers and just how serious a tragedy it actually was and I still did what I did, well, maybe I would feel differently. Remember, as far as I knew, it was only my aircraft involved. I think anyone else in the same position would have done the same too.

I truly believe that the pilot on our helicopter, Dave Burke, is a hero. He saved my life. He was able to, somehow, keep that helicopter under control enough to bring it in to land right side up. In doing so, he saved all of our lives. If he had panicked after we'd been hit by Black Hawk 1, I know I probably wouldn't be here now. I'd be just like the rest of the guys who didn't make it, never getting to see their wives and kids again.

Dominic Boyle lives with his wife, Carolyn, and their three children, Thomas, Jessica and Olivia, in Western Australia. He is no longer serving in the Australian Defence Force (ADF). He keeps in occasional contact with other survivors of the Black Hawk training accident, most of whom are also no longer members of the ADF.

'No one deserves to burn'

Corporal Gregory Clifton Kirkham SC

CITATION
STAR OF COURAGE

On the evening of Wednesday 12 June 1996, 2 Army Black Hawk helicopters from 5 Aviation Regiment collided in mid-air and crashed at the High Range Training Area, south west of Townsville, Queensland, during a training exercise with the Special Air Service Regiment. Corporal Kirkham ran to the wreck of Black Hawk 1 which was upside down and burning fiercely. He discovered a badly injured soldier in the doorway of the aircraft and using a pocket knife began to cut him free of his harness. He was soon joined by another member who assisted him in dragging the casualty clear of the burning wreck. Despite the great danger to himself from fire and exploding ordnance, Corporal Kirkham again entered the wreck in search of survivors. This he did on at least four occasions, each time clearing his way by removing bodies and throwing explosives clear. He found another survivor and assisted in moving him to safety. At one stage, Corporal Kirkham deliberately placed himself against the fire to shield other rescuers from the heat as they moved through the wreck. By his actions, Corporal Kirkham displayed considerable courage.

I WAS BORN IN SOUTH AUSTRALIA IN 1959 AND GREW UP WITH one brother, Lindsay, and two sisters, Lynette and Judy. We lived in a little railway cottage in a tiny place called Avenue Range, which was really just a one-shop town. Our nearest neighbour was about 300 metres away and the neighbour after that was another kilometre or so away.

Our family wasn't a military family like a lot of others at the time. Both my father and my uncle served in World War II, but we weren't military-minded. Joining the Army was just something I wanted to do. When I was a little kid my teacher asked the class what we wanted to be when we grew up. When it was my turn I said I wanted to be a war hero! What I meant was that I wanted to be in the Army because to me, all Army men were heroes.

I joined the Army as soon as I turned 17. I did only just over 12 months the first time before I was forced to discharge as there were family problems and I had to go home to look after my mother. I missed the Army a lot, so in 1981 I joined the Army Reserves and stayed on for six years, making Corporal by the time left. I was a pretty good shot, so I was always going away as part of the shooting team to competitions. I loved that. After a while I figured that if I was going to do so much with the Reserves part-time, then I might be better off getting back into the full-time Army again. They say you get green blood after being in the Army for a while! The Army was a good life and I never really settled after leaving in the first place.

When I re-enlisted, I had to redo elements of the Infantry basic course and it wasn't long before I was posted back to Infantry Corps and posted to the 1st Battalion, Royal Australian Regiment (1RAR) in Townsville. I started off as a Digger [private soldier] in Charlie Company. By the end of the first exercise in 1982, I was acting section second-in-command (2IC) and it was not long after that that I was fully promoted back to Corporal and running the heavy weapons section. I really liked that posting and stayed there until about 1990. But around then I was looking for something different and helicopters really appealed to me. I submitted my application to Corps Transfer for the Aviation Corps in 1989. At the time, I had wanted to be an observer on Kiowa helicopters. I did all the testing for that job and got through it all with no problems. One day, the career advisor for Aviation Corps told me he wasn't able to get me on the observer's course for nine months, which meant that I would have had to wait in my current job at 1RAR until the next course started. I was a bit disappointed but he said he was able to get me on a course as a loadmaster in a couple of weeks' time. Admittedly, I had no real idea of what a loadmaster did and whether it would be something I would like. When I learned about it, though, I thought it sounded fantastic. I agreed and did the course, and that's what I have been doing now for 15 years.

Being a loadmaster has got to be the best job an other rank can have in the Army. I love it; it's a real highlight in my career. A loadmaster gets quite a lot of responsibility, a lot more than someone wearing the same rank in some other corps. I love the fact that there is some freedom of action. There is no one standing over you, telling you what to do. The loadmaster looks after any internal and external loads, and any hoisting; that kind of thing. But perhaps the most important thing we do is ensure the safety of the aircraft. In a nutshell, it is our job to stop the aircraft from hitting anything. I know I have made calls where we would have taken off the top of a tree with the helicopter blades while we were tree-top flying had I not let the pilot know. Without those calls, there would have been collisions. It's a big responsibility.

There is not one person who can see everything from inside an aircraft. That's why we are called a 'crew'. Between us, the loadmasters and pilots, we ensure that the aircraft and everyone on board is safe. If you have ever watched a helicopter like a Black Hawk come in to land, you will have seen it go in with its back rotor down and its nose up in the air, so it is coming in tail down. When this happens, the pilot is basically looking straight up in the sky. He can look down through the chin bubble and through the side window to see what is going on below the aircraft to some degree, but essentially he is facing upwards to the sky. Where the loadmaster sits, in the back of the aircraft, we can see where we are landing because we can look down from our position. While we are landing, the loadmaster gives a running commentary on what is happening around and below the aircraft and where they want the aircraft to land because the pilot can't see. In effect, the pilot wants the aircraft to go where the loadmaster says it should go. When that responsibility is not shouldered by the loadmaster it can be disastrous.

On the night of the Black Hawk training accident, I was loadmaster on one of the six helicopters in the assault. I was in one of the two spotting helicopters that were tasked to cover the target site before the arrival of the four trooping helicopters flying behind us in formation. Our aircraft was on the right of the pair that crashed and I was sitting on the right-hand side of the aircraft. The target area was not on my side of the aircraft so I was calling the aircraft in to the site where we wanted it to stop. I didn't see what happened that night because of where I was sitting.

As we were flying, the emergency locator, situated on the right-hand side of the aircraft near me, went off. Initially that didn't trigger any concern for us on board because it would happen every now and again. Then, almost immediately after the locator went off, one of the guys on another chopper yelled across the radio, 'Helo down, check fire, check fire'. When I heard it, I looked out my side to see if I could see anything but there wa nothing. So I pulled my head back into the cabin of the aircraft and looked out the door on the left-hand side of the cabin. I could see that there were two balls of fire behind us. I don't know if they were in the air or on the ground as it was completely dark which makes it difficult to distinguish between ground and sky. And that was it, two Black Hawks had crashed in mid-air. It was something that we always hope won't ever happen – but it had, right behind us.

We were carrying medics on board as part of the safety element of the exercise, so the pilots wanted to get the aircraft on the ground to get the medics to the crash site. The other loadmaster and I called the aircraft in to a safe landing site about 150 metres from the crash site. The spotters from Special Air Service Regiment (SASR) on our aircraft were wearing infra-red night vision devices so as soon as our aircraft hit the ground, they took off towards the crash site. It was pretty dark and the area that we landed in was covered with huge boulders and ditches, so I said I would take the medics over to the site. I grabbed my big torch, which we always carry on the aircraft, and I led them across.

Once we got close enough, the light from the burning aircraft was enough to see by so the medics disappeared off to the first burning wreck. Just as I was going to head back to my aircraft, I noticed that there were heaps of people working on the helicopter that had come down first [Black 2] but there was no one at the other wreck [Black 1]. I ran over to that wreckage to see if I could do anything.

The wreck of Black 1 was upside down and on fire when I got there. The cabin where the passengers and crew sit was quite squashed. The top of the aircraft looked to be caved in and I thought to myself that there was no way there could be anyone alive in there. Nevertheless, I went around to the low side of the wreckage and one of the guys was lying there with his head hanging out of the loadmaster's window. I still had all my flying gear on because I hadn't thought to take anything off. I reached in through the window and tried to find a pulse on his neck but couldn't feel anything. Then I noticed I was still wearing my gloves. so I ripped them off and tried again. His skin was actually quite cold and I couldn't feel anything, so I began to crawl in through the broken window and as I went past, I tried for a pulse again. Thi time I could feel one.

When I tried to get him out, I noticed there was someone else lying across his legs, and they were holding him down. I went in further to get that guy off his legs and then pulled him around so that he was in the loadmaster's window. But I got to the point where I couldn't pull him any further out as he was a big guy and he seemed stuck. I started yelling at the top of my lungs for someone to come and help me, which got the adrenaline pumping, and then I managed to get him out a bit further so that I had his bum out but his legs and head was still inside the aircraft window.

Then Michael Williams (Willy) came around to where I was and began helping me. As we were pulling him, I noticed his harness was still connected and that was why I wasn't able to pull him out myself. Using my pocket knife, I began to cut through the harness. The spot where I chose to cut was the thickest part of the harness, close to four times the normal thickness of other parts of the harness. Under normal circumstances, it would have taken about half an hour to cut through that section of the harness with my pocket knife, but I had so much adrenaline going through me at that stage that I cut through it in one go with my little pocket knife! It was incredible. I threw the knife on the ground and dragged him out. We checked that he still had a pulse and dragged him away from the aircraft and lay him down on his side as best we could into the recovery position. Then Willy and I went back in to the wreckage for more people.

I crawled back in through the fuselage, looking for a pulse on every body I found. There were just so many piled on top of each other; we just kept dragging them out. Eventually, we couldn't get any more out from that side of the wreckage. I was in the process of running around to the other side of the aircraft when I tripped over someone who was lying outside the aircraft near the other loadmaster's window. I knelt down to grab him by the shoulders so that I could turn him over to check for a pulse, but as I did, I realised that there was no point because he was missing his head. Right then was probably the lowest I felt the whole time.

Willy and I dragged him away from the aircraft and put him down some distance away so at least he wouldn't burn. Then we tried to get in through the other side of the wreckage, but there were cables and all kinds of things blocking the loadmaster's window. I had to race back around to where I had dropped my knife earlier and then race back to Willy where he was trying to get through the mess blocking the window. Normally you never see wires, cables and other items inside the cabin of the aircraft, but they had obviously dislodged as a result of the accident and were hanging down from the walls and floor that was now the ceiling. Again, with my little pocket knife, I somehow managed to cut through steel tubing and pipes, got them out of the way, and began to get guys out from that side. The second last guy we got out was Gerry Bampton. He is now a paraplegic in a wheelchair, but he is alive.

The strange thing is that, from the moment I arrived at the aircraft to when the fire had gone all the way through the aircraft, fully igniting it, I was there for only four minutes. That was all it took before it was totally engulfed. When I got that first pulse, I wa pretty happy because I truly thought that there was no way anyone could have survived that crash; the aircraft was upside down, on fire, and there were bodies everywhere. I thought there was no way anyone was going to be alive. After that, it was just a case of getting them out. We needed to get each one out to get to the next one, and no one deserves to burn in something like that. Unfortunately, we couldn't get out one of the pilots and one or two of the guy from the back in the cabin area before the fire took hold, but we tried everything we could.

This was a live fire exercise so all of the troopers on board were loaded up to the teeth with all kinds of ammunition and it wa exploding everywhere. I could hear it popping all around me the whole time. Some of the guys were also carrying explosive door charges as well. These charges are about 40 centimetres wide and one metre long, designed to blow a hole in a door large enough for them to step through. The charges were primed up, ready to be used, so as we came across them, we would throw them out of the aircraft so they wouldn't go off while we were inside. We were trying to throw all the other ammo we came across as far from the aircraft as possible as well.

Even though everything was so chaotic and noisy all around us, I was able to forget about it because my main focus was getting the guys out. But towards the end, what looked like a big hand of fire burst through the loadmaster's window. Seeing it is something I will remember forever because it was such an eerie and strange sight. The fire just seemed to leap through the window and went straight to a magazine that was full of ammo, which caught fire instantly. Once that happened there was no way anyone could get back in there.

We stood back some distance from the wreckage and watched it burn. Then I looked around for something else to do. I went over to where some guys were treating Gerry. It looked like his arm was broken and he was clearly a bit of a mess but I helped out where I could. We tried to get a stretcher to get Gerry to the triage area that had been set up a little further away but by the time we managed to find one, it had been decided that he needed to be taken straight to the awaiting aircraft which then flew him back to hospital in Townsville.

After that, I just sat down on the ground, took my helmet off, and had a smoke. Until then I'd been in the process of giving up cigarettes but by the time I got back to Townsville later that night, I only had a couple left out of a full packet. Everyone was smoking. Even guys I know who don't smoke – who haven't had one before and haven't had one since – were smoking that night. What I find interesting now, on reflection, is that no one was talking about what had just happened. It was all very quiet; there wasn't much conversation at all. I think I asked how many survivors there were from Black 2, but no one knew how many had been killled or how many had got out alive. It was impossible to estimate because people were beng treated at the triage point and then being whisked off to hospital, or going straight from the crash site onto a chopper and back to hospital.

Sometime later, we decided we had better check further away rrom the crash site just to ensure that there had not been anyone who had been thrown away from the aircraft before they crashed. Fortunately we didn't find anyone. We swept the area out to about 60 metres before we all agreed that no one would have crawled any further than that, or have been thrown any further. All the aircraft were now ferrying the casualties back to Townsville until there was no one left who needed treatment. Once my aircraft came back, I jumped on board. I remember on the flight back to RAAF Townsville thinking about my wife, Narelle, and wondering whether she had heard about it. When we got back, the guys said that it had been on the news already and I cringed and thought, 'That's all I need!' I found a phone and rang her. She had been ringing the unit, but they were not able to tell her if I was alive or dead. They wouldn't even tell her whether I was involved in any way and I think that freaked her out even more. But she was extremely happy and relieved to get that phone call from me when I eventually got through to her.

As I've mentioned, earlier that night I had tripped over a decapitated body which I thought belonged to one of the loadmasters. Once I had rung home, I went back to the helmet room, and as I walked in, there he was, that loadmaster, standing right in front of me. I very nearly hit the bloody floor in disbelief. I was completely and utterly shocked to see him standing there because I'd been sure it had been him that I dragged away from the wreckage, dead. But it turned out it had been someone else. Little things like that happened a bit over the next 24 hours. Once we finally learned who had been injured and who had been killed, we all sat around and talked about the guys who were not coming to work that day. It was pretty sad because we lost a lot of good men that night.

About 12 months later, I received a letter stating that I had been nominated for the Star of Courage, which left me dumbfounded. I didn't know who had nominated me or who had seen me doing anything that night. I just figured that a lot of people had received similar letters saying that they, too, had been nominated. As it turned out, there were only three of us who got the Star of Courage (SC).

Without a doubt, I think it should have been more but I don't make those decisions.

The investiture at Government House was okay. It was good seeing the guys again but it brought back a lot of memories that were not very pleasant. I felt a bit strange to be getting such a high award when there were other guys there who should have been getting something higher than a Bravery Medal. I am not saying a Bravery Medal isn't a great thing, but I think they deserved more than that. I really had mixed feelings about the whole day and struggled to come to terms with why I was being awarded the Star of Courage. It just didn't seem fair to give such different awards to people. We were *all* there that night working our guts out to save lives.

I don't think being awarded the SC has changed me at all. I am still Kirky and always will be. I don't like wearing my medal because people see it and always ask what it is and why it was awarded to me. I guess I hate having to tell them the story over and over again because of the memories that come with it; I think it also makes me out to be something that I am not. I didn't do anything different to a lot of other people did that night. If you are as familiar around aircraft as I am you would have done the same thing. My actions were not something special. Rather, the circumstances meant that I had to do what I did.

Some people have said that I was the first one to the aircraft but wasn't. One of the Black Hawk crew members got there first and pulled one of the chicken stranglers [SASR troopers] away, but unfortunately he later died. I was the next one on the scene but I guess I screamed and yelled for someone to come and help me, and started getting people out. I would not have expected the chicken stranglers to get in there like me because they don't know the aircraft as well as I do. I don't think I went beyond what someone else would have done with my experience.

To me, courage and bravery is the same thing. Courage is when you know what you are about to do is going to be dangerous and life threatening and you think about those consequences and do it anyway. I have heard about people receiving the Star of Courage or the Bravery Medal and I think they deserve those awards so much more than me. They would have thought, 'I can get killed doing this' and done it anyway. That is courage – that is bravery. But that didn't really happen that night for me because there was no time to think about the consequences. It was just a case of Willy and me getting the guys out as quickly as possible. A lot of things happen where you don't have time to think about it. That night, I was too busy doing my job to think about any consequences at all.

I still don't like to talk about that night and I am surprised at just how emotional I get if I do. It was a pretty dramatic event and the saddest thing is that a lot of good guys didn't survive that night. We need to soldier on, but always remember them.

Sergeant Greg 'Kirky' Kirkham still lives in Townsville with his wife and children. The Black Hawk training accident of 1996 has not dampened his enthusiasm for flying, nor for Black Hawks, despite still suffering some lingering injuries. His home is adorned with prints, photographs and other aviation memorabilia and he talks fondly of flying and of his Corps. He is now posted to a training position in his unit and is responsible for training new loadmasters in the ways of the sky.

'I WANTED TO HELP MY MATES OUT'

Captain James Augustus Ryan BM

CITATION

BRAVERY MEDAL

On the evening of Wednesday 12th June 1996, two Army Black Hawk helicopters from 5th Aviation Regiment collided in mid-air and crashed at the High Range Training Area, south-west of Townsville, Queensland, during a training exercise with the Special Air Service Regiment. Black Hawk 1, on crashing to the ground upside down, burst into flames and quickly engulfed. The second Black Hawk, Black Hawk 2, crash landed and also rapidly exploded into flames. The situation was made even more hazardous due to live ammunition and explosives being on the aircraft at the time. Captain Ryan was one of the first men at the crash site. He showed complete disregard for his personal safety placing himself in great danger in his numerous attempts to remove those trapped and the bodies of those killed in the wreck of the burning fuselage. The added danger of exploding ammunition and devices did not dissuade him in his endeavours and he was directly responsible for the successful rescue of a number of the injured and the recovery of the bodies of those killed. Despite sustaining burns to his face during these rescue actions, Captain Ryan persisted with his efforts to save lives and free bodies. By his actions, Captain Ryan displayed considerable bravery.

I WAS BORN IN SYDNEY IN DECEMBER 1965. WE HAD A FAIRLY mobile family when I was young and we moved from Sydney to country New South Wales and then back to Sydney again when I was in early primary school. We didn't have a particularly military family. My father had been called up for National Service, but no one else in my family had served in the military.

I got into the Army way of things when I joined the Army Cadets at Waverley College. When I moved to St Joseph's College, I joined their Army Cadet unit as well. I really enjoyed it because it was a bit like the boy scouts in a way. It was always a lot of fun. I enjoyed being outdoors and doing all the things that cadets got to do. After I finished high school at St Joseph's College, I went to Sydney University where I spent the next four years of my life doing an engineering degree. I also joined the Army Reserve unit at the university, the Sydney University Regiment, because the Reserves was a great way to help pay my way through my degree and I could have a good time as well. Unfortunately, my university career came to an abrupt end when I realised that I wasn't going to pass! I liked the university's social side of life too much, I think. I was really interested in and enjoyed what I was doing at Army Reserves though, and decided I could probably make a career out of it. I decided to join the regular Army.

I applied and was accepted to begin training as a General Service Officer. I went to Royal Military College (RMC) at Duntroon and undertook the 18-month-long course there. Since then, my career has taken off. Looking back, I know now that I made the right decision. I don't see that I wasted four years of my life at university; I enjoyed my time there and I think it helped me mature. By the time I was at RMC, I was more focused on my future and a little older and wiser to the ways of the world too.

I enjoyed my time at RMC although it was a pretty intense course. I was fortunate, I think, by having spent so much time in the Reserves and Army Cadets prior to going – I knew how to polish my boots, how to march and do all those military things before I got there. Even so, it was still a huge shock to the system. At the end of my training, I was allocated to the Infantry Corps, which is what I certainly wanted. When I was in the Sydney University Regiment, it functioned as an infantry unit and I enjoyed all that kind of work; the lifestyle and the physical aspects. I don't think I would have enjoyed the other corps nearly as much.

Straight after RMC, I went to the Regimental Officers Basic Course (ROBC), which prepares newly commissioned officers for their corps appointment. The Infantry ROBC course is held in Singleton in New South Wales. When I completed that course, I was posted as a platoon commander to the 1st Battalion, Royal Australian Regiment (1RAR) in Townsville, which was where I was to spend the next two and a half years. I thoroughly enjoyed my time in 1RAR. There is something about your first platoon and your first battalion that stays with you forever. We didn't go on any operations overseas, but nonetheless I still had a great time. We had some wonderful company and battalion commanders so I was very fortunate.

It wasn't until I was settled in to 1RAR that I began to consider the Special Air Service Regiment (SASR). At the time, it seemed that everyone around me – my soldiers and other officers – were training for the selection course. The infantry battalion is a breeding ground for SAS soldiers. You could see just how hard the guys had to train, just to get to the selection course. I really liked that focus and figured that I should have a go at the selection course, too. There were a couple of ex-SAS guys who did their officer training while I was at RMC and they subsequently became good friends of mine. Next, it was a matter of finding the best time to start training because there are always other ongoing courses, exercises and commitments that can take you away from the preparation needed to get ready. When I was a young lieutenant I was pretty fit; I played football for the battalion. But I was never one of those super-fit guys who just seem naturally able to endure intensive physical training, so I had to train really hard.

Before I went on the selection course, an old ex-SAS Colonel gave me the best bit of advice. He said there were three key things that you needed to remember. Firstly, to maintain your sense of humour. Because nasty things are going to happen to you, you have to try to see the funny side of it. A sense of humour helps you to overcome adversity. I didn't realise just how significant that was until later in my career, after the Black Hawk accident. A sense of humour is very important to a soldier in the SASR.

The second thing, he said, was to look after your feet because the course itself is incredibly wearing on your muscles, but particularly your feet. There are always the most horrific foot injuries during the course, so if you don't take care of them, you won't be able to finish. And if you don't finish, you don't make it into the Regiment.

The third thing he said to me was to be there on the last day of the course. No matter how bad you feel, if you aren't there on the last day, you can't be selected. It doesn't matter what happens during the course, it's important to be there on that last day to give yourself the best shot of getting in. If you aren't selected, well . . . that is the way Special Forces operate.

In 1993, I completed the selection course and got selected, and then went straight on to the patrol course. It was pretty tough. At least half the guys failed that course, including me! I was invited to go back the following year to re-qualify and I passed it on my second attempt, and then did my parachute course straight after that, joining the Regiment in 1995.

Just after my parachute course, I had a knee reconstruction. I didn't try to hide the injury throughout the patrol course and the parachute course like some people do, and I did have some problems, particularly with parachute landings, but I would just try to ignore them so that I could complete the course. As a result of my operation, I wasn't available to do any serious work in the Regiment, so I was posted to the Operation and Support Squadron as the 2IC (second-in-command). I was there for six months while my knee healed. It was a very interesting place to work as it dealt with the inside workings of the Regiment itself and I learned a lot. At the end of June 1995, I was then moved to the squadron that was involved in counter-terrorism training.

One of the training exercises we took part in involved the Black Hawk accident. We were working with the 5th Aviation Regiment in a live fire attack on a simulated target in the High Range Training Area, near Townsville. Those on board were kitted up with massive amounts of ammunition and explosives, so the mission itself was inherently dangerous. What we do for a living is hazardous, and we have to make our training as realistic as possible so that if the proverbial hits the fan we all know that we are capable of responding appropriately. But the Regiment doesn't take high risks just for the sake of it, or without measures in place to try to minimise risk to life as much as possible. For example, I was employed as a safety officer for the live fire assault, as were four others, and we also had an officer-in-command practice and a safety net communicator. We were located on the ground to the south of the fire support base where the assault was to occur. Our job was to minimise risk of injury or worse to those conducting the assault.

At approximately 1845 hours, we could make out the aircraft approaching from the south. As it was a dark night with no moon, we couldn't see them, but could hear them approaching the target; I could hear the mortar rounds hitting about 500 metres from our position. There were six helicopters in total in the assault, but only four contained the troops. The other two had another purpose and they were further away from the main body of aircraft. When the helicopters were about 50 to 100 metres to our west and flying at around 50 metres off the ground, we saw the collision between two of the lead helicopters. As it was totally dark, the first thing we saw was sparks as the blades of one Black Hawk cut into the fuselage of the other, and then one dropped from the sky in flames. The second helicopter, Black 2, did not crash until a short time later when its pilot was able to crash-land it a little further away. The group I was on the ground with moved forward to the first helicopter as it was closest to us.

The first thing I remember when we arrived at Black 1 was that there was no noise at all. The tail was on fire and there was also a really strong smell of aviation fuel in the air. The helicopter had landed on its roof, and the side we approached from was crushed down to about knee to waist height. As safety officers we began to search inside the aircraft for any survivors with our torches, not really knowing what we would find.

Once inside, I could see equipment, bodies, and weapons strewn throughout what was left of the cabin. We were really worried because we knew that the explosives each of the teams carried on board were primed and ready to go, and combined with leaking aviation fuel we knew it was only a matter of time before the wreckage exploded. We began pulling bodies from the aircraft as quickly as we could.

I worked my way to the front of the aircraft and pulled a number of bodies out of the fuselage before dragging them clear of the wreckage site. Because of the impact of the helicopter landing on its roof, the interior cabin was squashed almost flat, which meant that we were literally on our hands and knees reaching well inside the cavity of the aircraft just to reach people. The whole time I was inside there were ammunition rounds going off, just kind of popping all around me.

I didn't find anyone alive, and most of the bodies I retrieved had quite severe injuries. The only body I recall in particular was one of our guys. He was one of the first we got out when we arrived. We dragged him 20 metres or so from the crash site in case the helicopter blew but he had such devastating injuries that we knew he was dead. Even so, we checked and rechecked him to be sure. Once we had cleared the aircraft and found no one alive, we moved away because the aircraft was now well and truly alight and there was ammunition exploding in it quite regularly by now. At this stage, I noticed that the other helicopter, Black 2, was about 20 metres in front of us and was also engulfed in flames.

Captain Wayne Bowen was the first member of the Army to receive the Star of Courage since its inception in 1975.

Captain Wayne Bowen receiving his Star of Courage in 1983 from the Governor-General, Sir Ninian Stephens.

Local Rwandans walk on a dirt track in the displaced persons camp in Kibeho, 1995. In the background are lines of makeshift huts constructed from sticks, mud and plastic.

An Australian Soldier of the Australian Medical Support Force standing amid the remains of the camp in Kibeho in 1995. Two weeks earlier it had been the site of the massacre in which over 2000 refugees were killed.

The Black Hawk Training Accident Memorial, The Palmetto, Townsville, Queensland: 'This plaque marks the dedication of the Black Hawk Memorial on 17 August 1997 as a community response to the tragic loss of 18 lives in an accident at the High Range Training Area involving elements of the Special Air Services Regiment and 5th Aviation Regiment on 12 June 1996 … It was unveiled by his Excellency the Hon. Sir William Deane AC, KBE, Governor-General of the Commonwealth of Australia, with the support of the Mayor of Townsville, Cr. Tony Mooney, and relatives of the soldiers who gave their lives in the peacetime service of the country. Lest We Forget.'

This poignant cartoon by Dean Alston appeared in *The West Australian* Newspaper within days of the Black Hawk accident. It is a moving tribute to the men of the Special Air Service Regiment.

Petty Officer Shane Pashley stands in front of a Sea Hawk, similar to the one used in the rescue operation during the 1998 Sydney to Hobart yacht race. He was later awarded the Bravery Medal.

Warrant Officer Murray Spriggs *(back row, far right)* and the rest of the crew who were involved in the rescue of survivors of the sunken yacht in 1994, 300 nautical miles off the coast of Queensland. *Back row, from left:* Sergeant Steve Carter (loadmaster), Captain Peter Tickner (pilot), Captain Davif Burke (co-pilot). *Front row, from left:* Sergeant Glenn McInnes (medic), Corporal Domenico Farina (medic). Springs was awarded the Bravery Medal for his tireless efforts.

East Timor 1999: Major John Scholl *(with back turned left)* and Federal Agent Paul McEwan *(with back turned, right)* surrounded by soldiers from the Indonesian Army as they try to make their way to the house of the UNAMET Regional Coordinator, which was under threat from a large group of militia.

Major John Scholl (left) and Federal Agent Paul McEwan (right) cross a river after the retrieval of the body of a student killed by a gun shot to the head during the bloody clashes in East Timor in 1999. School was awarded the Bravery Medal for his actions during this period.

Corporal Shaun Clements sitting on top of a tank similar to the one used in the exercise in which he risked his own life to rescue a colleague who had been crushed by the gun. Clements was later awarded the Star of Courage.

Above: The Lynx helicopter, the 'Ferrari' of the rotary-wing world, prior to contact in Iraq in September 2004 in which Scott Watkins and his crew came under enemy fire.
Right: Captain Scott Watkins in Iraq. He was later awarded the Distinguished Flying Cross.

This illustration shows the two routes taken by the helicopters under Scott Watkins' command on the day of the contact. The first leg departed Camp Dogwood, taking the route on the right to Baghdad International Airport (BIAP). The second leg shows where the contact occurred, some distance from both BIAP and Camp Dogwood.

The Bravery Medal.

GOVERNMENT HOUSE, CANBERRA

The Star of Courage.

GOVERNMENT HOUSE, CANBERRA

The Medal for Gallantry.

GOVERNMENT HOUSE, CANBERRA

The Distinguished Flying Cross.

NEW ZEALAND DEFENCE FORCE

It was right at that moment that I could hear what I thought was screaming and crying out coming from inside Black 1, but it seemed like it was coming from the other side of the wreckage. It's interesting now to look back because there is very little that I can consciously remember doing that night, but I remember this part very clearly. I ran around the other side and called out to see if I could pinpoint where the screaming had come from. There was no movement or noise so I began doubting whether I had actually heard anything. I decided to check again, anyway. Starting from the front, I moved inside the aircraft. Then I found someone. When I started to yank him free, he regained consciousness and called out in pain. He was tangled up in gear and webbing so I called out that we had a live person and needed to cut him free. A colleague came in with a knife and we cut him free and removed him from the wreckage. By this stage, the others who had been helping us had moved to the second Black Hawk and were removing more bodies from that wreckage. We were pretty certain there was no one else who could possibly have survived in the first Black Hawk so we moved away to Black 2 as well. About a minute or so later, a huge explosion engulfed the aircraft and we realised how well-timed our leaving was. We were pretty lucky. There was quite a large amount of charged explosives on board and it just went up.

When I went around the other side to search for whomever I had heard crying out, I knew the aircraft was going to blow, but I just thought, 'Stuff it'. I knew my face was getting burnt, but I don't think I stopped to think about it. I could feel the flames scorching me but I don't think the pain sank in. I wanted to help my mates out, so that urge took over, I think. Going in and out of the burning fuselage was simply what we had to do to help out people who couldn't help themselves at that stage. I think I was also trying to avoid the inevitable wondering that would come at a later stage as to whether we had left anyone behind who could have been saved. That kept driving us back to check again and again until we were 100 per cent certain that there was no possible way anyone else could be alive.

Black 1 was a total mess. As I've mentioned earlier, it was upside down, so the cockpit was crushed. The transmission that sits below the rotor had squashed through the top of the helicopter so that there was almost no room between what had been the roof of the aircraft and its floor. Of course, that was upside down, so the roof was now on the ground. The people we pulled out were the guys we could actually get to. We pulled one of the pilots out who was very badly injured, but the other side of the aircraft where the other pilot was sitting was completely destroyed. We knew there was no chance of him being alive or of us getting his body out until they lifted the helicopter off the ground. It was really hard not being able to do anything for him.

After we removed all the bodies we could find out of Black 2, I went over to the triage point to help out and then raided the ambulance for more first aid equipment. There were about 10 injured guys at the triage point being treated by the medics and most of them were seriously wounded. I was asked to get on the next helicopter that was being used to evacuate the injured back to Townsville General Hospital as they needed me to be the Liaison Officer back there. The chopper I got on, which I think was the third one to go back with wounded, also had two guys who received cardiopulmonary resuscitation (CPR) during the entire 25 minute flight back, as well as two walking wounded. The two walking wounded, Dominic Boyle and Gary Proctor, and I helped with resuscitating the two critically injured soldiers, even though we all had our own injuries. I know the other two [Boyle and Proctor] were in a lot of pain.

When we landed at the football oval near the hospital, we moved the injured into the ambulances that were waiting to take them to the Emergency Department. The two critically injured guys that we did CPR on from High Range were both pronounced dead at the hospital, which was really sad for all of us. It also turned out that more of the guys who had been evacuated had died during the flight back as well. That was pretty depressing because one of them was a good friend of mine. I had to identify his body, which was not pleasant. It was strange because he didn't seem to have anything wrong with him. He was dead, but he didn't have anything outwardly wrong with him. It turned out that his internal organs were a mess and that's what killed him.

More and more wounded kept arriving. I helped out in the hospital for another three or four hours and then I went back to join the squadron. My involvement in the whole incident up at High Range lasted about 25 minutes. It felt like a lifetime, but it was only that long: from the time the first helicopter crashed to the ground to when I was helping out in triage. There were a couple of really injured guys there and the medics worked furiously to save them. They were only young corporal medics and they didn't have a doctor there with them, yet they can be credited for saving so many lives.

It all sunk in – what had actually just happened up there – during the time I was at the hospital, but we still didn't know how many people had actually died. I know I personally pulled out five or six dead bodies, but I didn't know how many died in the crash itself, or how many died either on the way to hospital or after arriving in hospital. There were probably some bodies that we couldn't get out of the wreckage itself, particularly in the first helicopter where the transmission had come down through the roof when it landed upside down. We knew there had to have been guys sitting under that area, but we didn't know how many. The following day, they pulled Black 1 apart and they found two more bodies there. There was no way we could have gotten them out but just knowing they were there was still a terrible feeling for us. I spent that day helping to identify bodies, which wasn't a very pleasant task.

We spent another two days in Townsville after the accident during which the accident investigation team arrived. I had to go up to High Range to talk with them, as did a lot of others, in order to work out what had actually happened. Once our interviews had been completed, they loaded us all on to a Boeing 707 and we took our wounded back to Perth. Once we were home at Swanbourne. we simply tried to get on with our lives again. Training continued as normal. The only abnormal thing was the number of funerals I attended. It was a pretty weird couple of weeks; I even went as far as New Zealand to attend a funeral. We couldn't logistically go to them all as there were so many being held all over Australia, and we felt terrible about that, but someone from the Regiment attended every funeral.

As soon as all the funerals were over, the squadron started training again. The day after the crash, 15 new guys began training in Perth and they were to become reinforcements for our squadron to take over from the guys who had died. Helicopters flew to Perth and we continued training in them. This willingness for continued readiness came down to the strength of the individuals in the squadron. Losing 15 of their mates was pretty rough but the internal strength was amazing. The day after the crash, the squadron assembled and they read the nominal roll. Like after big battles in World War I, names were read out, and the silence after the names of those missing 15 men was incredibly depressing.

Afterwards, everyone dispersed into little groups to talk and I heard a few jokes being lobbed around about some of the guys who died. Not jokes in the perverse sense, but good-natured ribbing. One of the guys who died was notorious for being a bit of a scrooge when it came to money and one of his mates was laughing, saying that he died because he went back to the helicopter to get his wallet out. That kind of good-natured and harmless ribbing really helped to relieve the tension. We all knew that he had died on impact but it just shows the emotional strength of these guys to laugh in the face of adversity like that. They were not mocking those who died in any way – they knew that those who died would have appreciated the jokes. A sense of humour is one of the things that the Colonel had told me was essential to have in the Regiment before I attended the selection course a few years earlier, and clearly this illustrated exactly what he meant.

Since the accident, there has been a bit of debate about the awarding of medals to soldiers and officers for their actions on that night. Everyone who received a medal deserved it as far as I am concerned. However, there are so many other people who should have been decorated for their actions, but because no one nominated them or because no one actually saw what they did, they didn't receive any recognition. I remember that there were specific people who, while they were not involved in pulling bodies out of the wreckage, still performed actions that ensured that those wounded were evacuated out quickly; or set up good communication systems between us and Townsville; or set up the triage point extremely effectively; or set up the landing zone for the evacuation aircraft. These guys worked just as hard as we did and, unfortunately, they weren't given any public recognition.

I think everyone involved from both units should have received a unit citation so that everyone involved got recognition for what they did. Even though they wanted to get in there and help out next to us, blokes like the young medics and the officer-in-command practice guys had the discipline to stay away from the site and do their jobs. They made a conscious decision not to run into the burning aircraft because they knew it was more important for them to stay outside to do their jobs properly. As a result, the officer-in-command practice officer probably saved more lives by staying out of it than he would have had he got involved at the site itself. He told me afterwards that he was really cut up about not helping out more at the crash site itself. He found it really hard to stay back and continue to do his job. Bravery was simply everywhere that night.

We all did what we had to do. We were brave in that situation because we had to be. I didn't think what I was doing at the time was brave. The only time I consciously thought I could be at risk was when I made the choice to go back to the aircraft when I heard the cries of pain from someone on board. Even when I felt I was being burnt, it didn't register that I was doing anything unsafe or risky. I had to just go through the pain – a bit like being at the bottom of a rugby scrum! It's part of the game. In this case, it was just what I had to do to get everyone out, and I knew the pain wasn't going to last forever.

Life pretty much got back to normal in the squadron. We had plenty of counselling and debriefing sessions with the psychologists, but for most of us, just getting on with everyday life helped us get over it. Then, the following year, when I was training overseas, I received a letter informing me I was going to be awarded the Bravery Medal. I had to fly back to Perth midway through training in order to accept it. As there were a number of us from the Regiment who were being decorated in Canberra, a special flight was put on for us to fly over to the ACT together.

The investiture was held at Government House and we met the Governor-General, Sir William Deane, which was very nice. It was a special day, but also a sad day. We were all very happy to be decorated for what we did but it was a shame more decorations weren't awarded to others who also deserved them. The day after the investiture, we all flew back to Perth and, again, just got on with things. The medal itself hasn't changed me or changed who I am. A lot of people don't know what the post-nominal stands for, which never ceases to amuse me. I get really angry, though, when people who were not involved in the training accident in any way use it as an example of workplace health and safety gone wrong. But I also know that the accident had a significant impact on so many people.

Looking back at it all over 10 years later, I know that the strength of each of the guys from the squadron was the key to them getting on with life in such a positive way. It was a really horrible event but most people have put it behind them and are doing well now. We know the families of those who died would be getting on with their lives too, albeit with some difficulty still, especially those with young families. But the people who survived were not going to let this keep them down and all of them have gone on to bigger and better things, and put themselves in danger time and time again.

The Black Hawk Training Accident

As an officer it is incredibly humbling and rewarding to see those men behave like this.

James Ryan is now a Lieutenant Colonel and works in the Force Development Group, developing new capabilities for the Army. He is married to Krista and together they have a young son, William. Since receiving his decoration and being posted out of the Regiment at the end of 1997, Jim hasn't returned to the Special Air Service Regiment, but has had postings throughout Australia and overseas. Although not completely reluctant to talk about the events that took place in June 1996, he is still haunted by the memories on occasion. He keeps in contact with many of his colleagues from the Regiment.

SEARCH AND RESCUE AT SEA

F ROM TIME TO TIME, MEMBERS OF THE AUSTRALIAN DEFENCE Force are called upon to provide assistance or aid to the civilian community. At times this is at great risk to their personal safety. This has never been truer than the events surrounding the terrible crash on the island of Nias in Indonesia that saw the lives of nine men and women from the Royal Australian Navy and the Royal Australian Air Force lost in a Sea King helicopter crash during an aid mission after an earthquake and tsunami devastated the small region in South-East Asia. The tragedy served as a prime example to the Australian community of the risks that members of the Australian Defence Force take in order to provide service to civilians in peace-time missions. Throughout the years, similar missions have taken place, fortunately without the loss of life, but whenever the emergency dictates the rescue of people far out to sea, there is always a heightened element of danger.

In 1994, a Black Hawk helicopter and crew based at the School of Army Aviation in Oakey, Queensland, were called upon to carry out a dangerous long-range rescue of seven people at sea, in poor weather and fading light.

As that day was a public holiday in Queensland, it took some time to assemble crew and maintenance personnel, and even more time to adequately and safely prepare the aircraft for the long-range mission over water. This rescue is still a world record for an over-sea search and rescue in a helicopter. One of the crew in this rescue was Warrant Officer Murray Spriggs, who was awarded a Bravery Medal for his instrumental role in rescuing the seven men and women.

'I DON'T KNOW IF I WILL MAKE IT BACK UP'

Warrant Officer Murray Ian Spriggs BM

CITATION
BRAVERY MEDAL

Early in the evening of 2 May 1994, at about 300 nautical miles east of Brisbane, Warrant Officer Spriggs placed his own safety at risk to rescue the crew members of a stricken yacht, adrift on life rafts in dangerous seas.

Warrant Officer Spriggs was a member of an Army helicopter crew which had gone to the aid of the distressed survivors. Although untrained in such duties, Warrant Officer Spriggs descended into the ocean and swam to the life rafts where, over an extended period, he harnessed two survivors and had them hoisted to safety. During the rescue Warrant Officer Spriggs had to enter the sea on two occasions to right life rafts capsized by waves, and twice had to dive under the rafts to clear fouled hoisting cables. Despite the extremely hazardous and physically demanding conditions, Warrant Officer Spriggs continued until forced by exhaustion to desist.

By his action Warrant Officer Spriggs displayed considerable bravery.

I WAS BORN IN DARFIELD IN THE SOUTH ISLAND OF NEW ZEALAND in April 1954. We moved to Christchurch when I was about two years old, and I lived with my family until I was 22 years old. I left school just before finishing Year 10. At 16 I was a concrete batcher and had six guys working under me. I could tell very early on that I wasn't going to go too far doing that and I was lucky to be offered a carpentry apprenticeship by one of the firms that bought concrete from us. I took them up on the offer and did a four-year apprenticeship in commercial building, which was great work.

During that time, I met my wife, an Australian girl who came from Brisbane. I didn't like the cold so I thought that moving to Brisbane was a more attractive proposal than staying in cold New Zealand! Coming from a big family, I found it a little difficult to adjust to the move because I didn't know anybody and it was a bit isolating for the first year or so. My brother-in-law was into vintage cars and one of his mates was an instrument fitter on the F-111s, and I was playing competition squash with a guy who was an Iroquois helicopter pilot in the RAAF. Also, I knew a guy who was a reservist at Griffith University where I was doing some carpentry work. Being around these guys stimulated my interest in doing another trade. I looked into becoming a motor mechanic like my older brother, but then someone suggested to me that I should think about joining one of the armed services because you get paid while you are learning another trade. I liked that idea and the RAAF was the only service that I was interested in joining.

I joined the RAAF in November 1976. I went through Edinburgh in South Australia to do my basic training and went across to the RAAF School of Technical Training in Wagga Wagga in New South Wales after that. There was a six-week hiatus between arriving at the school and the start of my aircraft structural fitter course, so in the interim I spent time in the workshop making things like coffee tables. The others who were waiting for the course didn't have any trade skills behind them so those poor buggers had to paint rocks for six weeks! I finished my course in September 1978 and was posted to No. 3 Aircraft Depot in Amberley near Brisbane.

I had just under a year in that unit before I was posted to No. 3

Squadron in Butterworth, Malaysia, for two years. While I was in Malaysia I had my first exposure to flying in helicopters. I had already repaired them in the Depot, but hadn't flown until then. That experience made me think about getting in as an aircrewman on one of them but it wasn't possible in the short term. On my return to Australia in 1981, I went to No. 2 Squadron at RAAF Base in Amberley and only spent a few months there before I was promoted and posted back to No. 3 Aircraft Depot again for one year.

My next posting was to No. 9 Squadron, which was the Iroquois Squadron, and I spent three years there as an aircraft metal worker. I did a lot of bush pushes with them and really enjoyed that aspect of my work. At that time, the 8/83 Aircrew Scheme came out and I was lucky enough to be able to apply and re-muster to Load-master [responsible for passengers and equipment on board a fixed-wing or rotary-wing aircraft]. On my first application, I got all the way through the selection board but I had a minor health problem so I had to hold off for 12 months before doing it all again. I was selected to begin my training as a loadmaster on my second attempt.

I graduated from my course in July 1987 and was lucky enough to go back to No. 9 Squadron as a loadmaster. I was there until the end of the year and was moved up to Townsville in Queensland where I remained until the end of 1990. During that time, I had also qualified as a gunship loadmaster on Iroquois as well as a Load-master on Black Hawks so I was always busy. Because of an illness in the family, we needed to move back to Brisbane, so I was posted to Oakey where I remained for the next four years, working as a loadmaster instructor. I worked with a great bunch of blokes in Oakey, even if they were all Army!

In my final year in Oakey, I had a phone call at around 1000 hours from Dave Burke, one of the pilots. He said there was a search and rescue for a civilian yacht in international transit that had hit a submerged shipping container 303 nautical miles off the coast of

Brisbane. I was needed to join the crew for the rescue. No other civil aircraft had the endurance to fly that far out and back, so they called on the Army to do it. Black Hawk helicopters can fly further than civilian aircraft if they are fitted out with external fuel tanks.

Because of the distance we had to travel, Dave suggested we bring night vision goggles (NVGs) for the trip. Dave had been trying to get me qualified on NVGs for a long while, but the Army hierarchy denied my application for the training because I was going back to the RAAF at the end of the year. Steve Carter, who was the other loadmaster with me at work, was NVG qualified, so it was decided that I would be the one to go down on the hoistwire to rescue the survivors of the yacht.

It was unfortunate timing in a way because in the week prior, we had been doing navigation training on the Black Hawks, and the helicopters had been fitted with one fuel tank on each side. The week of the rescue, however, the jugs had been removed because we were now doing low-level tactical flying. It took some time for the aircraft to be reconfigured – the jugs needed to be put back on and the fuel lines checked. That hindered our response to the search and rescue by quite a number of hours. It wasn't our fault, the aircraft needed to be checked and cleared for safety. Given that we had to fly on it, I think that's fair enough.

We launched out of Oakey late in the afternoon and flew via Brisbane airport, where we fuelled up again. I remember thinking that 303 nautical miles is a really long way to fly; the pilots, Dave Burke and Peter Tickner, knew they needed every bit of fuel they could get for this journey. While we were at Brisbane airport, the ABC news crew gave us one of their cameras to take footage for their news broadcast, so, being the multi-skilled people that we are in the defence force, we did that too!

Even though I was 40 years old when this rescue took place, I was very fit. I was doing Tae Kwan Do two nights a week, and I was swimming with the Australian Masters team several nights a week. I didn't have any apprehension about being the one to go down on the wire. Admittedly, I had never done anything like it before, so perhaps it was ignorance on my behalf rather than courage! I felt quite calm on the flight out. As a kid I nearly drowned once, so I knew how fearful I could be about the water, but I had done a lot of swimming training since and I knew I was a very confident swimmer.

The helicopter training in Canberra used to train loadmasters to do lifts like this over water – and in nasty weather – but by the time I did my loadmaster training they had stopped. We wanted exercises like that to be part of the courses we ran in Oakey for many years, but it never came to be. Because the water reservoirs around Toowoomba were for drinking, the council was concerned they would be contaminated with fuel so we were never given access to learning their advanced techniques. Once I got the call though, I knew I should take something with me to keep up my energy levels because I figured we were going to be out for some time. I grabbed a chocolate bar, a can of Coke and a few Poppers. Then we all got on with getting ourselves ready. On board there were the two pilots, Dave Burke and Peter Tickner; two medics, Glenn McInnes and Domenico Farina; and the two loadmasters, Steve Carter and me.

The flight out was quite eventful. We were trying to work out how much fuel we were going to burn on the flight out, how much we would have when we arrived at the rescue site, and then how much we would have on our return, and that is all extremely complicated to do at the best of times. The pilots were pretty engrossed in their own planning, so anything extra Steve and I could do to help work out the calculations was really useful. Early into the flight out, the pilots discovered that there was fuel flowing out of one of the jugs into the tank and they couldn't tell how long this had been happening for, or how much fuel had flowed in. It meant that none of our calculations were going to be accurate, which was a bit of a concern because we didn't know how much fuel we had burned already, or how much we would have for our return leg back to Brisbane. Knowing that you have enough fuel to come home with when you are 303 nautical miles from land is pretty important.

We flew for what seemed like hours. Finally, we got to the area at around 1630 hours. This meant we only had about 30 minutes of light left. We had been briefed that we were looking for a couple of dinghies and a row boat. It's very hard to find a dinghy in the middle of the ocean under the best of circumstances, but it is even harder at dusk or in darkness. The row boat turned out to be something you wouldn't dare go out in on a flat dam, let alone be bobbing about in the open ocean in. The dinghy was a little inflatable one, with a roof on it. We didn't identify the dinghy until we were literally on top of it.

In the briefing, they said the water was calm. By the time we got out there, the swells were four to five metres high, and the wind was at least 20 knots. I thought it was pretty horrendous, to be honest. The pilots worked out which way the wind was going so they could approach and hover downwind so as not to tip the dinghy and row boat in its rotor downwash. The pilots then began their hover at around 70 to 80 feet above the surface of the water, which obviously alters intermittently, due to the swells. One of the hardest things for a pilot to do is maintain a stable hover over the ocean because there is no stable reference point. For example, when a helicopter is in a hover over land, the pilot can use a tree as a reference point and can remain stable for hours, but in the ocean there isn't anything like that and it is tough going. Identifying a ship can make it a lot easier, but with nothing like that on the surface of the water, it is a really difficult exercise.

Steve lowered me down on the wire and it went well. I got in the water and thought, 'Geez, I'd hate to see rough waters if this is supposed to be calm,' and then I started packing it a little bit. As soon as I entered the water I went under, so I inflated my life-vest to help me stay above the water – having a life-vest in a rescue is always a bonus! I backstroked over to the dinghy and the row boat, which was tough going because of the amount of rope floating around them; also, the swell kept knocking me around. When a good swell came through, however, I used it to propel me into the dinghy. There were seven people (four males and three females) – the captain of the yacht and six backpackers who were on the voyage as crew. They were all in shock.

One of the first things I noticed when I got in was that they all had their bags with them. I told them they would have to leave them behind because there wouldn't be room on the Black Hawk for them and it would make it too heavy because the fuel situation was still in our minds. The captain turned to me and said, 'I am the captain of this ship. You do as I tell you.' I was pretty angry about that and I pointed up at the helicopter and said, 'That pilot is the captain, and I am his representative. You do as I friggin' tell you, mate.'

Just then a big wave rammed into the dinghy and sent us all flying into the water. That was pretty horrendous. With all the bags and rope floating around, it was really dangerous. Getting back into the dinghy proved to be very difficult. Like every loadmaster, I always carry a knife and for this trip, I attached it to my Secumar strap. I'm pleased I did because there was so much rope in the water that I would have been stuck without it. While everyone clambered back into the dinghy, I cut bits of rope away to try to clear the area around us as much as possible.

I had taken an anti-rotation line down into the water with me, which is a line that holds onto the hoistwire and stops it from rotating and swinging during the ascent into the aircraft. Ideally, the loadmaster gets winched down and comes up with each person so that you can control the ascent and ensure that the survivor is safely harnessed during the lift. Steve and I worked out that I would not be able to go up and down with each lift because we would exceed the hoist cycles as the winch is supposed to be rested every 30 or so minutes. As there were seven in the dinghy, we knew we would be winching for much longer if I went up with each survivor and then down again, so I gave them all a quick briefing on how to position done it, very little else was said. I made some notes on the incident for my own records, as did Steve, and we just got on with our lives.

Quite a few years later, I received a letter from the Governor-General's office, letting me know that I was going to be awarded the Bravery Medal. Earlier in the year, some of the guys from 5th Aviation Regiment and the Special Air Service Regiment had been awarded bravery decorations after the Black Hawk training accident that had happened the previous year. I knew a lot of them, both the survivors and the guys who didn't make it, so for me the accident was terribly sad. My action was so different to theirs. I felt strange, in retrospect. I was very humbled to be decorated; and I was as equally pleased for Glenn McInnes being decorated too. It isn't about how many you rescue, it's about the circumstances. Glenn didn't hesitate in getting on the wire and going into the drink in just his uniform and boots in the dark, so he deserved to be recognised.

The day of the investiture was very humbling. I could only bring along three guests to the ceremony, so I flew my father over from New Zealand. Unfortunately my mother had passed away, so I was very heavy-hearted not having her there to see the ceremony. Three weeks before she died, though, I was in New Zealand when I received the letter saying that I was going to be awarded the Bravery Medal. It was wonderful that she was still alive to hear about it. Georgina, who was my girlfriend then, and another friend of mine, Cole, came along with my dad as my other guests. It was a very sobering experience to be among other people who had all carried out such incredible and diverse acts.

We were just normal people; we simply acted in a way that made us stand out as being 'brave', whatever that is. I am offended in some ways about the Order of Precedence and where the Bravery Medal sits in that order. I don't believe it is appropriate that someone can lose their life doing something that is considered considerably brave. which is what the Bravery Medal is awarded for, whereas someone else can be awarded the Conspicuous Service Cross or Conspicuous Service Medal for doing what is essentially their job, and they sit sent us all back into the water among the bags and ropes. This time, two others didn't come up and the only place that they could have been was under the dinghy, so I had to go under it, find them, and get them back into the dinghy again.

While all this was happening, the helicopter was still trying to maintain its hover and Steve was waiting for me to get the girl back into the sling. I had been in the water for some time by now and only two had been rescued. We finally got the second troublesome pair up on the next hoist. As Steve was hoisting up the third pair of survivors, one of them fell out of the sling as well, but Steve continued on with the hoist this time, bringing the remaining male survivor on board the helicopter. Then Dave Burke noticed that the person who'd fallen out of the sling was drifting away from the rescue site in the current, and the frightening thing was that it was now getting dark. The pilots made the call to stop any further hoisting and try to get this guy back. They could see where he was through the front of the aircraft so they aborted the hover and began trawling for him with the sling in the water. Miraculously, he managed to grab hold of the sling with his arms and they got him up and on board. They were bloody lucky to find him because it was pretty dark. Then they transitioned to NVGs but couldn't see anything because it was very misty and there was a lot of rain coming through as well. They came back for us with their lights on instead.

I couldn't see a thing by now. It was like being in one of those old movies with misty rain coming through; it reduced visibility enormously. It was horrendous. Also, I had been in the water for over 40 minutes now and I was knackered. I turned to the youngest guy who was left (with me and the captain) and said, 'Mate, I am stuffed. If this thing gets kicked over once more, I don't know if I am going to come back up. The captain looks like he is on his last legs. How are you feeling?' The young guy said that he was feeling fine, so we decided that I would go up on the line with the captain on the next hoist.

I didn't know it until later, but I was running purely on adrenaline and it was wearing off. I was coming down with a big thud; I was completely and utterly spent. I knew that if I went under once more, I wouldn't be any good to anyone. I promised the young guy that he wouldn't get left behind and then, the sling came down; I grabbed hold of it while I was sitting in the dinghy, readying the captain and myself to go up. What happened next was comical, really. Here was an 80-kilogram, dripping wet me holding on to an 18,000 pound piece of machinery on the end of a rope in one hand, and the dinghy in the other! The odds weren't in my favour. The hoistwire wasn't down low enough at this stage – it would only reach us when we were on top of a wave – so I was waiting for a swell to take us back up closer to the helicopter so that we could get ourselves inside the sling properly. When I grabbed the wire on the next swell up, I was also hanging on to the dingy; then the swell went down again. I got hurt doing that. Finally, on the next upward swell, I got the sling onto the captain and said, 'Righto mate, we're going,' and jumped out into the ocean with the loose cable so that once Steve hoisted us, we would be free of the dinghy.

Just as we were about to jump out of the dinghy, I looked at the captain and saw that some of the loose cable was wrapped around his neck and that he was still hanging on to his bag. I thought, 'You stupid bugger, let go of your bloody bag!' Then, as I was trying to get the cable from around his neck, I felt something around *my* leg. I thought, 'Shit, that's a rope!' Feverishly, I tried to get the rope off my leg as well as get the cable off and away from the captain's neck. Then I noticed that I wasn't in the sling. Somehow, and to this day I still don't know how, I got the cable off the captain with one arm, pulled the rope off my leg with the other, and managed to get the sling up under my armpits. Then, bang! We were lifted up straight out of the water. That screwed my back up and it needed treatment when I got home.

When we got up to the aircraft, the place was pure bedlam. There were people everywhere. I told Glenn, 'There's one more down there, mate. You've got to get him out.' Without a moment to lose, Glenn went down in just his camouflage uniform and boots, straight into the drink to get the last guy out of the water. Fortunately for Glenn, it went smoothly! Then we did a head count to make sure we had everyone on board before heading back to Brisbane. By this time, we had been gone for nearly six hours. Once I got back into my seat, I started to take off my wetsuit, and went through a six pack of Poppers in about a minute or so. Then I had a huge cry. I have no idea why. The guys reckoned it was because I was coming off the adrenaline rush, but whatever it was, I was just shattered. I am not a cry-baby by any stretch of the imagination so it shocked me, too.

On the trip back, Pete Tickner told me that, at one stage during the rescue, they were getting a bit worried about the fuel situation and they had contemplated leaving me behind with a couple of the survivors overnight in the dinghy and coming back the next day to get us. I was pretty bloody glad I didn't know about that at the time because I would have had something to say about it! On the return journey the weather was deteriorating. We didn't have weather radar on the Black Hawks, so a Queensland Government aircraft came out to fly ahead of us and vector us through the bad weather. We landed back at Brisbane airport because these people still had to go through customs, quarantine, and immigration. As it turned out, we had used up pretty much all of our fuel with very little to spare.

I don't know what time it was when we got back to Oakey but I was back at work the next day, business as usual. In the months after the rescue, we had some 'round table' discussions about the rescue itself and the conditions that the rescue took place in. A lot of the other loadmasters said they didn't think they would have had the endurance to do what I had to do. As I said, I was really fit at the time, so I know that that helped me immensely, but even still, I was completely knackered at the end of it. Apart from some of the other guys saying they couldn't think of anyone else who could have done it, very little else was said. I made some notes on the incident for my own records, as did Steve, and we just got on with our lives.

Quite a few years later, I received a letter from the Governor-General's office, letting me know that I was going to be awarded the Bravery Medal. Earlier in the year, some of the guys from 5th Aviation Regiment and the Special Air Service Regiment had been awarded bravery decorations after the Black Hawk training accident that had happened the previous year. I knew a lot of them, both the survivors and the guys who didn't make it, so for me the accident was terribly sad. My action was so different to theirs. I felt strange, in retrospect. I was very humbled to be decorated; and I was as equally pleased for Glenn McInnes being decorated too. It isn't about how many you rescue, it's about the circumstances. Glenn didn't hesitate in getting on the wire and going into the drink in just his uniform and boots in the dark, so he deserved to be recognised.

The day of the investiture was very humbling. I could only bring along three guests to the ceremony, so I flew my father over from New Zealand. Unfortunately my mother had passed away, so I was very heavy-hearted not having her there to see the ceremony. Three weeks before she died, though, I was in New Zealand when I received the letter saying that I was going to be awarded the Bravery Medal. It was wonderful that she was still alive to hear about it. Georgina, who was my girlfriend then, and another friend of mine, Cole, came along with my dad as my other guests. It was a very sobering experience to be among other people who had all carried out such incredible and diverse acts.

We were just normal people; we simply acted in a way that made us stand out as being 'brave', whatever that is. I am offended in some ways about the Order of Precedence and where the Bravery Medal sits in that order. I don't believe it is appropriate that someone can lose their life doing something that is considered considerably brave. which is what the Bravery Medal is awarded for, whereas someone else can be awarded the Conspicuous Service Cross or Conspicuous Service Medal for doing what is essentially their job, and they sit higher in the Order of Precedence. At my investiture I was only one of two people who received bravery decorations who did not die as a result of their act. Everyone else was dead, and yet on the Order of Precedence, someone who simply does their job sits higher. I think what I did was part of my job but I think the circumstances made the actions brave. We were 303 nautical miles off the coast doing that rescue. I could have carried out the rescue in the same horrendous weather in a river and it wouldn't be the same thing, because if things had turned to clay, you knew you could always swim to the shore. The crew of the helicopter didn't have that luxury. If anything went to clay, they would have had to ditch the aircraft into the water, and then we would all have been stuffed!

I don't think I feared for my life during the rescue, but someone who does something in which their life is at risk is certainly a brave person. A bloke diving into the broken window of a car that is on fire is an incredibly brave person. Someone running into a burning house is also brave. In both circumstances, those people know that the act might kill them. I didn't think I would be killed doing the rescue. To me, bravery is something that is governed by circumstances. Certainly, the rescue that I was involved in was one of those situations, but what choice did I have?

Warrant Officer Murray Spriggs is still serving in the Royal Australian Air Force. He is currently the Airmen Aircrew Manager for the Air Lift Group. He is responsible for providing advice on matters relating to promotions, postings and other personnel matters. His son, Alex, is 25 years old. He lives in Sydney where he and his wife, Georgina, hobby-farm alpacas.

The 1998 Sydney to Hobart Yacht Race Tragedy

IN 1998, THE 54TH ANNUAL SYDNEY TO HOBART YACHT RACE began like any other. Crews and their craft were lined up awaiting the starter's gun on a clear and relatively calm Boxing Day afternoon in Sydney Harbour, watched by an estimated 300,000 onlookers around the shoreline and in the hundreds of boats jostling for a better view on the water. However, the race that covers 630 nautical miles was to be shrouded in tragedy and become the most disastrous event in the 54-year history of this classic Australian yachting race. By midnight on that first night, atrocious weather with near gale force winds began battering the middle of the fleet. During the first night alone, six yachts were forced to retire from the race with rudder, rig or hull damage and by the end of day two, over 20 yachts had retired from the race and two people were confirmed dead. By race end, of the 115 boats that lined up to start the race, only 44 were to finish it. Six people died and more than 50 others were rescued as their boats encountered destructive winds and torrential rain.

While the nation watched the events unfold on television, members of the Royal Australian Navy were called upon to assist in the rescue of some of the survivors. The media reported the tragedy hourly and brought footage of the sailors being rescued in stormy, vicious seas into our living rooms each night. One scene that is burned into my memory forever was from the footage of a man hanging below a Navy helicopter being buffeted by ferocious winds. He was being dunked and dragged along underneath the struggling aircraft as he tried to carry out the rescue of a couple of yachtsmen in a tiny life raft. At the time it reminded me of a human tea bag and I remember hoping that the poor bugger was all right. One man who was filmed carrying out these rescues, Petty Officer Brian Shane Pashley, was to play such a significant and courageous role in the rescues that he was awarded a Bravery Medal for his actions at sea.

Petty Officer Pashley was also a recipient of a Group Citation for Bravery stemming from his rescues, along with the rest of the crew of the Seahawk helicopter: Lieutenant Commander Richard Neville, Lieutenant Aaron Abbott and Lieutenant Nicholas Trimmer. This citation follows Petty Officer Pashley's story.

'THE HUMAN TEA BAG'

Petty Officer Brian Shane Pashley BM

CITATION
BRAVERY MEDAL

On the night of 28 December 1998, Petty Officer Brian Shane Pashley was involved in the rescue of yachtsmen during the 1998 Sydney to Hobart Yacht Race. Petty Officer Pashley was a crew member of the Royal Australian Navy Seahawk 875 Helicopter that was tasked to identify a light source observed 80 nautical miles south east of Merimbula. On arrival at the scene, the crew noted that the wind was coming from the south east at some 30 knots, the swell was 10 metres, the wind chop was at two metres and visibility was reduced to 2000 metres. Petty Officer Pashley observed two men, one of whom was injured, in the remains of a life raft. Petty Officer Pashley was then winched into the sea to rescue the injured man, and was buffeted by strong winds on his way down. Despite the darkness and the large swell, Petty Officer Pashley managed to reach the life raft and attach the winch strop to the injured man. At this point, the aircraft's auto pilot system malfunctioned causing the aircraft to abandon its hover position and, consequently, dragging Petty Officer Pashley and the injured man some 50 metres through the sea. It was a further 15 minutes before they were winched to safety and, during this period, Petty Officer Pashley maintained a grip on the injured man. The crew, realising the increased danger caused by the technical problem with the aircraft, decided to rescue the second yachtsman in a single lift. The unmanned winch was lowered into the sea and, on the second attempt, once he had secured the winch strop to himself, the remaining yachtsman was winched safely aboard the helicopter. By his actions, Petty Officer Pashley displayed considerable bravery.

I WAS BORN IN GLADSTONE, QUEENSLAND, IN MARCH 1965. My school years were fairly uneventful. I was an average student and had a small group of good friends. I played representative level soccer, played rugby league, was a member of the local Sea Scouts, and was also in the school Army Cadets. At primary school I was also quite good at athletics, regularly winning or placing in sprint races, high jump, and long jump. As a family we used to go camping during the holidays, mostly on the islands around Gladstone, so most of my childhood was spent on the water, fishing and camping. School became harder for me as I got older. The school work was not really a challenge in itself, but I was unhappy at home. My dad was fairly strict. But in hindsight, his discipline wasn't such a bad thing as I have never been in trouble with the law and I would like to think I have good moral and social values!

In 1980, I was in Year 10 and the opportunity of getting away from school and into the workforce was too strong to ignore. My neighbour had joined the Navy the previous year and my best friend's elder brother was in the Navy so I thought I'd follow suit. Like most people when they joined the forces, I had no idea what I was getting myself in for and knew little about the Navy, except for seeing a few patrol boats coming into Gladstone. I applied once I had received my Junior School Certificate.

In February 1981 I went to Brisbane to do my enlistment interviews and was accepted into the Navy. I signed the dotted line on April 1981 and was then flown to Perth to start my training as a junior recruit. Recruit training consisted of 'advanced level academics', general service subjects, learning to march, first aid and that kind of thing. Throughout the nine months of training, we were also being assessed on which branch we were suitable for on completion of training.

By the end of our recruit training in December, I had been given my first choice and was posted to HMAS Albatross to begin my training as Aircraft Technical Communications sailor. HMAS Albatross is the home of the Navy Fleet Air Arm at Nowra in New South Wales. I think the only reason that I chose to go into this stream was that it was the only job in the Navy I had heard of! I figured it would do for me, especially since I had always had a passing interest in electronics, mainly from fixing my own record player or cassette deck growing up.

After six months training, I was posted to 817 Squadron, which is at HMAS Albatross, to work on Sea King helicopter radar, sonar and radio equipment. During my seven years at 817 Squadron, I went on various detachments and advancement courses around Australia and was promoted to Leading Seaman in August 1988. This job was okay but I find I get into a comfort zone and am content to stay somewhere as long as possible. I did my job, promotions came around at the right time, and I enjoyed my social life. It was all so simple then.

In 1986 I met a girl from Mackay and started a long distance relationship that lasted for just over two years. When we split up, I decided that I might as well have a professional change as well as a personal one so I volunteered for changeover to Aircrewman. At the time, I had a couple of friends who were aircrewmen and they seemed to enjoy what they did. Additionally, when the aircraft came back from a sortie, we maintainers would notice the aircrew going home while we had to stay behind long into the night, maintaining the aircraft. Aircrewing seemed like a pretty comfortable and easy job to me! Of course, in reality there is a lot of work to be done when we aren't flying – all flying does is put off the paperwork until you get back. If I'd had any drive, I would have applied for a commission and tried my hand at becoming a pilot. Anyway, how cool does it look hanging out of the back of a helicopter – who wouldn't want to give it a go?

Late in 1988, I met Kay. We moved in together into a group of units with four other couples. We had a great couple of years there. Eventually, we all got married, moved into our own homes, but I still count all of these people as my closest friends 16 years later.

In March 1990, I was back at the training centre at HMAS Albatross for the start of the aircrewman course. It lasted four months and once qualified, the four of us who were on the course would be able to fly as aircrewmen in Squirrel helicopters, conducting utility operations. Utility operations consist of winching, load lifting, basic navigation, search and rescue, and first aid. Another qualification we earn on basic course is that of Surface Swimmer. When we go out on an overwater rescue mission, one of the aircrewmen will go dressed in a wetsuit and has the job of either being winched into the water or jumping from the helicopter, if necessary, to effect the rescue. Like most things in life, you can be told what it will be like but you need to experience it for yourself to gain a true appreciation. The requirement to be a surface swimmer doesn't worry me – jumping out of a helicopter is fun – but I am not a big fan of swimming in the open ocean. If I can't see the bottom, I have no idea what is coming up to eat me – and I don't like that at all!

In August 1990, I was posted to 723 Squadron, also at HMAS Albatross, for flying duties in the HS748 Electronic Warfare Training aircraft. The 748 is a large, fixed-wing aircraft, and my duties included looking after passengers on transits, and operating electronic training equipment. My helicopter training was not going to get much use for a few years.

The only exposure I had to helicopters in those two years was as surface swimmer in a Seahawk for a search and rescue just off Nowra in late 1992. The situation was that a boat had capsized in Jervis Bay. When the police launch went out to investigate, they found two lifejackets, so we were launched to help search for what they believed were two people. Eventually, the police found one body and he turned out to be the only person on board. They recovered his body, so we weren't required for anything more than to assist with the search.

In February 1993, I was dragged kicking and screaming out of my comfortable job on the 748 to start flying with 816 Squadron, still at HMAS Albatross. The Seahawk is a large, 10 tonne helicopter used for anti-submarine warfare. The Navy had only been operating them for four years at that stage and they were in use in the first Gulf war on guided missile frigates. They were also in use at Nowra for training new aircrew. Initially, the plan was for me and one other Leading Seaman Aircrewman to be trained only as utility aircrewmen, and the officers would continue with their training to become sensor operators (they operate the radar and sonar gear). I completed my utility conversion back to helicopters without much trouble and started my new life as a helicopter aircrewman. I suppose I saw this job as a new challenge for me. I remember getting a bit bored at 748 Squadron and was always trying to go out helicopter flying with the other guys, without much success.

There had not been any aircrewmen on Seahawks up to this point – it had been decreed that the job of sensor operator would be too hard for non-commissioned aircrew. It was all new ground for the Navy and there was a fair bit of pressure for Leading Seaman Aircrewman Shane Paton and myself to do well. Up to this point, the aircrewman branch was in danger of folding as we are a small branch and therefore hard to justify and sustain. These days, all sensor operators are aircrewmen. We have gone from 'no aircrewmen required' to taking over the officer's position in the back of the Seahawk. Pretty cool.

In January 1994, the Squadron were on leave, but by 0100 hours on 8 January, we were flying to RAAF Richmond to help with the Sydney bushfires. For six days, we had Seahawks, Sea Kings, and Squirrels, as well as a number of Army and civilian helicopters, dropping water all over Sydney trying to put the fires out. It was exciting, if not dangerous flying, as there were lots of aircraft to avoid. We were lifting and carrying 1300 litres of water in big buckets suspended beneath the helicopters in hot, smoky conditions. The buckets were loaned to us by the New Zealand government and arrived by Hercules on the first day of the outbreak. We hadn't flown them before so we rigged one up to a Seahawk and took it flying to see how it would work. We didn't hurt ourselves so we went fire fighting.

In December 1994, I was on leave again, but we received the call to go out on another rescue, this one getting worldwide media coverage. The BOC Around the World Solo Yacht Race had entered Australian waters, and one of the sailors, Isabelle Autissier, had gotten into trouble. Six of us were flown to Perth on a Qantas flight, driven to Fremantle and then taken out to HMAS *Darwin* by boat. As Isabelle was so far to the south of the mainland, we needed to be ferried to the area by ship, so HMAS *Darwin* was deployed from its base at HMAS Stirling in Western Australia and sailed south towards Adelaide. As we sailed south, a Seahawk was being flown from Nowra to Adelaide.

Once the aircraft landed on the ship, we sailed south, towards Antarctica. During the transit south, Chris Young, who was Chief Aircrewman, and myself went over the procedures we would use during the rescue. The most difficult part would be trying to do the job we had come to do – a relatively easy winch from a yacht – while controlling all of the passengers we had in the aircraft. It wasn't known if Isabelle was injured or how well we could communicate with her so we had a doctor and an interpreter on board, plus a cameraman from Channel 10 in Perth. There was also a newspaper photographer from *The West Australian* on the ship, but there was no way we could fit him into the helicopter as well so I was given a quick lesson in using his new digital camera, and I was to take photos during the rescue. Fortunately the photos turned out but I was happy to stay in my job in the Navy!

We launched at just after 0300 hours on New Year's Day 1995. The rescue itself was fairly straightforward because we do a lot of winching training to small boats. Once we found the yacht, I was winched down on to what remained of the deck and hooked Isabelle up into a strop, and Chris winched us back into the aircraft. It probably only took about 10 minutes. During these kind of rescues, most of the time is spent getting the aircraft into a good position over the moving object, then getting the wireman down onto it. It only then takes a moment to put a harness on the survivor, then winch off the vessel.

Isabelle was fine; we landed back on the ship, and sailed back towards Adelaide. We spent the night at RAAF Edinburgh, then flew back home for a belated New Year's celebration. As usual, there was lots of media coverage and interest but we really didn't see what all of the fuss was about. It was a fairly simple rescue. Having said that, I think the level of media interest was proportional to the amount of interesting stories they had to fill their 30 minute news slot. It must have been a slow news day. Still, it was probably the biggest marine rescue carried out in Australian waters in years. The cost, the logistics, and a solo woman on a disabled yacht 900 miles south of Adelaide all makes for dramatic reporting. The Navy and Seahawk helicopters backed up a year or so later with the rescues of Tony Bullimore and Thierry Dubois. The logistics of that rescue became a major talking point by the media, especially the cost, which was estimated at $2 million.

In July 1995, I was posted back to 816 Squadron and home again. It was great. I was volunteered to become an instructor. In a small unit like ours, there is volunteering and there is 'volunteering'. It was part of the plan before I went to sea with HMAS *Darwin* that I would come back to start instructing after six months. Most sensor operators get posted to sea for three years so I figured I was lucky to be coming back so soon and would happily take on the instructor's position under the circumstances. In October 1995 I completed the instructor's course, which consisted of three weeks at HMAS Cerberus outside Melbourne, Victoria, where we learned the basics of planning and delivering lectures and in the use of training aids. Then it was back to the Squadron to be checked out on airborne teaching. This consists mainly of leading the students through the flight brief, intervening at appropriate times during a flight (before it gets unsafe), and debriefing the student. Once we are qualified, our civilian qualification is Certificate 4 in Vocational Training (Instruction).

In June 1996, we got called out for another yacht rescue, this one about 100 miles east of Lord Howe Island. An American couple, George and Diana Goodwin, had been smashed around by a large storm and needed to get off their sinking yacht. We spent a night in Port Macquarie then flew out to Lord Howe, refuelled, then out to sea. The yacht was so far from land that two aircraft were deployed, so we could look after each other. When we got there the yacht was still afloat and all the rigging was still intact so we were hesitant sending me down on to the yacht as the risk of straining me through all of the rigging was too great. As a single crew we make joint decisions. We came to the consensus that I would go down but we got George and Diana to board their life raft and I picked them up from there once it had moved far away enough from their yacht.

The rescue sounds pretty straightforward, but I guess being winched out of an aircraft into the ocean 100 miles from land might not appeal to everyone. It is also quite difficult to winch a person from a moving raft. We usually hover at about 60 to 70 feet so small movements by the aircraft cause the wireman to swing around like a pendulum. I was flying past the raft so much that I began to make a game of it to keep the survivors amused. Each time I went past, I would pretend to swim or fly through the air. I believe I was hanging around down there for around 20 minutes but it felt a lot longer but the antics kept everyone amused. Even the crew in the other aircraft were in fits of laughter watching me.

A few weeks later while on a domestic flight, I read a magazine article in *The Australian* about the rescue. It said, '. . . dangling in space, Pashley plays some sort of cross between Superman, the Thunderbirds, and Bill and Ben. It eases the tension. Just as they land him in the dinghy, it falls off a wave, and speeds away. The wire goes taut, and Pashley goes overboard. 'I'll be back in a minute,' he yells . . .' I would never say that we find humour in someone else' misfortune – we don't think their circumstances are amusing – but I suppose being a bit silly does release the tension a bit, particularly on the flight home or over a beer afterwards. I think most us would prefer to tell a funny story about something that happened to us during a flight as opposed to telling how 'good' or 'brave' we were.

I spent the next few years training students and going on detachments – usually to Western Australia, Victoria or Queensland. Our training relies heavily on other Navy assets. For example, when we are doing anti-submarine warfare, we need a real submarine to work on; when we do deck landing practice, we need a real ship. Quite often we go to where the asset is, usually during a major exercise. We will fly the students there and operate out of the airport, the RAAF base or off the ship to achieve the training events needed to progress the students.

On Boxing Day in 1998, Kay and I were on holidays and were enjoying our usual Christmas–New Year holiday break with the family in Berry. We saw the start of the Sydney to Hobart yacht race on television and commented on how it might get interesting because the weather reports were starting to indicate a rough trip. I received a phone call the next evening: I was required to come into work on 28 December to fly down to Merimbula with the Seahawk and crew from HMAS *Melbourne*. Their sensor operator was on holidays in Western Australia so I was required to fill in for him. Squadrons 816 and 817 take year-about turns to be on recall over Christmas; whoever is staying in the local area will generally be on 12-hour recall, which means no drinking or going too far away and always being readily contactable.

Our initial employment was to take a new winch cable to Merimbula for the crew of HMAS *Newcastle*'s Seahawk. They had winched nine survivors from the yacht *Sword of Orion* the previous night and had damaged their winch cable in the process. Merimbula airport was very busy with several civilian helicopters and fixed wing aircraft, as well as Navy Sea Kings and Seahawks, which were all there as part of the search. Aircraft were constantly departing for the search area then returning for fuel. Hundreds of people had lined the fence at the airport to watch the spectacle and most probably to catch sight of any survivors. It was quite calm with little wind to speak of so it was hard to believe there was so much carnage only a few miles away.

We received tasking to search an area approximately 60 nautical miles from Merimbula and I got into a wetsuit in case I had to go into the water. As soon as we left the coastline, the weather deteriorated and we were faced with a strong south-westerly wind at around 40 knots and seas as high as 50 feet. Being inside a chopper in this kind of weather is not too bad, really. The most noticeable thing is how slow it feels travelling into a strong headwind. It was a bit bumpy but we were in a large helicopter so it didn't feel too bad. I would hate to do it in a little helicopter like the civvies do! The further southeast we travelled, the worse the weather became. We searched our area but with no luck. Staring into the water for long periods of time is very tiring. It would be great to go to the briefed position, see the person, pick them up and go home, but I doubt that ever happens. If our job is to search, we search. If we come up empty it isn't good, but we have played our part by reducing the size of the search area.

After about one hour searching our area of operation, it became clear that there were numerous Emergency Personal Indicator Rescue Beacons (EPIRBs) transmitting but there was little information available as to whose beacons they were. As the Seahawk is capable of direction-finding to a beacon, we were retasked to locate the beacons. The first one we found was onboard the yacht *Business Post Naiad*. After hours of looking into large seas seeing all manner of flotsam, it was good to finally discover what we had been searching for. We were informed that all survivors from *Business Post Naiad* had been recovered the previous night, but there were two bodies on board. It was a sobering sight for us and really drove home the point of how severe the situation was becoming. You always hope you can go out, do a fairly basic rescue, and bring people back healthy and happy. Seeing bodies and wreckage brings you back to reality a bit.

I reckon one of the worst things was the sound of the EPIRB going off - it is a really freaky noise. It makes the hair stand up on the back of my neck. We continue our search and ended up around 120 nautical miles to the east of Merimbula. HMAS *Newcastle* was in the area, so we landed on her deck to refuel. The sea had become so rough that we were unable to launch at first, so the ship sailed north to try and find us some smoother water. Once the conditions improved, two of our maintainers were transferred by Sea King to inspect our aircraft. The ship was rolling and pitching so much that there was a risk of the aircraft being stressed by the movement. The limit is 26 degrees roll, which was exceeded that night. One we had the all clear from the maintainers, we manned up and launched to investigate two radar contacts held by HMAS *Newcastle* and then transit back to Merimbula.

During the transit back, a RAAF P3-C Orion aircraft reported a contact about 60 miles to the south of our position. There were no other aircraft available so we diverted to assist. The P3 was investigating a light in the water, which later turned out to be John Gibson's torch. Once we reached the area the P3 dropped a flare for us to home in to. As we approached, we turned on all of the aircraft lights and located a life raft.

Weather conditions were bad for night hovering over water as there was low cloud, no visibility, wind of around 30 knots, and a swell of around 40 feet. Our lights were barely penetrating the dark and the raft was little more than a ghostly spot at the edge of the light. We could make out two people in the raft and as there was no way of communicating with them, there was no option but to go into the water to assist them. After spending a lot of time during the day looking into the water, seeing sharks and bits of boat, plus being fatigued from searching for nearly 12 hours, I didn't really feel like going for a swim. Another turn-off for me was that we were about 70 miles from land, it was dark, and there were big waves rolling through.

The pilot set up for the approach to the raft and we settled into a hover over the raft trying to stay about 60 feet above the waves. After a wave went through, it meant that we were sitting about 100 feet above the water. The aircraft was able to sit in a stable hover because the autopilot was using radar to measure the height. As I was being winched into the water, I was spinning around on the wire.

In one second I would be looking into blackness, and the next I would be looking directly into the aircraft's lights. Needless to say, I had no night vision by the time I entered the water. It all seemed so surreal. There I was, hanging beneath a big helicopter, miles from nowhere, nasty winds and big seas all around me. I entered the water about 20 or 30 yards from the raft. Everyone has seen the television footage of the wireman being pounded by the seas during the day rescues; all I can say is that it wasn't comfortable and I don't really know how bad it looked while I was doing it because I couldn't see anything. Each time I would get near the raft, a wave would come through and push me back. The winch wire would go tight and I would be pulled through the wave, out the other side and back into mid-air. It was like being in a washing machine. After what was probably only five minutes, I made it to the raft and pulled myself up over the side, hoping to have my legs out of the water because sharks were still on my mind. The raft had a big tear in the floor so I went staight back into the water. I figured that if these two guys hadn't been eaten by now, I should be fine, too!

Over the noise of the aircraft and the sea, I asked the guys if they were all right – hypothermia or back injuries can really complicate rescue by winch. They said they were fine so I put the strop over Gibson's head and shoulders. At that exact same time, the radar on the helicopter couldn't cope with the large differences in the size of the swell and it tripped itself off. The aircraft lifted up. Luckily, I had managed to get the strop all the way over John's head. Otherwise we might have broken his neck. We punched through a few more waves before the pilot regained control of the aircraft. All I could do was keep hold of John ans wait for the guys to fix the problem and get us on board. Everything was moving around so much. John was obviously pretty tired so I was holding him up and trying to keep the winch cable from wrapping around us. I held John up in the water for several minutes as the aircraft was repositioned, and then we were finally winched into the cabin.

The rest of the crew decided that it was too dangerous to send me down again, so while Wal Abbot guided the aircraft, I winched out the strop to pick up the remaining sailor, John Stanley. He put the strop on and I started to winch him up. Th raft started to come up with him so I put him back in the water so that he could untangle himself from the raft. I winched him up again, but at about 30 feet above the water he fell out of the strop. I was getting ready to go back into the water because it looked like he needed some help but we decided to give it one more go. We put the strop back into the water and this time John was able to get himself into it. Then we were able to pull him into the aircraft.

A lot of the details of that night are forgotten. I am not even sure how long the rescue itself took. The general consensus was that I spent about 15 minutes in the water and then maybe another 10 minutes fishing for John Stanley. We were concentrating on the job so we weren't aware of anything else around us. It's the kind of thing we had trained for so there was no need to panic or be frightened. I am really hard pressed to describe my feelings during the rescue, simply because I don't think I really had any. I don't think I was feeling anything at the time. All I wanted was to get the guys out of there and get home in one piece – and not leave Kay a widow. At an awards night at the Cruising Yacht Club of Australia a few months later, other wiremen who went into the water during the day resues asked me what it was like doing it at night. They were awestruck that we (the Navy) were even flying during that weather, let alone hovering, and conducting winch resues. But it is what we train to do, so we just do it.

After we got the sailors on board, we flew back to Merimbula where they were put into an ambulance and taken to hospital. We went to find somewhere to sleep for what was left of the night. While I was getting out of my wetsuit, for the first time I noticed some soreness in my right knee and that my diver's knife was missing. As I was dragged out of the raft, I think my knife became tangled and was ripped off completely. Also, somehow my leg got twisted as I went over the top, and I ended up with some cartilage damage. This injury was fixed with an arthroscopy and several months of physio.

The next morning we went back out to the search area to try and find the missing sailors from *Winston Churchill*. Another Navy helicopter returned to Merimbula with the bodies of two crewmen and at 1600 hours the search was called off. We went home to continue with our leave.

Life went on as normal until one day when I was in Darwin on a flying exercise. I got back and one of the guys told me that the commanding officer who was back in Nowra at the Squadron was after me. All I remember is going cold. But I didn't have a guilty conscience, so I knew I wasn't in trouble. All I could think was that something had happened to Kay. When I called him he told me about the nomination for the Bravery Medal over the phone and that he was faxing me the forms to accept it. A few weeks later, I received confirmation of the award. You have to keep these things quiet until they are printed in the *Commonwealth Gazette*, so only Kay and I knew about it for a while. Once it was published, I received letters of congratulation from admirals, ministers, and the Premier of New South Wales. It was all quite surreal. John and Jane Gibson had sent us all letters of thanks just after the rescue.

On 23 September 1999, all the crews attended the investiture ceremony at Government House and received awards for their efforts. There were a lot of other people receiving awards of all kinds: doctors and professors getting awards for their research or discoveries or work, couples who had raised hundreds of children getting awards for that, and then there were all kinds of people being awarded Australia Medals and Order of Australia Medals. There were a couple of civilian bravery awards as well. Each recipient is brought forward and presented with their award as their citation is read out. I was told later that the biggest rounds of applause were for our awards, and lots of recipients came up to congratulate us. One fireman, who had also received an award, said, 'I just want to shake your hand.' I still don't understand why. I mean, don't these guys do this sort of thing every day, with no big fanfare?

Since getting the Bravery Medal, nothing much has really changed for me as a person. A couple of friends always introduce me as 'the hero', which embarrasses me and means I have to tell the story again. Doing the rescue has probably helped me acknowledge my abilities and boost my confidence and experience levels, but I don't think I needed to receive an award for that. My nephews and nieces think I am a cool uncle because I have fast cars and bikes and fly in helicopters. That is more important to me than wearing a medal. I think anyone who is trained to do what we do would say that we are not brave. We just do what we have to. People rely on us to help and we have the training and the equipment to do it. It's as simple as that. I think true bravery is the one person out of the crowd of onlookers who, untrained and unprepared, will put themselves in danger to help someone. I would not hesitate a second to do the same thing again, though. I have done it in the toughest conditions now, I trust the people I work with, and all my affairs are in order.

Shane is now Chief Petty Officer posted to 816 Squadron at HMAS Albatross in Nowra. Since receiving his decoration he has been called upon to assist in fighting the bushfires that destroyed parts of Canberra in January 2003. He continues to be an instructor in Seahawk Sensor Operations. Shane now lives near Nowra. He has no plans to leave the Navy and still enjoys the occasional detachment and deployment to other parts of Australia.

FOLLOWING IS THE GROUP CITATION FOR BRAVERY AWARDED to Shane and the crew of the Seahawk helicopter after their efforts in the Sydney to Hobart rescue.

GROUP CITATION FOR BRAVERY
Lieutenant Aaron Seaton Abbott RAN
Lieutenant Commander Richard Duncan Neville RAN
Petty Officer Brian Shane Pashley
Lieutenant Nicholas Mark Trimmer RAN

On the night of 28 December 1998, the crew of the Royal Australian Navy Seahawk 875 Helicopter rescued yachtsmen during the 1998 Sydney to Hobart Yacht Race. The crew were tasked to identify a light source that had been observed 80 nautical miles south east of Merimbula. On nearing the given location, the lack of visibility forced the crew to fly slowly with the cabin door open. On sighting a light, the helicopter was placed in a hover position and the crew identified two people in a life raft. Despite the crew facing conditions involving winds up to 30 knots, a swell of some 10 metres, and poor visibility, they decided to attempt the rescue mission. The aircraft was placed in a hover position 80 feet above the stranded yachtsmen and a crew member, Petty Officer Pashley, was winched down to assess the yachtsmen's physical condition before attempting a rescue. On reaching the life raft, Petty Officer Pashley attached the winch strop to one of the yachtsmen. Unfortunately, before he and the yachtsman could be winched aboard, the helicopter's auto pilot system malfunctioned, dragging the pair some 50 metres through the sea. Through team effort and determination, the helicopter's position was corrected after some 15 minutes and the winching operation was then successfully carried out. The crew, realising the increased danger caused by the technical problem with the aircraft, decided to rescue the second yachtsman in a single lift. The unmanned winch was lowered into the sea and, on the second attempt, once he had secured the winch strop to himself, the remaining yachtsman was winched safely aboard the helicopter. For their actions, they are commended for brave conduct.

EAST TIMOR

EAST TIMOR, A NATION NOT UNFAMILIAR TO INTERNAL VIOLENCE, has been on the United Nations General Assembly international agenda as a country in turmoil since 1960. Then, East Timor was administered by Portugal, however in 1974 Portugal effectively abandoned East Timor, leaving the country to declare itself independent. Civil war broke out between those who favoured independence and those who advocated integration with Indonesia. Indonesia intervened with military force and later incorporated East Timor as its 27th province with an estimated death toll of 60,000 East Timorese and almost half a million more displaced by February 1976. The United Nations never recognised this integration, and both the Security Council and the General Assembly called for Indonesia's withdrawal from East Timor.

Throughout the 1980s and 1990s, the United Nations held talks with both Indonesia and Portugal in an attempt to resolve the status of the territory. In May 1999 a set of agreements were signed by both governments to allow the UN to organise and conduct a 'popular consultation' to determine what the people of East Timor wanted: independence from Indonesia, or integration with Indonesia.

To complete this consultation process, the United Nations Assistance Mission in East Timor (UNAMET) was established on 11 June 1999. The mission deployed some 900 international staff members, including Australians, to carry out its mission, including up to 280 civilian police officers to advise the Indonesian Police, as well as 50 military liaison officers to maintain contact with the Indonesian Armed Forces. The role of UNAMET was to oversee the process of the referendum and the transition period pending implementation of the decision of the East Timorese people. The people of East Timor voted for full independence from Indonesia amid violent clashes, primarily started by pro-integration militia groups. Unable to handle the violence, UNAMET ceased to function on 25 October 1999, and peacekeepers were sent in.

Australia's major role in East Timor began on 20 September 1999, with the formation of INTERFET (International Force East Timor). The purpose of INTERFET was to restore law and order to East Timor after the failure of UNAMET. The 9500-strong Australian force, the largest deployment of Australian troops since World War II, led the multinational force, securing East Timor and engaging a defensive position on the Western Border with Indonesia. The West Timor Enclave of Oecussi was also secured by the 3rd Battalion, Royal Australian Regiment (3RAR).

Making up a small, yet significant, component of the INTERFET force was a Squadron from SASR. Initially, their role was to assist in the security of points of entry in Dili and Baucau for the rest of the force. Later, the squadron featured heavily in operations throughout the province, providing force commanders with situational awareness, or the gathering of intelligence. During an intensive three weeks, various sized patrols undertook numerous operations, many of which proved quite unnerving due to the constraints of the INTERFET rules of engagement. On 13 October, a small patrol, led by Sergeant Steve Oddy, was tasked with a reconnaissance of an area near the border of East Timor in which intelligence suggested a large militia force was located. For three days, the patrol moved undetected towards their target. As the patrol was establishing their observation post, a small group of militia stumbled upon them. What was to follow saw Sergeant Oddy decorated with the Medal for Gallantry in April 2000.

Following Steve's story is another account that demonstrates great bravery and presence of mind. During the process of preparing East Timor for the referendum that was to decide their future, a small group of Australian civilian police, military personnel, and public servants joined the UNAMET mission. One of those Australians was Major John Sholl, an Army intelligence officer. Working as a Military Liaison Officer in the district of Viqueque, he witnessed first-hand the violence between pro-independence and pro-integration groups as the date for the highly charged referendum approached. Two weeks before the vote was to be held, Major Sholl intervened in what would have become a deadly clash between a mourning group of East Timorese people and an unarmed senior Indonesian police officer. His role in averting the danger saw him decorated with a Bravery Medal in May 2000.

'A LOT GOES THROUGH YOUR MIND IN A CONTACT'

Sergeant Steven Oddy MG

CITATION
MEDAL FOR GALLANTRY

For gallantry on 16 October 1999 while leading a patrol in the vicinity of Aidaba Salala, East Timor, during Operation WARDEN.

I WAS BORN IN GERALDTON IN WESTERN AUSTRALIA IN 1967, and grew up in Margaret River, south of Perth. I come from quite a large family as there are step-siblings, half siblings, and then my own siblings as well. In total, I have four brothers and three sisters. Margaret River isn't a large place, so my school years were great. There were only ever around 100 kids at both my primary and my high schools. I formed some really great friendships and even now we are still in contact with each other.

My father was a cray fisherman, with his own boat. Growing up, I guess I just expected that I would become one too. I loved fishing and thought crayfishing would be the best job I could get. We fish out off Geraldton and the Abrolhos Islands. Cray fishing wasn't as easy as I had hoped. Getting out of bed every day before dawn wasn't fun so things changed after working with Dad for a year! At age 17 I began to reconsider my future. When the cray season ended, I found myself working as a brickie's labourer for my brother-in-law in Margaret River. While I didn't mind the labouring work, I wasn't satisfied. Out of the blue I told my mum I was going to join the Army. The first two jobs of my life were very physical and strict, and although I didn't realise at the time, they set me up well for my new career.

The Army was something I had never considered before. I didn't know much about it at all. In fact, I didn't even know that there was a Special Air Service Regiment in Perth. My grandfather was in World War II but I didn't know that either, until I joined the Army. He never spoke about it. Mum and my stepfather thought that joining the Army was great. Dad was obviously disappointed because I am sure he had hoped that I would help him until I could take over from him. But he was always proud of me and he understands the choices I made. Once I made up my mind to join the Army, things moved pretty quickly. I made enquiries in October 1984, had my interviews in November and by January 1985 I was at Kapooka, New South Wales doing my basic training. I didn't have much time to think about whether I was doing the right or wrong thing.

Army training shocks everybody; there is no question about that. I don't think too many people would say that they weren't a bit overwhelmed in the first few weeks of walking through the gates at Kapooka. It is tough coming from a civilian lifestyle where things are pretty carefree and relaxed, to military training where you are told what to do every waking moment. Admittedly I was used to getting up at four in the morning to go fishing and I was fit and strong from labouring. The physical stuff didn't bother me at all. I coped with that really well. I struggled more with the initial discipline. I was an 18-year-old kid who didn't take too well at being told what to do! But after the first three or four weeks, I began to love the training.

Mum, my stepfather Victor and my youngest sister Jodie drove all the way over from Margaret River to watch me at my march-out parade at Kapooka. I was awarded the trophy for Best at Physical Training. Coming to my march-out parade was one of the happiest times of their lives and they were immensely proud of me. I was allocated to Infantry corps and went to Singleton to do my initial employment training after marching out of Kapooka. Although I didn't know much about the Army, I really liked being in the bush and all the physical work, as well as the shooting and patrolling, so I couldn't think of any other corps that appealed to me more than Infantry. Most of my platoon was also allocated to Infantry, so it was a great few months with a great bunch of blokes. I was getting paid, I was active, seeing different parts of Australia and I had a fantastic time.

After I finished my training in July 1985, I was posted to Delta Company, 2nd/4th Battalion, Royal Australian Regiment (2/4 RAR) in Townsville. I was thrilled to be going to that unit because I didn't know anything about any of the towns along the east coast and Townsville was such a big Army town. I was just glad to be going somewhere new that was by the ocean and wasn't cold like Singleton! After six months in the company, I went to Reconaissance platoon where I stayed until I went for my selection course.

The funniest thing about the way my career has played out is that I didn't have any idea what Special Air Service (SAS) was when I went for the selection course. My platoon commander, Lieutenant Bill, came to work one morning and said, 'Steve, you are doing the selection course next year,' and like a good soldier I simply said, 'Yep, no problem.' After a few weeks of constant training, I asked, 'So what is this selection course anyway?' I honestly had no idea what it was all about.

In retrospect, not knowing much about this selection course worked to my advantage. I didn't have any expectations so I just trained according to what Lieutenant Bill outlined, and I trained really hard. Mentally, there were some really tough parts to the selection course but I was extremely fit because Bill had worked us extremely hard. I think I was the second youngest bloke to get into the Regiment since the Vietnam War. My age and fitness really worked in my favour. Seven out of the 14 of us that Bill selected for the selection course got in, including Bill.

I quite enjoyed the selection course. It was only 28 days long back then. A lot of the staff who ran the course were Vietnam veterans. Rumours went around about what some of them did in the war, but we didn't have much to do with them personally. As a student it wasn't like you could sit down and have a chat with them about it. To be honest, I didn't really know much about the Vietnam War. I didn't look at them and think, 'Wow', because I didn't fully understand what it was all about. However, six months into my training in the Regiment, I began to understand what these guys had done and the experiences they'd had. After that I was really in awe of them. They were great instructors and good blokes. They were around in the Regiment for the next six years or so before they started retiring, so we all got to learn a lot from them.

I felt like I had a home in the Regiment. I settled in really quickly and we were extremely busy during my first year. We did courses and exercises back to back, but because I was young, I adapted really quickly. Being single also worked in my favour as the guys who were married had to lead two separate lives; their home life with their wife and family, and their Regiment life. Juggling the two was tough. My life simply revolved around the Regiment, initially. Then I met Lisa in 1989 and we were married in 1991. Our first child was born the following year. I sincerely thank Lisa for her understanding as there is no way I would be where I am now without her. While I had to have two lives like the other guys, she is so supportive of me and so capable. I know I can go away and that she will manage. I didn't have to constantly worry about whether she is going to be all right or whether she is coping. It has made my life and job a lot easier.

My years in the Regiment prepared me to be a good leader. I gained immense experience from the people, exercises, and operations we were involved with. By the time our squadron was deployed to East Timor, I had been in the Army for 14 years, 12 of which were in the Regiment, and I was a sergeant. Our time in East Timor was very busy right from the beginning. We were involved in Operation SPITFIRE, which involved the evacuation of Australians and United Nations (UN) personnel from East Timor in September 1999. Then we were part of INTERFET and Operation STABILISE immediately after that.

Because we had a good understanding of the problems in the country we knew it was always a matter of when something was going to happen, rather than if, and we approached everything with that understanding. I was involved in the Suai incident [an ambush of INTERFET troops by militia in October 1999], along with a couple of other incidents.

There were a lot of militia pockets around the West near the border; there were rumours circulating that large groups of militia were throughout the area. After speaking with Squadron Commanding Officer, Jim McMahon, in mid-October, I discovered that a reconaissance patrol would be sent out to see what was in the area before we went in and did whatever we had to do. I said that I wanted to do it and about 12 hours later, we were flying in to the region of Aidaba Salala and our patrol was inserted. Another patrol had already been through and had observed militia groups in the region.

Ours was a six-man patrol, which included one non-Australian who was in the Regiment on exchange, and was made up from the troop that I was Troop Sergeant for. We had been training together as a troop continuously for three months leading up to our deployment so we knew each other extremely well. I had a very close connection with all the guys. Essentially, we were going in for a set period of a couple of weeks with the capability of staying for longer if we had to. There was a certain amount of flexibility, though: if we found what we wanted in 24 hours, then we could come out, but if we needed to stay for longer we could do that, too.

The patrol itself was really interesting as we had several close calls with the enemy before our contact. After we were installed, we patrolled very slowly in the direction of our target, which was the village of Aidaba Salala. During the first night, we crossed over a dry river bed around four kilometres from the village. It was a really foggy night and our vision was severely hampered. We needed to cross the river bed by night so that we could lay up by day. When we got to the other side, I sat the patrol down. For a reason that I can't explain, I wasn't comfortable where we were so I picked them up and moved them another 50 or so metres before sitting them back down again. During the move I had noticed some foot prints along a small track. Again, I wasn't happy with our position so I picked them up again. The guys were probably getting really annoyed with me moving them so much but I just wasn't happy; I didn't think we should stay where we were.

I moved them in to a thick, scrubby area. As daylight came on, the fog started to lift and we began to hear a lot of voices very close by. By the time the sun had come up and the fog had fully lifted, we discovered we were right in the middle of a village, and we didn't know what it was because it wasn't on our map. We knew the militia were displacing a lot of villages and rounding up the men to make them fight with them. Where we were now holed up just happened to be one of those newly formed villages, and it was heavily populated. We stopped counting at 300 men, but there were certainly more than that there. We found out later that a lot of the men in this village were from surrounding villages that had been displaced and were effectively taken against their will to fight for the militia.

Throughout the day, the villagers were often walking past us no more than two metres away. We were in very thick scrub so we were quite happy that they couldn't detect us. Throughout the day, I got our signaller to send messages back to headquarters letting them know what was going on. We stayed there the whole day, remaining completely undetected. Occasionally, little pigs and dogs would come up and sniff around us, but they weren't interested in us, fortunately. Despite being right in the middle of the village, I felt so comfortable where we were hiding that we took it in turns to have a kip!

We waited until nightfall and then moved out using our night vision goggles (NVGs) because it was a completely pitch-black night. By now everyone in the village was asleep – once the sun goes down, they just go to bed. We could see where they were sleeping around their little fires so we patrolled our way in among them.

The problem with wearing NVGs is that you have limited depth perception, which makes it hard to see things on the ground, particularly when it is pitch black. As a result, one of the guys in the patrol fell into a hole camouflaged with branches. Obviously the sound of him falling into this hole was deafening when we were trying to be sneaky! We froze and waited but nobody in the village moved. We saw a dog lift up his ears and have a bit of a sniff but he put his head down and went back to sleep. To this day, I still don't know why that dog didn't bark.

After that our hearts were pounding and we were even more hyper-alert. We continued to follow the windy track that ran through the village so we could get out of there. We probably got 100 metres or so further along this track and one of my scouts stopped dead where he stood. Through my NVGs, I could see he was bringing his weapon up to his front. Then I heard footsteps about 15 metres or so in front of him. Right around then, I saw five militia-men who appeared to be going out on patrol, walking on the track towards us.

The scout could tell they hadn't seen us so we slunk back into the jungle and they walked past us. The track was only two feet wide and we literally just stepped back into the vegetation on either side of it. As they moved past us they were no more than 10 centimetres from our chests. It was really frightening to be that close to the enemy and not know if we were about to be detected. I think we all just held our breaths and hoped that our camouflage continued to work. The fact that they didn't sense us or smell us still amazes me now. Then again, perhaps they did see us. Perhaps they held their breaths as they walked past us and once they were past, said 'Phew, did you see those guys back there?'! In any case, we didn't want to compromise ourselves so we went back on patrol out of the village once they'd gone past.

I think a lot of what happens with us in the Regiment is luck. You can do all the planning in the world but when it comes down to the crunch, I think luck has a part to play. Stumbling across this village was a good thing in hindsight, as we gathered a lot of intelligence that might have helped in planning future operations. There were plans to send large groups of our guys through the region because it was thought that there were only small groups of militia in the area. They could have easily had quite a nasty clash with this village because of the large numbers of militia it contained. For all we know, it might have been another Somalia where they just came out of everywhere and attacked when they were least expected.

We patrolled the whole next night, moving towards our target area, and stopped at around 0200 hours to rest for an hour. Then I and two others went forward a few hundred metres to ensure our location was accurate. After we found the creek which I had planned for us to cross, we rejoined the patrol and moved out under darkness back to the creek. As it started to get a little bit lighter, I noticed some fresh footprints on the bank of the creek. I decided to set up an observation point. Fom the map, I knew the creek flowed from the border between East and West Timor, and that there were villages along the way. We assumed that any militia crossing the border from the West to the East would follow this creek bed because it would be easier for them to navigate.

The observation point was on higher ground in among lantana and scattered scrub, and looked down into the creek bed and along it. The dry bed was only around 15 metres wide but it had steep banks on both sides. I had only positioned the patrol for around 10 minutes when I heard the first shots ring out. I don't remember the exact time the contact began, but I think it was around 0600 hours. We didn't see the enemy when we were crossing the creek bed earlier – where we crossed gave us a good view. They weren't walking slowly, though. I couldn't say whether they knew we were there or not; it wasn't obvious in the way they were patrolling. For all I know, they could have been sitting 300 metres away and saw us cross over and decided to try to find us.

When the initial contact began, I was right in the middle of the lying up point doing a final navigation check and getting ready to send a situation report back to headquarters to let them know what was going on. We were quite prepared to stay there at that observation point for as long as we needed to. Our job was to find out if there was anyone in the area, and as I had already noticed footprints, I knew there was. I figured it would be a long couple of days, watching what was going on. We weren't going in there to hunt anyone down so ideally we wanted to remain undetected. It didn't surprise me when the enemy appeared in the creek bed, but I think I was surprised how soon after our arrival they were there. In retrospect, it shouldn't have been too surprising because it was first light. In East Timor, the middle of the day is really hot so they tend to move in the cool of the morning or when it begins to cool down later in the afternoon.

I think we were lucky that we were already in our position when the contact began. I heard the shots ring out across the back of my right shoulder, which was where I had positioned one of my scouts. My immediate reaction was to help him out. When I got there, we could see the enemy patrol of about six or seven guys coming up the creek bed at a distance of 100 metres or so. I found out later that the enemy scout and our scout saw each other simultaneously. The enemy scout put his weapon up in the direction of my guy, who had just finished clearing his area so that his view was unimpeded but his concealment was intact. Whether the enemy scout was going to take an aimed shot or was using his weapon to point in our direction, we'll never know. We don't know if they saw or heard something or were just a little jittery, but when our scout saw the enemy scout bring his weapon up aggressively, he didn't hesitate to open fire. He was well within the rules of engagement given to him before we went out on the patrol and he did the right thing.

A lot goes through your mind when a contact like this begins. It isn't like things move in slow motion – things are quite clear. As soon as I returned fire, I looked back at the rest of my patrol. Obviously they knew we had a contact but as they weren't in direct line of the enemy, they weren't involved in the fire fight. They couldn't see much at that stage because of the positions I had just put them in. Only my scout and I were firing.

The enemy withdrew immediately. We don't know how many were killed or wounded in that initial contact, but we do know that one enemy, presumably dead, was left in the creek bed when they withdrew. They continued shooting in our direction as they withdrew but none of their fire was effective. You could see their rounds going into the trees above our heads. We felt pretty safe; their withdrawal was very disorganised. They continued shooting at us, some shots ringing out from even as far as 300 metres away. Once that had quietened down, I figured that they would probably try to come around in a flanking attack so I repositioned two of the guys to a higher point so they could see further down the creek bed.

About five minutes later, the enemy came back up the creek bed and tried to flank us just as I predicted. The two guys I repositioned for that purpose repelled that attack fairly quickly. One of the guys was the machine gunner and he killed another person in the creek bed. I could hear some of the enemy coming around the far side of the two patrol members so I put in covering fire and pulled them back, sitting very still, just listening. My thoughts shifted to whether we should move out now and in which direction we could go. I could hear a lot of movement all around us. It sounded extremely disorganised but I didn't know where we could go without running into them. To the left was some high ground but it was very open so I knew there was no point going that way. To the south was the target village, which was where the enemy had come from. This village was only probably 500 metres away so that wasn't going to be an option. I knew that there was a track to my east but I definitely didn't want to go out on that. As I was contemplating our withdrawal, I heard a lot of movement in the direction of the track so we knew then that they were going to attack us again.

Once again, I was faced with the decision of what to do next. I didn't want to move from our position because I wasn't sure of the number of enemy we were facing. I knew we were safe where we were because none of their fire was effective. Clearly, they didn't know where we were exactly. I got my signaller to tap out a contact report on his radio. He was able to send it within three minutes, ████ was good on his part. Then we went back into all-round defence again.

As I said, I could hear a lot of movement coming from the direction of the track. I pushed my second-in-command a little bit further out so that he was on a mound, and we could hear them mounting another attack towards us from the track. It sounded a little more coordinated this time. We couldn't understand everything they were saying but you could tell by the tone of their voices that they were confused about our position. We had a linguist in the patrol who could understand them perfectly. He and I were looking at each other throughout the moments leading up to each of the attacks but he wasn't sending me any alarmed looks to indicate that it was all going to hit the fan. Rather, his look was very calm; and if he wasn't worried, neither was I.

They began to attack us in an extended line, but only five of them were in our area. We waited for them to come within about two to three metres of our position and we shot at them again. Because they were closer, we were able to throw grenades as well. Their firing and moving slowed down very quickly after that. At that point, I knew that we had to use this lull to make a withdrawal. We broke contact and ceased firing. As we weren't receiving effective fire, I didn't see the point in continuing to waste ammo. They were still firing at us but it was going well above our heads so we withdrew on our stomachs and knees for about 400 metres without firing back. The enemy didn't understand where we had gone and once we had pulled back across the creek – it was the only way we could go – I could still hear them firing but it was not directed at us. While we were on our stomachs, I knew they wouldn't be able to see us. If we stood up, though, they probably would have seen us. Earlier that morning I noticed a possible landing zone so we were heading for that. Almost two hours after the contact began, we made it to the landing zone.

The concerning thing for us was that the Quick Response Force (QRF) hadn't shown up. It had now been about 90 minutes since our initial contact report had been sent. The plan was that on any contact, the QRF would be despatched to help out. While we were back at the observation point, we saw four Black Hawk helicopters flying past us towards Dili about five miles away. Initially we thought they were the QRF but later on we found out that boys from the Squadron were on board those Black Hawks but the QRF were still back in Dili. Some of the guys on board the helicopters said that they heard our contact (the grenades and the M203s going off) as they were flying past but obviously they didn't have any idea what was going on.

At the landing zone I got our signaller to re-send the message. Then I asked him to get on the other radio to get them up on voice to explain what had happened. It turned out that although our radio had sent through the message, headquarters didn't receive it. Nobody else knew what was going on and no QRF was coming. But once they received word that we had been in a contact, the QRF arrived at the landing zone within 15 minutes. We got on one chopper while the other one circled the area.

Before we withdrew, I got the guys to leave their packs so that we could get away more easily. We grabbed our radios and any other mission-essential equipment and took them out with us. When we got on the chopper, the pilots said that they hadn't seen much activity apart from some people scattering off towards the village. None of them were carrying weapons. Discarding weapons was a common thing among the militia because they knew we couldn't do anything to them if they weren't carrying any – we could round them up but couldn't shoot at them. I asked the pilots to fly over the area of our contact and we could clearly see that there was nobody there. We could see the enemy killed in action but there didn't appear to be anyone else around so I asked the pilot to land near our lying up point so that we could collect our packs. Two of us jumped off, grabbed the packs, then climbed back in. Then we flew back to Dili and went into debriefing.

The total time taken from when the first contact took place to when we were back in Dili being debriefed was around two and a half hours. Everything happened really fast. The enemy mounted four assaults on us and none of them were effective. Only the last assault had any kind of control. The rest were disorganised and chaotic.

Another patrol went back to the area around three or four weeks later and they interviewed the head of the village about what he recalled of that day. He said that there were over 100 militia hunting us down during that contact. It certainly didn't sound like over 100 guys attacking us, though. Afterwards, 11 of their guys were missing. They recovered five bodies, which were the five that we knew we had killed, but there was still another six guys they couldn't locate. I personally couldn't account for 11 killed. I saw three to four killed and that is what I reported, but none of our figures added up to the possibility of 11 dead. The figures from the other patrol members added up to six or seven killed.

When they heard the noise of contact from the village, they banged drums to rouse all the militia in the area to conduct an assault on where they thought we were. I knew in the last attack that there were probably more than 20 of them because they were spread out and you could hear a lot of voices. In our area alone there was five enemy, so if you multiply that out, they could have had around 25 in the line, but they did have some depth. At the time we thought there was possibly up to 30 of them on a concentrated attack on us but all I was concerned about was the safety of the patrol, so whether there was 30 or 100, it didn't matter. Perhaps, if we had been receiving effective fire on our position, I might have felt differently. There was certainly a lot of fire coming towards us – definitely a lot more than we were putting out – but it was all going at least a metre above our heads.

The thing that I feel really strongly about is ensuring that the other guys in the patrol get some credit for their conduct on that day. They were so well disciplined. There was one guy who didn't even fire a round. No enemy came within his arc of responsibility so he didn't fire his weapon. He maintained courageous battle discipline to have fought off the instinct to leave his post and join in the fire fight. That was brave to me. I always use his action as an example when I am training with anyone, whether it is with Australian or foreign forces. In the movies, whenever there is a contact, the guys just shoot off wildly, going through magazine after magazine. I think I shot the most rounds out of anyone in the whole series of contacts, apart from the gunner, of course, and I only shot 47 rounds. Only shooting off 47 rounds in a series of four contacts over a period of an hour and a half is extremely good. That's something that shocks people when we talk about it because of the number of casualties, and the time we were in contact, outweighed far and beyond the amount of ammo used.

Everyone in the patrol should receive accolades. The non-Australian soldier in our patrol was outstanding. He had a wife and children and I could see that he was very apprehensive at times. He would look back towards me as if to say, 'What are we going to do now?' I would just say, 'Sit there and wait', and he would immediately turn back and wait. We knew the enemy was going to be coming from his direction in one of the assaults, so he was going to be the one to hit the enemy first just over two metres away from him, but he just sat there and didn't argue. He trusted me enough and was brave enough to stay there when I told him to. He didn't become agitated or fidget; he just got on with the job.

Another guy who was on the other side of the lying up point was also really good. He also knew he was going to be the one facing the enemy in one of the assaults and he stayed there, unflinching. The rest of the guys in the patrol were great, too. Not one of them said, 'Come on, we've got to go' or anything like that. They stayed in their positions all the way through four assaults. We were all in eye contact throughout the fire fight so that helped. As Patrol Commander, I didn't have to worry about them; I could just get on with my job and make decisions to stay one step ahead of the enemy's movements. They didn't catch us off guard once, so not having to worry about the patrol contributed to us getting out of it as well as we did. The guys are not thinking about what we will do next, where we will be escaping to, and that kind of thing. That's my job. It is all about trust and fortunately, they trusted me enough to let me do my job. They knew that I am a calm guy by nature and that I wasn't going to get flustered. Even when we were being shot at, I watched the rounds going overhead and it didn't faze me. That was the first time I had been shot at, so I was interested in how I would respond to that. At one stage early on in the shooting, I sat up and took my carotid pulse just to see how my body was reacting! My signaller saw me and gestured for me to get down. I sat back down again and he just shook his head. Funnily enough, my heart rate had only elevated to 80 beats per minute!

Everyone in the patrol made the correct choice. I was not disappointed with any aspect of it. We all got out safely and unharmed, which is ideal. We also gathered good intelligence, which meant that we achieved our mission. Obviously, not to have had the contact would have been even more ideal as it may have meant that we gathered even more intelligence, but the contact meant that our intelligence was right. The guys in the patrol talked about the incident a bit with their close mates, but I can't say that I really did. I was given another tasking very quickly after that, so I never really had much opportunity to think about it or dwell on it. It isn't as though it brings up bad memories; I just can't be bothered talking about it.

About five months after I came back from East Timor, I received the letter to say that I had been awarded the Medal for Gallantry.

Admittedly I didn't even know what it was. I asked CJ, the second-in-command of the Squadron at the time, who explained what it was and what it was for. I don't read a lot of military books and I certainly never read anything written about the Regiment. I had no idea what this medal was all about or why I would be getting it. As a unit we are quite happy to do what we do and not be noticed for it. Then suddenly, two or three books came out about us and now everyone is interested. I accept that people are interested, but I didn't want to be a part of those books.

In all honesty, the day of the investiture was a fairly stressful day. My wife and children went over to Canberra to be there with me and, as none of us had been there before, the day before the ceremony we got into our car to do a reconaissance of where we had to go the next day. The last thing I wanted was to get lost or be late! We did the reconaissance and figured we would be fine the following day. Then, on the day of the investiture, we approached Government House from a different road and missed the exit completely! I made sure that we left the hotel early enough that we would have arrived at Government House with 30 minutes up our sleeve. As it turned out we ended up rushing in with only 10 minutes to spare because we got completely lost and then couldn't get off the road we were on. We ended up driving over a median strip so we could get back to where we needed to go.

Despite that incident, the day was fantastic. The Queen was there to present us with our medals. Our kids were telling their friends at school that they were going to meet the Queen but no one believed them. Meeting her was really an honour. She took time after the ceremony to talk to us all. She was a lovely lady, just like a grandmother; she seemed genuinely interested in what we had to say. She spoke a fair bit to Lisa and the kids, which they got a kick out of.

I guess it didn't really sink in until a few hours later that we had just met and talked with the Queen. It was quite an honour. Everything is so formalised and at the time I didn't take it all in. I was more concerned with ensuring that I did everything I had to do correctly. I certainly didn't want to be remembered as the one who stuffed up! Later, though, I reflected on it and I think that was when I could relax and enjoy what had happened.

Within the Regiment we don't talk about the awards. I never found out who nominated me. The guys in the patrol were really happy for me. After the incident, I did get a lot of thanks from the guys but we don't talk about it anymore. If you receive a medal in the Regiment, you know that you didn't receive it because of your own individual actions. I have made that clear all along – that if it hadn't been for the five other blokes in the patrol, there is no way I would have received that medal. It is quite embarrassing to wear it in front of them. They are happy for me and whenever they come over, they like to have a look at it. I very rarely take any notice of it other than when I have to wear it. I don't think it has changed me as a person in any way and I don't think it has affected my career. I knew what I wanted from my career before I was awarded the Medal for Gallantry and I have been working towards that ever since I started in the Regiment. A year or so after being awarded it, I did end up in the US on a posting for a few years, so perhaps that was a bit of a reward.

I don't think what I did was as brave as some and that was why my initial reaction upon receiving that letter was to go and ask CJ what the medal was for. I didn't think I did anything gallant in the true sense of the word. I re-read the letter more thoroughly and I saw that the medal is awarded for leadership under fire as well as gallantry. My actions were the reaction of a commander of a patrol and I responded in the way that any other in the Regiment would have done.

To me, bravery is what the Victoria Cross gets awarded for. If you do something above and beyond your job that is so courageous that it saves other people's lives, regardless of whether you put your life in danger or not, that, to me, is brave. What I did on that day was carry out the actions of a soldier and commander.

Now a Warrant Officer Class 2, Steve Oddy has served for just on 20 years in the Australian Defence Force. Since being awarded the Medal for Gallantry, he has taken part in numerous operations and exercises both in Australia and overseas, and was awarded the Bronze Star for his service with an American unit. He lives in Western Australia with his wife and family, and continues to spend what little spare time he has showing his children the joys of life.

'I WAS WAITING FOR THE PAIN OF HIS BLADE'

Major John George Sholl BM

CITATION
BRAVERY MEDAL

On the afternoon of 11 August 1999, Major Sholl was serving in Viqueque, East Timor with the United Nations Assistance Mission in East Timor (UNAMET), when he participated in the rescue of an Indonesian police officer who was being attacked by pro-independence East Timorese villagers.

While on patrol, Major Sholl and a fellow UNAMET officer encountered a group of East Timorese villagers retrieving the body of a man who had been killed by pro-Indonesian militias. The arrival of the police officer provoked anger in the villagers who menaced him with their machetes and spears. Major Sholl and his companion placed themselves between the police officer and the hostile crowd and prevented them from pressing their attack. Some of the villagers who tried to strike the police officer were wrestled away by Major Sholl and his companion. Fearing for his life, the Indonesian police officer broke away and ran into nearby bushes. He was pursued by some of the villagers who attacked him with their machetes. Major Sholl followed and placed himself between the police officer and his attackers so as to prevent the police officer from being killed. Moments later Major Sholl was able to lift the injured police officer to his feet and carry him to safety.

I WAS BORN IN REDCLIFFE, IN QUEENSLAND, IN MAY 1967. MY father was a horse trainer and he died when I was four years old. After his death, we moved to New South Wales to be closer to my mother's family. When I was 13 years old, I moved back up to Queensland to live with my paternal grandparents while I attended high school. During high school I got involved with the Navy cadets and Army Reserve.

I enjoyed it so much that I looked at making a career out of the Army and I applied, and was accepted, to become an officer. After completing Year 12, I went to the Australian Defence Force Academy in Canberra where I completed an Honours degree in history. After that, I went over the hill to the Royal Military College, Duntroon (RMC), for a year and upon graduation, I was allocated to the Infantry Corps. I served five years as an Infantry Officer. My last appointment was as the Intelligence Officer (IO) in the 2nd/4th Battalion, Royal Australian Regiment (2/4 RAR) and that was where I got my taste for intelligence work. I found it very interesting. I decided I would make a great intelligence officer, so I transferred to the Intelligence Corps in 1996.

My first appointment in Intelligence Corps was to go to the School of Languages so that I could become fluent in another language. I really wanted to study French. I had ancestors who were French so I had been learning it myself. In its wisdom the Army said that I couldn't do French because they didn't need French-speaking personnel. This was at a time where engagement into Asia was the topic of the day so anyone who was going to the School of Languages could be assured of learning an Asian language. Obviously Defence relations with areas of Asia were beginning to become a significant focus. However, the decision for me to learn Indonesian was to go on to have great consequences for me a couple of years later. I am now highly knowledgeable in all facets of Indonesia.

From the School of Languages, I was posted to Army Headquarters in Canberra and then to Land Headquarters in Sydney.

During that period I had been involved in working with the training teams in Indonesia as their interpreter, as well as planning conferences and exercises and those kinds of things. I had worked at the Australian Embassy in Indonesia on a short-term secondment in the defence section as a relief member so that the defence personnel could take leave. That was one experience that I enjoyed immensely.

In 1999, the Army began calling for nominations for personnel to go to East Timor to assist in the election process. Initially, we understood that these personnel would go over as Military Liaison Officers (MLO) as part of the United Nations Assistance Mission to East Timor (UNAMET) mission. When I first saw this call for nominations, I thought I was the ideal person to go because of my background. I had a quick conversation with my boss to say that with my background, my fluency in their language, and my understanding of the Indonesians, I was the perfect person to go. He agreed and put my name forward. Eventually five Australians were selected to go over as part of the UNAMET team and I was lucky enough to be one of them. Initially, the number of candidates who were suitable was around 20. However, all of the five who were eventually chosen to go had in-country experience.

I joined UNAMET in Darwin in late June 1999 after completing 10 days' training in Sydney for the mission. On 2 July 1999, we arrived in East Timor and I was shocked to say the least. I thought Dili would be a larger city, much like a Javanese city. It was anything but! As I looked out the window of the minibus, I thought the place was a dump. I think I expected a city in the true sense of the word, but it was backward even for Asian standards. It was dusty; almost like something out of Africa. The irony was, after a month away from Dili, the thought of going back there was extremely appealing as it was entirely better than where we were sent!

I was paired up with an officer from the New Zealand Army, Major Philip Morrison. We were informed that we would be sent to Baucau, which was quite an exciting prospect because it was quite a large town by Timorese standards, and it had better infrastructure and facilities. It was also supposed to be relatively peaceful compared to the rest of the country. However, the following day, we were informed that there had been some unrest in Viqueque, a small district in the south east of the country, between UNAMET and militia, in which a civilian UNAMET member had been threatened with death unless they left town. The house in which the UN people lived had been attacked and all the staff had left and refused to go back, leaving the electoral coordinator there on his own. So on 4 July we were sent to Viqueque to bolster the numbers there.

Our job in Viqueque was to act as liaison officers between the UNAMET electoral officers and the Indonesian military (TNI), as well as liaison officers with FALINTIL (the Armed Forces for the National Liberation of East Timor), and the militias as well. The term 'Military Liasion Officer' came about because the commander of the Indonesian military, General Wiranto, refused to have United Nations Military Observers (UNMO) present in the country. He said that as there wasn't a war, there was no place for military observers, even unarmed military observers, in the country. He saw having UNMOs present was an affront to Indonesian sovereignty. Our role had to be further clarified – that we weren't going to be there as military observers but as liaison officers for the purpose of the election. The title Military Liaison Officer was acceptable to him, so that is what we were. I think the term UNMO has some serious negative connotations to it because they are always present when there is a war or clash going on. This wasn't a war between nations. To the Indonesians, this wasn't even a civil war. General Wiranto agreed to allow a small number of us in; in total, there were about 30, six of whom were from Australia. There were others from nations like New Zealand, Russia, UK, Germany, Austria, and a lot from Latin-American countries.

Originally, Viqueque was not considered worthy of having a MLO presence so early. It was considered a low priority; generally, it was a calm place. But the day before we arrived, they recovered the body of a man who had been hacked up with a machete and his body dumped in a swamp. On arrival, we were delighted to learn that there were four Australian Federal Police agents serving as UNAMET Civilian Police (CIVPOL) in Viqueque. We quickly established a good rapport with them and even established our daily operations as joint MLO–CIVPOL.

The UN essentially gave us a bag of money and told us to find our own accommodation, so Philip and I leased a house in a village known as Monumento, which is in the main part of Viqueque town. It was called Monumento because it had a large monument in the middle of a roundabout that was the focus for the village. We were the only UNAMET personnel living in this part of town apart from the UNAMET Regional Coordinator, Paul Guerin, who was an Irish national, and his staff. The remainder of the UNAMET staff lived some distance away in the village of Beloi.

Once we had arrived in Viqueque, a normal day was very mundane in the beginning. After breakfast of some sweet toast or cake, we would front up to the UN headquarters in Viqueque to attend some morning meetings with CIVPOL or with some of the personnel who were running the election effort in the region. After that, we would usually head out to some of the surrounding areas to conduct some liaison visits. Two weeks after our arrival, our numbers were bolstered with the arrival of Lieutenant Colonel Manuel Lima Neto of Brazil and an American, Major Kerry Larrabee, who has become a very good friend of mine.

A lot of our work involved jumping in one of our UN vehicles to visit electoral roll registration sites in the district. Initially, we got out to meet as many people as we could, from the civilian population through to the Indonesian military, CIVPOL, and even the militia groups. We briefed them on who we were and what our mission was about. After four weeks of doing this, we would find that we just needed to get out and make our presence felt. Often we would try to make our visits friendly, so we'd stop and have a cup of coffee with people, check that the polling sites were running and check whether there had been any incidents. We wore the uniform of our country so they knew who we were, but we wore the UN beret or cap and brassard, and we were unarmed. We were always trying to establish and maintain a rapport with the locals and the UN stakeholders, so we kept these visits as sociable as we could.

Meeting with the militia was always problematic. Sometimes they would meet with us and sometimes they would refuse. Generally, they were very reticent to talk to us. A lot said they didn't recognise the UN's presence and they didn't need to talk to us. Some of them said that, because we were talking to the Indonesian military, they didn't have to talk to us. Most of our meetings with them were very tense. In Viqueque, whether you were pro-independence or pro-integration was based very heavily on tribal and class beliefs. The impression I got was that the higher class – the aristocrats and tribal leaders – were almost overwhelmingly pro-independence. These were the people who had been educated by the Portuguese and had sympathies to Portugal. The militia, though, were like the people from the fringes of society, I thought. They were the dispossessed people in their tribes. Every culture has them, and in East Timor, these kinds of people tended to wind up in the militia because it gave them an identity, rations, a wage, and somewhere to belong. For the most part, they tended to congregate in an area called Beobe.

Major Kerry Larrabee and I went to one meeting in Beobe that was extremely tense. There were men with machetes talking very angrily at us. It was a very interesting experience and I know I walked away feeling exhausted from being constantly on alert. We went back two days later and no one would talk to us because they had been told not to speak to us any more. These meetings were somewhat frightening. The militia had a propensity, and a track record for that matter, for violence. We knew from history that these guys had been guilty of some pretty horrendous violence in the past so meeting with them was pretty scary. I knew they were more than capable of committing a similar act against us if they so chose. The other thing that played on my mind was the death of 10 Belgian peacekeepers in Rwanda in 1994. I had no illusions that the blue beret would protect me, just as it hadn't protected them. I was very conscious of the fact that we were unarmed when we went in to these meetings. However, would I have preferred to have been armed? At the time probably, but with the gift of hindsight, I see that it was almost certainly better not to have been. A side arm wasn't going to save our lives if we had have found ourselves in such a situation. Simply carrying one would have got us into a lot of trouble. I think we knew deep down that we would have to rely on our good looks and charm to get us out of any trouble!

Meeting with FALINTIL was even more problematic. We had one key meeting with one of their commanders, Sabica, when he brought a group of his fighters in to register to vote. We sat down with him and had some sweet biscuits and warm beer. As a non-drinker I didn't join in but Manuel, the Brazilian colonel, did. It was quite an interesting meeting because Sabica couldn't speak English and he wouldn't speak Indonesian, so Manuel and he spoke to each other in Portuguese.

Within a fortnight of our arrival, tensions in Viqueque really quietened down. Throughout early July, it was a model mission. We had high electoral enrolments, low violence, and the militia were keeping a low presence. People began going out in the evenings.

Then, in early August, a group of militia, whom we suspected had come from Dili, had been seen in the area. We think they told the locals they weren't carrying their weight and that things were too quiet. The locals were '59/75 Junior' or 'Sons of 59/75'. The 59 was a reference to a 1959 anti-Portuguese rebellion and the 75 referred to the 1975 invasion. Also around this time, a group of pro-independence supporters known as the Student Solidarity Front (SSF) were in the process of opening up a representative office. None of us wanted this because we knew that they could be really provocative in their actions. Their plan was to campaign against the autonomy option in the upcoming ballot. Paul Guerin, the regional coordinator, had already counselled them that the effect of their presence would be counterproductive, because most voters in the region had already decided how they would vote. Even at this stage, we sensed a strong pro-independence sentiment. Unfortunately, they chose to ignore Paul and the SSF office was scheduled to open on 11 August.

After 11 August, an eerie feeling settled on the town and people stopped going out after dark. In their culture, it is quite normal to spend the evenings strolling around the streets, visiting friends. For there to be nobody out of an evening and for the streets to be deadly quiet was not a good sign. To me, it was worrying.

The National Council of Timorese Resistance (CNRT) had already opened up an office in Viqueque without incident. The CNRT were clever operators, though. These guys knew how far they could push their political agenda before they invited retaliation. They were old hands at the independence game. The SSF worried us. Our preference was to stop them doing what they wanted to do but we had no legal basis to do that, or do anything else about it. The Indonesians didn't particularly want them there but allowed them to open up regardless. You can imagine the response of the international media if the Indonesians hadn't allowed them to open up, so they did the only thing they could do. To me, the student presence was the problem.

Things really started to go wrong on the evening of 10 August. It started with a number of shots being fired at the SSF office with homemade weapons in a drive-by shooting. Also, two SSF members were reportedly kidnapped. When we heard the shots, our drill was to stay in our house and the CIVPOL would go to investigate. They took some statements and that was the end of it. The shooting died down just as quickly as it started so none of us were particularly worried. Having said that, it wasn't unusual to hear the occasional shot being fired so we never concerned ourselves about it, unless of course it was outside our house! The militia were usually responsible for this show, whether they were making a display of bravado or intimidation, or simply hunting.

The next morning we got on with our normal day's activities. By this time, part of my normal daily duty included a monster of a trip to a little village called Dilor. As a crow flies, the village is probably only 60 kilometres north-west of Viqueque. However, as I had to go by vehicle, it was a horribly long trip over the worst road in the district that took almost two hours one way. I would have to get up early so that I could get there and leave again before it got dark. Dilor was also a militia stronghold and every visit was very stressful. It was an oppressive place that could quite easily over-whelm you. You could see that the people in the village were genuinely frightened. We had wanted to have a permanent presence there but the UN security office wouldn't allow it. I had even volunteered to go there; I hated the journey so much that I was prepared to go and live there in among all that oppression and unease. I had nothing but admiration for the two UN Electoral officers, one from America and the other from Czechoslovakia, who worked there every day during the registration period for the ballot. In any case, I had been going there every day for a week and was really exhausted. I told my boss that I needed a break and he agreed, believing that I would be better off spending the day in Viqueque catching up on paperwork and having a bit of a rest.

My plan for 11 August was just that – rest and paperwork. In the afternoon, I would try to go for a run. That morning, Manuel and Philip were going down towards the coast as they had been told that there were some explosives planted on a disused pipeline that they wanted to have a look at. It was fairly quiet for most of the morning and I had managed to catch up on a lot of my paperwork. I certainly felt rested.

By 1245 hours, I was having a nice lunch of rice, tuna and sweet chilli sauce while listening to the portable radio we all carried so that we could communicate with each other. I heard a large number of gunshots somewhere in the distance. A CIVPOL came on the radio to say that there had been a shooting over near the SSF office and instructed all the UNAMET personnel to stay where they were. I continued eating my lunch when I heard my call-sign being called by the CIVPOL telling me that they needed my help because the TNI were involved.

As I didn't have a vehicle, Federal Agent Paul McEwan had to come by to pick me up. I got quite excited at the opportunity for some action when the call came through. I also remember some trepidation too, but that was certainly not an overwhelming sense. I remember being quite annoyed that my lunch was being interrupted though, and I hastily shovelled in as much as I could before the vehicle arrived! I wanted to make sure I had some energy reserves for whatever might come. Our first stop was the police station in Beloi, where there were a lot of police officers doing not very much at all. Our understanding was that the POLRI [the Indonesian Police] had the lead in this incident, but when we checked in with the TNI, they said that they had the lead for it. With all that confusion, we drove around trying to get closer to where the shooting occurred to see what was really going on. Throughout this whole time, I was sending reports back to my headquarters in Dili on my satellite telephone. However, we kept getting turned away at the militia checkpoints. We would go up one street, get turned back, and try another street only to get turned away again.

Eventually, we worked our way right around the edge of the village until we were stopped at a checkpoint manned by some TNI soldiers and two officers. One of the officers, Lieutenant Yusef Tandi, was someone I knew. The other officer was particularly agitated and was waving his pistol about as he spoke with us. Lieutenant Tandi seemed quite calm so I asked him what was going on. He told us that the TNI Officers' Mess accommodation had been attacked by the SSF with guns and machetes. I suggested that I try to make contact with the TNI liaison officers, who were essentially doing what we were doing, except that they were from the TNI. I indicated that I needed to contact them to find out if they needed anything, so Lieutenant Tandi agreed that we should go to Beloi to check with the liaison officers. We were ushered through their checkpoint and were stopped once again by another checkpoint, this time operated by militia. I was able to explain that Yusef Tandi said we could go through to the Mess and they let us through.

When we arrived at the TNI Mess, I spoke with the liaison officers about their version of the events. They said that they had been attacked by a large group of youths throwing stones, supported on the other side of the river by more students who were firing M-16s. The M-16 story had been coming up for some time as the TNI had been claiming that someone had been giving M-16s to radical pro-independence groups. I was a little sceptical about that but I wasn't going to say anything at the time. The other thing that made me doubt this story was that while I heard several hundred shots fired, none of them sounded like incoming rounds. An incoming round has an unmistakable 'crack-thump' as you hear the round shot followed quickly by the sound of it hitting something. I didn't hear that at all that day. I really didn't think there had been any incoming fire at all. To me, it sounded like outgoing fire or firing into the air. The two locations were about two to three kilometres apart, but in line with where the firing was alleged to have originated from.

The significant thing about that period was that, as we were driving around trying to get a sense of what was going on, I found my infantry training coming back to me. The Army prepared us really well. I can always remember being told, probably at RMC [Duntroon], that when you are on the radio, don't get excited regardless of what is happening around you. As an officer, the soldiers don't want to see you panicked or flustered. Always be cool, calm and collected and it will instil confidence in those around you. I remember at one checkpoint having these scraggy-haired, red-eyed militia men pointing guns at us and felt terrified, but as I had to transmit back to headquarters what was going on, I had to stay really calm, despite being utterly frightened that these guys would think nothing of shooting us. I didn't want to panic anyone else who might be listening in to my messages so I really concentrated on staying calm while relaying those messages.

Not long after 1400 hours, Paul and I returned to the main part of the town. As we drove past the TNI headquarters, which was directly opposite the POLRI headquarters, we noticed that there was a large number of militia milling about near the home of the regional coordinator. These guys were carrying home-made firearms in plain view of TNI and POLRI and behaving in a provocative manner. Over the radio, I heard that the regional coordinator and several other staff members were still inside the house unable to leave because of the militia congregating outside. This really worried us because the militia had been to the house before to issue death threats. One night, at a function at the house, the militia came by and threw rocks at the roof and windows. Understandably, we were very concerned for the safety of the UNAMET staff that were trapped in the house.

We pulled up outside the TNI headquarters, and I went over. I asked the Commander, Lieutenant Colonel Djoko, and two TNI liaison officers why the militia were being allowed to carry weapons unchecked. Their answers were evasive, claiming it was a POLRI matter and nothing to do with them. I was becoming increasingly frustrated with the TNI officers and decided to leave before I said anything I might regret. As I walked back to the vehicle, Paul called me over to the POLRI headquarters where he needed my help in persuading someone there to clear the militia off the street. However, the officer declined, saying he could not help us, even though the militia were firing indiscriminately in the air.

Paul and I were becoming increasingly concerned about the safety of the UNAMET personnel at Paul Guerin's house, and even more frustrated by POLRI and TNI's inaction. We decided that we had to attempt to do something to relieve the situation. The only thing we could think of as we got back into our vehicle was to attempt to drive our way through the group of militia to the house.

If we approached the militia, the Indonesians might actually do something. As we drove off, the Indonesians suddenly became very animated and chased after us, just as we hoped they would. I can remember looking out of the side mirror and having a laugh at the 20 or so Indonesian police officers chasing after us wildly, waving their arms about.

As we neared the militia, they aimed their weapons in our direction, forcing us to reverse back to the Indonesians who were now running down the street after us. Satisfied that we had at least elicited a response from them, we continued on foot, walking towards the militia. We played the card that the Indonesians would not allow us to be hurt; our intention was to force them to intervene by placing ourselves in the vicinity of the militia. The Indonesians surrounded us and animatedly told us to go back the way we came; then, though they were very half-hearted in doing so, they eventually cleared the militia from the streets. It seemed like a really good thing for us to do at the time, but in hindsight, it was a tad crazy. We were eventually able to get through to make sure Paul Guerin and his colleagues were okay. Fortunately for them, the militia hadn't turned their attentions to them at that point. They were just hanging around on the roundabout, stopping traffic and being disruptive. The house was about 20 metres away, so they were probably lucky.

After that, we returned to the UNAMET office and took stock of what had just happened. A Dutch journalist and her Irish photographer had approached Paul to say that they had come across a body; we were to find out later it was a student involved with the SSF. Paul and two other CIVPOL asked me to accompany them to retrieve the body and return it to his family so that I could interpret. It was the first time I had ever seen a body of someone who had died in violent circumstances. Although I tried really hard to maintain my composure when we found him, there is a photograph of me that clearly shows my sense of disgust. This young man had died from a single gunshot wound to his head. He was still holding on to a rock in his right hand and he was lying on top of a rusty iron bar, which we presumed he had been carrying in his other hand. It appeared as though he had been shot at very close range with either a .38 callibre weapon, or even a 5.56 mm round at some distance. It was difficult to tell. Earlier, the TNI liaison officers mentioned that these students were carrying M-16 rifles – but if this guy had an M-16 rifle with him, he must have been carrying it with his feet, because he was still holding the rock and, until very recently, the rusted iron bar in his other hand. There wasn't a rifle to be seen, nor were there any expended cartridge cases nearby.

The POLRI became agitated that whoever did this might still be around, and made actions for us to leave and take the body with us. The body was carried back over the river to the local health centre where his family was called to pick him up. As the family carried the body away, Paul and I stood at the roadside, in silence, caps off with our heads bowed in respect of their grief. We might have saluted according to the drill manual, but we chose a mark of respect the family would understand. We were both revolted by the complete lack of compassion or respect displayed by the POLRI troops, who milled around smoking and talking, before mounting their vehicles and forcing their way past the family's procession. Seeing the body of this young person got to me; it all seemed so pointless. Actually, the whole situation was pointless. The incident got me feeling extremely angry at the waste of life. As far as I was concerned, I didn't want to see any more wasted lives.

After the family had left with the body, we went back, yet again, to our headquarters. Because of the turn of events throughout the day, the security officer, Gordon Prentice, made the decision that all UNAMET staff would spend the night in the UNAMET office rather than being allowed to go back to their houses. We knew it would be cramped, uncomfortable, and a bit unpleasant, but there was safety in numbers. Gordon felt that keeping us to together was far better. The militia were using drugs and alcohol that they brewed up themselves and they could be unbalanced in their behaviour. We figured that while they might be prepared to kill two or three of us who were alone in our own houses they would probably hesitate at committing an act of violence on our large group where there would be plenty of witnesses. Additionally, the military police station and the Indonesian military headquarters were directly across the road, so we counted on their proximity if anything were to happen during the night. If we were all together we knew it would be much easier to account for everyone and if we had to, we could evacuate to the nearby soccer field to be picked up by helicopter.

At around 1600 hours, Paul and I realised that the two foreign journalists who came across the student's body were still wandering around alone and we became concerned for their safety. We were certainly under no legal obligations to offer them protection or to be worried about their well-being, but I felt we had a moral obligation to offer our assistance in the very least. There was still a fair bit of shooting going on, at least a shot or two every minute or so. Paul and I left for Beloi to try to find them.

We went back to the family of the deceased man because that was where the journalists remained after we left. The group said that the journalists had left to go to the hill behind Beloi, so we got back in our vehicle. About a kilometre from Beloi, we came across a group of approximately 10 men carrying spears and machetes. As we got closer, they motioned for us to slow down. My first thought was that they were militia and, given the time and distance we were from assistance, I began to feel extremely apprehensive. I guess it wasn't abnormal to be wary of anyone carrying a weapon! When we got closer, they identified themselves as FALINTIL auxiliaries or sympathisers who had formed a sort of village home guard. We were able to communicate with each other in Indonesian, and they told us that the two journalists had located another corpse on top of a nearby hill. They agreed to take us to the area.

The walk itself took about seven minutes and I was very much aware of how it might not be such a good idea to go wandering off with these people. Paul had a hand-held radio but I didn't because UNAMET had insufficient stocks to issue all of us with one. I was carrying a first-aid kit! When we reached the top of the hill, we saw the journalists and close to 60 Timorese men, women, and children standing around the corpse of another young man. Most of the group, however, was male and they carried traditional weapons. At this point, Paul, being the police officer, did his best to take control of the crime scene and begin his investigation. The female journalist introduced us to a man known as the *Comandante*, or commander. We assumed he was the FALINTIL commander for this group who in the main seemed to be civilians or Internally Displaced People (IDP). He was very friendly and certainly appeared to be in charge of the group. He was bearded and wearing a beret – a sort of symbol of office.

After examining the body, Paul concluded that the young man had been shot in the chest by a single large calibre weapon, probably a 5.56 mm or a 7.62 mm round, and had bled to death. There were some other young men around who also had some wounds. I gave them some bandages from my first aid kit and let them take care of each other. Some of the group said that Indonesian police had shot the victim earlier that afternoon. When we spoke with the two journalists about their safety, they said that they already had accommodation for the night and that they felt safe to stay there. I suggested that they really ought to go there now and stay there until morning because we believed that further violence was likely overnight given the amount of tension in the air throughout the district. They left, taking a track that was almost at right angles from where we had come up from the road.

Some of the FALINTIL group approached us to say that there was another man who had been wounded in the shooting and asked if we could help him. Under our mandate, we were not permitted to provide any assistance to any armed groups. There wasn't a doctor in Viqueque anyway, so we couldn't have done anything more than basic first aid. We said that all we could do was transport him to the local hospital but they declined, saying that he would be at risk from the TNI, POLRI, or militia.

By this time, it was getting quite dark and we really didn't want to be out after dark in the current situation. Paul and I offered our condolences to the victim's family and friends, explaining that we had to leave. As we made ready to leave, I noticed a POLRI Lieutenant Colonel, a young priest, and a young Indonesian Foreign Affairs officer coming up the track that the two journalists had taken earlier. I recognised the Foreign Affairs man as I had already met him on a visit to Dilor, but I had never seen the POLRI officer before. I assumed that he was the Viqueque POLRI commander, Lieutenant Colonel Abdurachman. I started to get quite concerned because I knew this visit would spell trouble of some kind as his very presence might enrage the crowd behind us.

I took off down the track to cut them off before they got too much closer. I saluted him and shook his hand, saying hello to the priest and the Foreign Affairs officer. I could see that they were unarmed and I asked them if they thought it was safe to be coming up here. The POLRI commander simply smiled and walked past me towards the Timorese group. The Foreign Affairs officer explained that they were going up to talk to the villagers because they wanted to stop the cycle of violence that was going on in the district. There was nothing I could say to stop them, so Paul and I stood off to one side to observe. As far as I could tell, the POLRI officer was a good guy and he was simply trying to do the right thing, but I just didn't think that it was going to be a welcome visit by the mourning group. Given our very strong mandate by UNAMET, Paul and I were in a difficult situation. I knew that if I became involved, I could jeopardise the mission. However, I was also aware that if I stood by and did nothing, I could very well be criticised for that too. Our radio wasn't working anymore because we were out of range, so we couldn't even notify CIVPOL of our whereabouts or the situation. By now, my gut was really beginning to churn and I had a terrible feeling that something was going to happen.

As soon as the POLRI officer got near the group, they became extremely aggressive towards him. He tried to speak to the group but some of them started kicking and punching him. I thought, 'Okay, here we go.' Paul and I moved in and stepped in between him and the group. The priest and the *Comandante* joined us and we held our arms outstretched to the side to form a barrier to prevent the mob surging forward. Because the *Comandante* was there with us in the line, I think it gave us some authority with the Timorese. Without him there, I was confident that they would have simply run right over the top of us. Given the emotional state of the crowd, I think it was inevitable that things were going to go wrong. In my experience, the Timorese tend to suppress their emotions and then, when they can endure no more, they explode with rage and emotion. For now, they were staying behind the human barrier we had formed but I knew it would take nothing for them to get out of control.

The POLRI officer and the Foreign Affairs officer then used this time to try to move away from the enraged group. At first, they took a couple of walking steps, but these eventually quickened until Abdurachman, the POLRI officer, was running back down the path. When he was about 10 metres from the group, five or six young men broke from the crowd and ran after him. One guy with a large machete was rapidly closing in on the POLRI commander. At the same time, I noticed that another man with a spear had broken away from the crowd on the left flank, which was closest to Paul. It wouldn't take him long to take aim and use his spear.

At this point I think I might have momentarily frozen. I was very afraid of becoming involved in the altercation, not only because of any injuries I might receive, but also because I might breach the UNAMET charter by any involvement. In hindsight, that last concern was ridiculous but at that moment in time, it was a real worry for me. At that point I believed that the Timorese men intended to kill Lieutenant Colonel Abdurachman in retribution for the deaths of their friends and kin.

After what seemed like an eternity, but in actuality was probably only a millisecond, I came to the decision that whatever else might happen, it would be wrong to allow a human being to be killed. Adrenaline is a crazy thing. Things seemed to be moving in slow motion. It felt like I had minutes to make decisions, but afterwards, when talking with Paul about the event, I realised that I was making these decisions in split seconds. Once I made the decision to act, I remember feeling immensely relieved. It's a strange sensation, but it felt fantastic making that first decision to act and become involved. Now that I was committed to a course of action, I no longer worried about the repercussions or consequences. But once I moved away, Paul and I were separated, which in hindsight wasn't a good thing.

My memory of the next 30 seconds is incomplete. It's like watching a movie when you're walking in and out of the room. I can remember running down the hill at great speed and pushing past several Timorese men as I did so. As I got closer, I could see that the POLRI officer was now on the ground and the Timorese man with the machete was swinging it wildly at him. I saw the Timorese man change his grip on the machete so that he was now thrusting it down in a stabbing motion while Abdurachman squirmed on the ground to avoid the machete thrusts. He was clearly panicking and wailing in a high pitch voice, as was the Foreign Affairs officer, who was standing off to one side.

When I was within few steps of this attack, I paused to evaluate what was going on. Again, it felt as though I stood there for a few minutes but in actuality, it was probably not even a second. I was still extremely committed to stopping this attack but there was the infantry part of me who was assessing the situation to minimise the risk to myself. There was no alternative other than to step between the attacker and Abdurachman.

I stepped in front of the attacker with my arms outstretched while trying to appear as non-confrontational as possible. I put my hands on the man's shoulders and gently kind of pushed him back, keeping my arms outstretched. I figured that at least this way, he was at arm's length from my body and I could observe his machete! He had a ferocious attitude and he glared at me. I am quite sure that he was very ticked off at me for interrupting his attack and he began brandishing his machete at me. Out of the corner of my eye, I could see that the POLRI officer was still on the ground in a confused and frightened state, while the priest and Foreign Affairs officer attempted to lift him to his feet, albeit unsuccessfully.

My mind was working overtime at this point. I felt that the longer I did nothing more than hold this guy back, the greater the risk was of him starting his attack again. Additionally, he now had a lot more support from some of the crowd who now reached us. All it could take was a shout from the crowd and it would all start up again, with me in the middle of it. I was afraid to turn my back on this guy because he was still glaring at me and swinging his machete wildly. Nevertheless, I figured that inaction was the worst choice, so with great trepidation I slowly dropped my arms and turned my back on him to assist Abdurachman to his feet. The whole time I had my back turned, I was waiting to be struck myself. I suppose I was waiting for the pain of his blade. He was shouting abuse at us but seemed to have stopped swinging his machete. Maybe the pause in his action was enough for his anger to subside a sufficient amount for rationality to set in. Despite his hatred of the Indonesians, he probably didn't want to attack a priest and a member of UNAMET.

Much like packing down next to him in a rugby scrum, I grasped Abdurachman and pretty much carried him down the hill in the direction that they had come from. I had a pretty good look at him, despite the dangerousness of the situation, and strangely, he appeared to be free from wounds. His uniform was shredded across his chest, but he didn't appear to be bleeding. He had a notebook and pen in one of his pockets, and it appeared that they took most of the brunt of the attack. He was a bloody lucky man. I remembered from first aid training that casualties suffering from shock take comfort from physical contact with others. I also knew from my time in Indonesia that they are a tactile people and it is common for men to hold hands. To keep him calm and manageable, I held his hand or had an arm around him until we were at the bottom of the hill and out of danger.

Paul joined us about five minutes later. He told me that the *Comandante* had managed to control the crowd but that it was highly advisable that we all got out of the area as quickly as possible. I certainly had no desire to stay in the area, even once we got rid of Abdurachman, because as far as FALINTIL were concerned, I was now associated with their enemy – an Indonesian. There was no way I would have gone back up the hill to say anything further to the group. I didn't even think it was safe for me to stay in Viqueque any longer.

On our drive back to Viqueque, Paul and I became really concerned that Abdurachman would return with his troops and that there would be a violent retribution from the POLRI towards the Timorese in the area. As we neared our office, we saw Lieutenant Colonel Abdurachman talking with a CIVPOL in the street. Abdurachman asked us not to mention the incident because he knew that his troops would run amok in revenge for the attack on their commander. With immense relief, we both agreed and drove off still shaking our heads. The sporadic gunfire seemed to stop at around 1830 hours and the rest of the evening was quiet.

That night I found myself going through a whole range of emotions. I recounted the events in a phone call back to our headquarters in Dili and then spent the night in my office. I recognised each stage that I went through from some of the training I had been involved with when I was an Infantry officer. I felt euphoric because I knew that I had survived something that could have come out quite badly. Part of me felt concerned because I made a decision that went against the orders that I had for my mission, but there was absolutely no way that I could have done anything else but intervene. Nothing came out of it so I was relieved that I hadn't done any lasting damage to the UNAMET mission.

Later, Paul was to hear that the militia were planning to kill an Australian Military Liaison Officer in Viqueque to try to force UNAMET out of the area. As I was the only Australian military liaison officer in the area, clearly they were referring to me. After some discussion, we decided to ignore the threat, believing that it was intended to frighten us into leaving voluntarily. Given that if we were wrong I could be killed, it was probably a bit of a gamble!

Life went back to normal. Relationships between UNAMET and the TNI, FALINTIL and the militia continued on a rocky path. Of course, once the elections were held, our mission was completed and we were able to return home.

I don't think I did anything brave. My boss at the time, Lieutenant Colonel (now Brigadier) Paul Simon spoke to me and the gist of his advice was that I did what any good officer should do, and that I should take pride in knowing that I had been tested and passed. I would like to think that all officers who found themselves in my circumstances would have reacted the same way as I did. Who knows, maybe they could have dealt with it better than I did? I think that the Army prepares its soldiers very well. I was only acting on instincts gained from 12 years' service in the Army.

I also believe that the traditions of Australia's armed forces should be maintained. In this time of rapid change, I would hate to see our systems ditched in favour of a more modern Army without traditions or a sense of cohesion. What it boiled down to for me on that day is that I didn't want to be the one who broke the link in the chain between the Army of our past and the Army of our future. We talk about the ANZAC legend as being something intangible, but every day soldiers conduct themselves in ways that have tangible links to that legend. Whether it is overseas on operations or helping out in the community in times of natural disaster, both in Australia and overseas, Australian soldiers go about their business, just as the ANZAC legend says our soldiers did on the beaches of Gallipoli or on the Western Front. It is happening all the time.

Since his time in East Timor, John Sholl has continued his relationship with Asia by attending the Indonesian Command and Staff College in Jakarta as well as going back in the wake of the devastating tsunami in 2005. He has seen overseas service in the Solomon Islands and more recently in Iraq. Now a Lieutenant Colonel, John plans to discharge from the Army in late 2006 and use his knowledge of South-East Asia in the civilian business world. He lives in Brisbane with his wife, Christine, and young daughter Grace.

Runaway Tank

MANY ASPECTS OF THE NECESSARY TRAINING FOR AUSTRALIA'S defence force can be inherently dangerous. Practising for war often takes our forces to the very edge of their capability. Many tasks and actions of the arms corps (infantry, armoured and artillery) demand degrees of speed, stealth, precision, accuracy and lethality beyond those required of any other division of the Army. Through the use of live ammunition, real equipment, and real soldiers, 'war' comes to life and risks must be taken so that actions and reactions under duress are honed and become instinctive. But this kind of training also demands a careful balance between safety and realism and it can only be achieved through meticulous military preparation and planning, and staged training sessions which reflect the difficulty and danger of the task to be achieved.

The modern Australian military is risk-averse. It doesn't seek to cause injuries or deaths as part of training, nor is it considered acceptable for them to happen. However, what training often can not necessarily take into account are unexpected and freaky events such as vehicle accidents and equipment malfunctions. These kinds of accidents happen without warning, and the fate of those involved in the accident is left to chance and good fortune.

One such accident occurred in May 2001 at the Shoalwater Bay Training Area, north of Rockhampton, Queensland. Corporal Shaun Clements was a crew member of a tank that was taking part in an Army training exercise. As his story tells, he rescued the driver of his tank who had sustained life threatening injuries and prevented further injury to troops around him and the destruction of millions of dollars worth of equipment. Shaun was seriously injured during the rescue and spent several weeks recovering in hospital. Extremely humble about his actions, Shaun downplays the rescue as simply one mate helping out another. For his courageous actions, Corporal Clements was awarded the Star of Courage.

'GEEZ, YOU WERE LUCKY, MATE'

Corporal Shaun Clements SC

CITATION
STAR OF COURAGE

Late in the afternoon of 5 May 2001, Corporal Clements rescued the injured driver of a runaway army tank during a training exercise and prevented the tank crashing into two occupied tanks. Corporal Clements was a crew member of a tank taking part in an Army Training exercise at the Shoalwater Bay Training Area in Queensland when he heard the tank driver screaming. The turret of the tank had been moving erratically, and the tank driver's head was caught between the gun and the outside edge of the exit hatch, Corporal Clements, who was in the turret with the tank commander, immediately pulled himself out of the turret to go to the aid of the driver, who had suffered serious head injuries. The tank suddenly accelerated and sped down a heavily-wooded gully. While holding the driver's head in one hand, Corporal Clements tried to apply the handbrake with his other hand, and attempted, unsuccessfully, to turn off the engine. The tank continued to pick up speed, crashing into trees that covered the terrain. Corporal Clements could see the tank was on a collision course with two other tanks at the bottom of the gully. He again reached into the driver's compartment and managed to steer the tank up a slope, narrowly avoiding one of the stationary tanks. Eventually he was able to bring the tank to a halt by using the gradient of the slope and the trees. Corporal Clements sustained broken ribs, a collapsed lung and considerable bruising during the incident. However, he remained on the tank to help with the medical evacuation of the driver. By his actions, Corporal Clements displayed conspicuous courage.

I WAS BORN IN 1968 IN ROCKHAMPTON, QUEENSLAND. MY parents had emigrated from Northern Ireland and when I arrived my father was working in the meat works there. A few years later, my father found a new job at the meat works in Townsville, and I did all my schooling in Townsville. I never enjoyed school, even from a young age. At 16, I left home to become a stockman, and I found work all over Australia. While I was working in New South Wales, I met my wife. At around this time, my family left Townsville and moved to Tasmania, so I followed them down there. It was one place I hadn't seen before. I spent six years in Tasmania, continuing to work as a stockman.

A mate of mine thought it would be a good idea to join the Army. I was between jobs at the time and I had always wanted to enlist. Growing up in Townsville you'd see Army presence every-where. I liked watching armoured personnel carriers drive past on their way up to the High Range Training Area for their exercises, and seeing Army vehicles on the roads was commonplace. I thought it looked like a pretty good life. I was 26 when I joined up, so I was like a grandfather to some of the kids who went through Kapooka [in New South Wales] with me as most of them had only just turned 18. I was the eldest by a good few years and these kids looked up to me for advice. If there was a problem, they'd come to me and then I'd go to the section commanders and tell them what the problem was and try to sort it out for them. That wasn't the way it was done in the Army, though, so I found myself getting into a bit of trouble!

I think my parents were a bit put off when I joined up because I suspect they wanted me to take over the running of their property in Tasmania when they couldn't do it any longer. At the time, things weren't too good at home so there was no way I wanted to take that on. My dad thought my wanting to join up was just a passing fad because my mate had joined up, but when I finished my recruit course and marched out of Kapooka in front of them, they were more than proud of me – especially my father.

Towards the end of the recruit course, everyone starts to think about what corps they hope to get allocated to. Back then, recruits didn't get a choice. Everyone had their preferences but that didn't mean you would get what you wanted. The instructors decided where each recruit would be allocated according to where they thought you were suitable. It seemed to me that it was a bit like, 'You 10 here are going to Infantry, you three over there are going to Armoured, and you two go to Catering', that kind of thing. I think I was quite lucky with my allocation. When I first joined up, I wanted to go to Engineers but looking back on it now, I am really glad I was allocated to Armoured corps.

When I left Kapooka, those of us who had been allocated to Armoured corps were told that we were all going to become Australian Light Armoured Vehicle (ASLAV) drivers. However, when we got to our initial training course in Puckapunyal in Victoria, the corps decided they only wanted six of us to go on ASLAVs and the other four to go to the tanks. I was one of the four who went to the tanks. After Kapooka, I had a couple of days off before I needed to be in Puckapunyal on Christmas Day. We then had to wait for three months before the course started. That meant that we had three months working in the hangars as lowly recruits with the other trained soldiers. Interestingly, that time was pretty well spent as it gave us a chance to get an appreciation of the ASLAVs and the tanks. I discovered I was glad to be going to the tanks.

I was relieved when the course finally began, though. I thought we would spend more time out in the field than we did and being a stockman, I really liked being in the field. I don't like barracks life much. If we aren't out bush, then we are back there cleaning. I don't mind fixing the tanks at all because I am mechanically minded, but cleaning wears thin after a while. Back then, when I was a private soldier, I'd really look forward to going out bush, but because of my current job and my buggered up knees, I don't get to do that so much any more.

After finishing my driver's course in Puckapunyal I was posted to Darwin where I spent the next seven years. Usually, it's normal to spend only between 12 months and two years as a driver. After that you get to move up in responsibility. The normal progression is from driver to gunner to loader to crew commander. I spent four years as a driver. At the two-year mark, I did the gunner course but because I was an exceptional driver, they left me in the driver slot for longer. I won an award, the Brad Robinson Memorial, where I was given an $1800 gold watch as a prize for the best driver of the year for the Regiment. It's presented for the good work you do in the field and also in barracks, but it was a surprise and a pretty big honour, really. I would be happy if I was still just a driver today. However, after those four years I had to move on.

They put me in the gunner spot, but I didn't like that because I suffer from really bad motion sickness. As a gunner, you are inside the vehicle the whole time. In Darwin, it gets up to around 65 degrees Celsius inside the tanks, so I got pretty crook. I endeavoured to get to crew commander as quickly as I could, which I did four years ago. After 12 months as the crew commander, I got my own troop and then did two years as a troop corporal in 2 Troop B Squadron in the Regiment. After that posting, I was posted back to Puckapunyal as a driving instructor at the School of Armour.

One of the great things about our job is the mateship and camaraderie that exists between us. It's drummed into us from day one at Kapooka. You've got to have that sense of teamwork and mateship, otherwise it isn't going to work as it should. At Kapooka, everything is taught in a basic infantry style, but when you become an Armoured corps soldier, that sense of mateship becomes even more important. There are three other people with you inside a tank and you are with them 24 hours a day, seven days a week. You spend three months out in the field and you are together that whole time. You eat, sleep, and work in the tank together; and obviously you fight and – if need be – you die together.

We were on an exercise at Shoalwater Bay in Queensland when the accident happened. It was much like any other exercise except that in this case, our Regiment was split up. 'A' squadron went with the visiting Americans who had a squadron of their tanks with them and this combined squadron were tasked with performing beach landings and that kind of thing. They were also tasked to be the enemy for the exercise. 'B' squadron (my squadron) and 'C' squadron were tasked with defending a piece of ground. Basically, the scenario was that we were fighting the American 'invasion'.

I went in to the exercise with the advance party a week earlier than the others. We sent a brigade's worth of tanks, ASLAVs, and vehicles around to Shoalwater Bay from Darwin by ship. The ship docked in Gladstone, Queensland, and we took all the vehicles to Shoalwater Bay where we set up a regimental hide while we waited for the rest of the Regiment who were flying in from Darwin by Hercules aircraft. For the first two days of the exercise, we were doing lead up training to get all the bugs out of the system as we, and the vehicles, had been in the barracks for quite a while. Late in the afternoon of day two of the exercise, we received a message over the radio that we had to go to a particular site for orders. We turned the tank off the main road in the training area and got onto a track where a ground guide met us. He was going to guide us to where we needed to go for orders. The track went up a ridgeline and at a certain point along the ridgeline, we needed to turn off and steer down into the low ground. Because we were being ground-guided, I didn't have to navigate on this occasion. I was inside the tank using the time to get my maps and traces ready for the orders briefing.

While I was getting this stuff together, I heard someone scream-ing loudly. It is really noisy inside the tank when the engine is running and I also had my helmet on which dulls the noise a bit. Even so, I could hear the screaming over the top of it all. My first thought was that we had run over the ground guide. I put my head up through the hole and saw that the ground guide outside had a terrible look on his face, so I knew then that something was wrong with the driver, Rick.

I jumped out of my hole, which is further up the tank. Once I was on top of the tank, I ran across the top of the turret and down to the driver's hole where he sits with his head poking out. I knelt down in front of Rick and cradled his head. Blood was going everywhere. Within seconds, my hands were covered in it. I held his head upright and realised it was like mush behind his ears. The whole back of his head had caved in. It was horrific.

It was pretty obvious to me that the gun had somehow moved and squashed the back of his head as it swung around. It had squashed his head first with his helmet on and then Rick must have gotten stuck between the gun and his turret, so he pulled his head out of his helmet. The gun must have then come back around the other way and squashed his unprotected head against the other side of the turret. The damage was pretty terrible. When I was there with him it was an awful time. If you have ever heard anyone or anything die before, you know that their last few breaths are terrible – the death rattle. That's the sound he was making. By the time I got to him, he wasn't moving and I truly thought he was about to die or was already dead.

The vehicle was still moving at this time, but I don't remember it. We had just come off the ridgeline and we were rapidly going downhill. As the gun barrel squashed his head, Rick had passed out and his foot stayed on the accelerator. I was sitting on the front of the tank with my back facing the front trying to hold his head still. It was a really heavily wooded area. The tank was running into trees and Rick was getting bashed around by trees and falling branches. I heard people running beside the vehicle telling me to jump off, but there was no way I was going to leave Rick. I leaned across him, using my body as a shield, and continued to hold his head.

I started looking around trying to think of something to do when I noticed that we were heading towards a massive tree. I learned later that it was over 90 centimetres in diameter. I remember hoping that the huge bulk of this tree would stop us, so I grabbed Rick's head in a headlock and shielded him more with my body. A few seconds later, we hit the tree, but unfortunately, the tank just sheared it off at ground level. The whole tree came down on top of me and apparently that is how I sustained my injuries. I didn't know I was injured at the time, though, because the adrenaline was just coursing through me.

After the tree was felled, the tank continued moving rapidly down the hill. I looked at the direction we were heading in and noticed two other tanks at the bottom. It looked like we were heading straight for them. There were guys sitting on the ground in front of the tanks having a brew and a smoke while they waited for us to turn up for orders. I don't know why they didn't move; they just sat there, staring at us racing down the steep hill towards them. I can clearly remember watching one guy who was calmly sitting there, watching us. I don't know if he was in a state of shock or if he thought we were just mucking around but he was frozen to the spot. I really thought we were going to run them over or, at the very least, smash into their tanks, which I knew wouldn't be too good for me and Rick.

I reached down past Rick's body and tried to pull on the hand-brakes. With all the adrenaline running through my body, I pulled the handbrake clear out of the vehicle, completely breaking the cables and rendering them useless. I tried to switch the engine off but I couldn't reach the ignition button as it was too far inside the tank for my arms to reach. In hindsight, I don't know what that would have done anyway.

Then I remembered something my father said to me when I was working as a stockman in Tasmania: that if you are ever on a tractor that is running out of control, try to turn it back up a hill to stop it. I figured I had nothing to lose. I manoeuvred myself around so that I could grab the steering handle while still holding Rick's head in my arms, and put my weight down on the handle. Somehow I managed to steer the tank back up the hill and away just in time. It was like a movie, where the tragedy is averted with only seconds to spare. The tank stopped with its engine still running and the tail-end of the tank was only about five metres away from the other two tanks.

When we hit the big tree earlier, Rick's foot had came off the accelerator so the momentum of going downhill was all that had kept us moving. But before we hit the tree, we were travelling at 40 kilometres per hour in a 42 tonne tank down a relatively steep hill and it was still in gear when it eventually stopped. Everyone started running towards us but I yelled at them to stay back because I wasn't sure what would happen next. I was concerned the tank might roll backwards or start going back up the hill. I knew that if I tried to turn the engine off, it would just roll backwards down the hill and we would hit the other tanks or run someone over. I didn't have any handbrakes as I had already broken them, so I tried to keep everyone back while I got someone to chock the tracks. It was only when that was done that we were able to switch the engine off safely.

Next, we had to get Rick out. By this stage, he was coming in and out of consciousness and bleeding profusely from his head wound. There was no way I was going to leave him until I knew he was all right. The medic passed me a neck brace to put on him and then I stayed there, holding his head and talking to him. They climbed inside to put a back brace on him and about 30 minutes later, he was lifted out of the vehicle. By the time we got him out and had loaded him on to the stretcher, the armoured carrier that acts as an ambulance arrived. We put him inside the carrier and then they took off to evacuate him to hospital.

Once he was gone, one of my mates asked if I wanted a brew. I sat down near his tank and while I waited, I lit up a cigarette. When I drew back on it, I could taste blood. I looked at the butt of my cigarette and it was covered in blood. Then I coughed and all this frothy blood came up. I realised then that I was hurt.

Immediately, there was a mad dash to get me to the landing zone (LZ) as well to get on the Black Hawk helicopter that was called in to take Rick to hospital. While this was going on, two tanks were making an LZ by knocking trees down to make a clear area wide enough for a chopper to land safely.

By the time I got to the LZ, I was having some problems. I found that I couldn't breathe and I was coughing up a lot of blood. When the chopper landed, the pilot said he couldn't fly me in to the hospital because I had injuries to my lungs. They took off with Rick in the helicopter and I went by road to the Army field hospital that was set up in Shoalwater Bay. Fortunately, they were also on exercise, too, and their hospital was fully set up. They took me in straight away. I spent three days in intensive care in that field hospital before I was well enough to be moved to Rockhampton Base Hospital. It's funny, in a perverse sort of way, but I spent longer in hospital than Rick did! I had broken all my ribs, punctured a lung, ruptured my spleen, ruptured a kidney, and then I developed pleurisy in the lung while I was in hospital. I was a bit of a mess. They were contemplating removing my spleen at the time but thankfully they decided against it in the end. Fortunately, I am fine now.

The whole thing, from the moment I knew something was wrong, until it was all over, only took about six minutes. I was aware of what was happening; the trees bashing into me, where everything around me was. In that time, we travelled about 600 metres, most of which was down a steep gully. I was outside on the front of the tank the whole time, sitting in front of the driver's hole. When the big tree fell and landed on me, I nearly got pulled in under the tracks. I can distinctly remember that. I think I contemplated jumping off then, but something inside stopped me from leaving Rick. I guess it wasn't until I sat down to have a smoke at the end of it all that I realised what had just happened and it began to sink in. The adrenaline was starting to wear off and I looked back up the track that we had just come down and thought, 'Holy crap!' There was a massive path of destroyed trees where we had come down out of control.

We'd knocked down everything in our way. The huge tree, the one that I thought would stop us, was all smashed up. My mate, Garp, sat down and said to me, 'Geez, you were lucky, mate,' and I thought then, 'Yeah, I am.'

It still affects me now, talking about it. I get upset thinking about it sometimes. I suppose the time I spent in hospital meant that I reflected on it quite a bit. I didn't think it affected me too much at the time. Remembering the whole incident doesn't worry me except for when I think about holding Rick's head and feeling that the back of his skull was mushed. Seeing my mate like that is the only thing that still gets to me.

After the accident and my recovery, things went back to normal and I went back to work. Once the investigation was completed, no one in the Regiment talked much about the accident. In November 2003, I received a letter from the Governor-General's office telling me that I had been nominated for the Star of Courage. That was really unexpected. In February 2004, I received another letter saying that it had been awarded to me and that it would be gazetted in March. I don't know who nominated me for the award. But what I did, I did because a mate was in trouble. I didn't do it to get an award, so I was, and still am, a bit embarrassed by all the fuss that was made of the accident. I have actually been ordered by my commanding officer to wear my medal because I wasn't wearing it.

I don't think I deserve such an award for doing what I did and I am really self-conscious that I have been singled out like this and given an award. Mind you, on the day I was given the award at the investiture, it was a pretty big honour. It seemed that every man and his dog was there. The whole experience was a little overwhelming. Unfortunately, my parents weren't able to come, as I was only permitted two guests. My wife was there, of course, and my commanding officer wanted to come, too. My kids couldn't come along, which I regret. On the day, there was a young boy who was awarded a civilian Bravery Medal for his actions in an accident. He and another kid were walking along the side of a road when a car lost control and swerved towards them. In the split second that it took for the car to veer towards them, this boy had the choice of getting out of the way himself, or pushing his mate out of the way of the oncoming car, which meant that he would get hit himself. This brave little kid chose to push his mate out of the path of the car and ended up being hit. He truly deserved an award for his actions because he knew what was going to happen – and he still did it anyway. That, to me, is brave. What I did was not brave or courageous; it doesn't even compare to something like that little boy's act. I did what I did, not knowing that I was going to get injured by that tree. It never entered my mind, even when the tank was going full bore down the hill towards it. What else could I have done in the circumstances? I expect that someone would have done the same for me, too. But to me, that isn't bravery. It's just helping a mate out. That is what mates do for each other.

Rick's doing okay now. He doesn't drive tanks any more; he has transferred to another corps. He has never been back in a tank since the accident. He has had some problems since the accident – he has metal plates in the back of his head, he lost his sense of smell, he can't hear out of his left ear. He and I have never spoken about the accident itself. We are still in contact with each other but it's an unspoken thing between us.

Quietly-spoken Corporal Shaun Clements is fiercely proud of being in the Army and despite how difficult he finds talking about aspects of the accident, he never turns down an opportunity to talk about his award if it means that it will raise the profile of the Australian Defence Force. He has been invited to talk to large audiences about the accident on several occasions since being awarded the Star of Courage, including being invited as a guest speaker at a lunch put on for the members of the Essendon Football Club. A career soldier, Corporal Clements is still working as an instructor at the School of Armour in Victoria.

Helicopter Under Fire

T HE AUSTRALIAN DEFENCE FORCE PROVIDES MANY opportunities for its members: to learn skills or a trade, to travel, to develop and utilise essential leadership skills; and these are just a few. Another example, and one that is highly sought after by many members of the military, is the opportunity to go on a posting to work as part of an international defence force. As part of an international defence force, the soldier becomes part of a new unit, participating in all that it has to offer. On occasion this includes active service.

A young pilot, Captain Scott Watkins, was given this very opportunity in 2003 when he was offered an overseas exchange with a British aviation unit. Not only was he given the chance to fly a different aircraft, the Lynx – known among those who fly them as the Ferrari of the rotary-wing aircraft – but he also experienced several exercises in exciting and unusual locations. Within 12 months, Captain Watkins found himself on active service in Iraq, flying alongside his British comrades, and soon faced the ultimate test that any pilot could ever face: coming under fire while on a routine mission in a war zone. On more than one occasion both Captain Watkins' flying skills and personal courage were put to the test.

'I HAVE NEVER FELT SO EXPOSED IN MY LIFE'

Captain Scott Warwick Watkins DFC

CITATION
DISTINGUISHED FLYING CROSS

Captain Watkins is an Australian exchange officer, serving with 1 Regiment Army Air Corps in Germany. In September 2004 he deployed for four months on Operation Telic as the Lynx Flight Commander of the Army Aviation Detachment that is part of the Joint Helicopter Force (Iraq). Between 8 and 15 November he deployed to the Forward Operating Base Kalsu as the commander of a Lynx and Puma formation that were tasked with providing aviation support to the Black Watch Battle Group in a very high threat environment. During that time he twice came under effective enemy small arms fire. On both occasions he behaved in a courageous manner, remaining cool, calm and collected.

During a routine mission on the morning of 10 November Watkins' formation was engaged by small arms fire from two firing points of two to three men each. The Lynx was struck by three rounds, one of which hit his co-pilot, Captain Keith Reesby. He broke away from the contact area and put out a full contact report before successfully recovering the aircraft back to the Black Watch Main Operating Base at Camp Ticonderoga from where Reesby was evacuated. Throughout the incident Watkins remained calm and professional, providing encouragement to his very seriously injured co-pilot while ensuring that everybody was informed of the incident. That afternoon he had another close shave when a rocket landed thirty metres away from him, further damaging the helicopter he was inspecting. Despite being given the opportunity to recover back at Basra Watkins elected to stay to the end of his scheduled rotation.

Two days later B Company Black Watch call signs were contacted by rocket-propelled grenade fire on the east bank of the Euphrates. The Lynx and Puma pair identified a suspected illegal Vehicle Check Point. Both aircraft were then engaged by sustained small arms fire from two different locations. Watkins positioned his aircraft to provide mutual support to the Puma. With tracer rounds passing on either side of the aircraft his door gunner returned fire at three men at one of the firing points, forcing them to break off the engagement. At that point Captain Watkins ordered his door gunner to cease fire, as they were no longer a threat. As the situation developed, he was instrumental in identifying a further suspect car that was tracked to a mosque where it was intercepted by ground call signs. A quantity of rocket propelled grenades, shells, detonators and bomb-making equipment was found and two men were arrested.

During his week long rotation flying in support of the 1 Black Watch Battle Group, Watkins proved himself to be a cool and courageous pilot. After the shock of seeing a fellow pilot shot he rallied his crew and kept them focused on the task of supporting the Black Watch to the best of their abilities. Despite the very real threat to his aircraft, he repeatedly placed himself in exposed positions in order to provide mutual support to the Puma and the ground call signs he was supporting. In the opinion of the Commanding Officer of the Black Watch, Watkins' actions undoubtedly saved the lives of a number of soldiers in the Battle Group. His example and courage set the benchmark for those who followed.

I WAS BORN IN TOOWOOMBA, QUEENSLAND IN MARCH 1971. I spent the first six years of my life there before my dad got a promotion and we moved to Brisbane. I grew up there, doing all my primary and most of my secondary schooling in a suburb called The Gap. In 1986, my dad got another promotion that saw our family relocating to Sydney, and I completed the rest of high school in Baulkham Hills.

After high school, I found myself at Macquarie University for a short time undertaking a Bachelor of Science with a Diploma in Chemistry and Industry. That was a pretty full-on course and an absolute nightmare. I never felt right doing it; I just fell into it. While I was at university, I became extremely interested in flying. There were a number of degrees coming out at the time that were aviation related, but I couldn't get into those, primarily because they were very expensive degrees to undertake. I left university after about eight months and got a job working in a computer company in Sydney. The sole purpose of that job was to earn some money to pay for flying lessons. I began taking private tuition out of Bankstown Airport towards the end of 1989.

Growing up, all I wanted to do was fly. When I first left high school, I applied to be a pilot in the Air Force. I was destined not to get through that selection process then because I think I put so much pressure on myself. I was only 17 and I was really nervous during the interview and selection process. When I was learning to fly with the school in Bankstown, one of the guys on staff was an Army pilot who was doing some part-time work as an instructor. He encouraged me to give the Army a go, so I soon found myself going through the same rigorous selection process again. Interestingly, even after going through the recruiting process for a second time, I still didn't pass the pilot aptitude test, but I did pass everything else so I was given the option of going to Royal Military College, Duntroon [RMC], to become an Army officer.

At the time I remember thinking that Duntroon was only for guys who had been school captains of exclusive private schools, and I certainly was never one of those! But I took up the option of going and I enjoyed it. Infantry looked particularly attractive to me as a career path. I decided that I would give the pilot aptitude test one more try, and on the third go, I passed it. Strangely enough, I think I passed only because I wasn't putting myself under any pressure this time around. I had a career now as an Army officer and I was pretty content in where my life was going. When I passed the pilot aptitude test, I was in a bit of a dilemma because I was faced with the choice of going in one direction as a pilot, or in another as an Infantry officer. In the end, I decided not to go with the flying option, knowing that I could probably do it later down the track if I wanted to.

After graduating from RMC at the end of 1993, I was posted as Infantry Officer to the 5th/7th Battalion, Royal Australian Regiment (5/7 RAR) in Sydney. I spent two years there as a platoon commander and as a mortar line officer. In 1996 I was posted to the headquarters of 1st Brigade as the liaison officer working in the operations cell. There, I decided that now was the time to give flying a go, so after speaking with my corps adviser, I requested to be transferred to Aviation corps into a non-corps flying position.

In 1997 I found myself finally flying in the Army, almost 10 years after I first began flying. In my case, having an Infantry background was great because I had an insight into how that part of the Army works. It also gave me a bit of credibility among my peers because I had commanded soldiers and I had a greater understanding of how our role fits in with theirs. The pilot's course was 18 months long, and split into three courses, located in different parts of the country. The first six months of training was in Tamworth, New South Wales, the second six months was in Canberra, and the final six months was in Oakey, Queensland.

During the training I streamed myself as a reconnaissance pilot because I thought that, with my background in 1 Brigade, I would have a better understanding of operations. While reconnaissance is a great job, the helicopter we used, the Kiowa, wasn't particularly good. Having said that, I think our work on the Kiowas was far more interesting than the work that Black Hawk pilots do, so I was very happy with my choice.

My first posting as a pilot was to 161 Reconaissance Squadron in

Darwin where I remained for three and a half years. I enjoyed that posting immensely. While I was there, I went on three operational tours in a very short space of time. I was Aviation Liaison Officer in Bougainville during Operation Belisi for about five months at the beginning of 1999; and then, when INTERFET kicked off later that year, I spent two months in East Timor as part of that mission. Then, in 2000, I went back to East Timor under the banner of UNTAET and remained there for almost four months.

On the whole, the experiences I gained from those three operations were quite good. Flying over jungle isn't particularly rewarding because you can't see what is happening on the ground; in fact, you have to work extremely hard to see anything. Obviously, as a reconnaissance pilot, I want to see what is going on down there! But when we got to operate in the northern parts of the country, like in the Australian area of operations for example, it was great because the vegetation was a little more sparse and I was able to see enemy movement going across the border between East and West Timor, as well as a little bit of what was going on in West Timor. That was pretty rewarding because I felt that I was providing a service, through information and intelligence, to the guys on the ground. Having said that, flying in general is quite rewarding but providing intelligence and information makes it even more so.

After my posting to 161 Reconnaissance Squadron, I was posted to a position as the Aide de Camp (ADC) to the Chief of Army, who was General Cosgrove at that stage. I was with him for around six months before he was promoted to Chief of the Defence Force, and then I became the ADC for Lieutenant General Leahy when he took over as Chief of Army. That posting was great and I met some very interesting people, and witnessed a different side of the Army. While I was the ADC I was advised that my next posting was to the United Kingdom on exchange with a British Army aviation unit. Postings like this are highly sought after so I was more than thrilled when I finally got word about it. I'd always wanted to get this kind of posting. The chance to fly a different helicopter, live in a different country, and enjoy the experience of working with the Brits was something I had always wanted to do.

When we first arrived in England in 2003, my wife and I lived in the south of England near Salisbury because I needed to attend the Army Air Corps school to convert to the Lynx helicopter. After five months we moved to Germany where I joined up with my unit, 1 Regiment Army Air Corps. The squadron I went to was 652 Squadron, which is one of the oldest in the Army Air Corps. It has a lot of history so it was quite exciting to be posted there.

I had an amazing tour; everything seemed to fall into place. For the next 14 months after arriving in 652 Squadron, I went on numerous exercises to various parts of Europe like Norway and Bavaria. We also did some flying in Kenya in support of a large British exercise. As it turned out, the exercise in Kenya served to prepare us extremely well for our tour of duty in the Middle East, which we had been notified about at the beginning of 2004. As a result of the Kenya experience I got to know the aircraft better, particularly because Africa is a hot, dry and high environment, much like the Middle East, which severely degrades aircraft performance. In Kenya we really pushed the aircraft close to its limits, so it gave me confidence that I would do just fine when it mattered in Iraq. My squadron didn't rotate in to Iraq until September 2004 and I stayed with my squadron group until the unit rotated back to Germany on 14 January 2005.

We departed Germany on 1 September and arrived in Iraq a day later. We had a week of acclimatisation that consisted of things like in-country briefings and area orientations. We didn't do too much, though, because we had come from a northern European autumn to autumn in Iraq, which, in reality, is exactly like an Iraq summer! We were working in temperatures averaging 49 degrees Celsius from the moment we arrived before they tapered off about two months later, when it gradually moved into winter. That in itself was a shock to the system.

At the end of the first week, we started to get stuck into the flying. Wherever the Army Air Corps pilots are needed to fly in a new area, they are required to re-qualify on the aircraft because each environment is different. We spent a bit of time flying around with an instructor who was very familiar with the Middle Eastern environment and he pointed out important aspects in the area of operation, natural phenomena that might affect our flying, like landing in sand and dust or flying at night under zero illumination. It's all good training that limits the likelihood of things going wrong. Once that was finished I was free to command missions and do all the normal tasking that was required as a Lynx pilot.

When we first arrived in Iraq, we were based at Basra Airport with the Joint Helicopter Force, which is a tri-service organisation. The British have rotary wing aircraft in all three services, the Army, Navy and Air Force. This organisation received its tasking from the multi-national division and then allocated the missions to the relevant helicopters. Up until November, the Lynx helicopters had been working in the multi-national divisional area of operation in the south of the country, watching over convoys or reacting to contacts. In these, I would sit over the top and provide information to the guys on the ground as to what was going on.

Our tour coincided with quite a contentious period for the British Army in Iraq. The Black Watch Battle Group, which elements of our squadron group were to be attached to for five weeks, had recently been informed that their tour of duty was to be extended. It was early November and the Black Watch were moved from their area of operation in what was considered a relatively safer area in the south of the country, to a more hostile environment to the south of Baghdad to a base called Camp Dogwood (aka Camp Ticonderoga). The British media felt that the lives of the men in Black Watch were going to be put at greater risk now. The insurgents knew that if they were able to kill or wound men from the Black Watch when they were supposed to be safely at home, it would cause a lot of problems back in the UK.

Obviously British commanders were adverse to all this publicity because you don't exactly want every man and their dog knowing where units are moving to, but by the time the unit moved to their new base, it was all over the press. Initially it was understood the Americans would provide all the rotary wing support that the Black Watch was going to need, but in reality they were only able to provide medical evacuation support. After the Black Watch sustained casualties in some early attacks, the unit decided that one of the things they really needed was additional support from the 'eyes in the sky', so that was when we were tasked to provide information and intelligence from the air for the unit from Camp Dogwood, which was situated on the western side of the Euphrates River.

In the four days prior to our arrival, the Black Watch had sustained six killed-in-action (KIA) and of those, five were killed by suicide vehicle-borne improvised explosive devices (SVBIED). They also had had two wounded-in-action (WIA) at that stage, both of whom lost their lower legs due to the SVBIED. The British public wanted them home. Tony Blair went on television in the UK and promised the British public that he would have the Black Watch unit home by Christmas and I guess after that, the unit received a lot of attention from the enemy. The insurgents weren't stupid; they knew that anything they could do to cause death or injury would cause further contention back in the UK so they continued to attack members of the Black Watch.

We were sent up on 8 November and operated from a US Marine Corps base which was near Dogwood; Dogwood didn't have the infrastructure for us to base our rotary wing aircraft there. The US Marine Corps base operated their own rotary wing aircraft from there so we were able to use their facilities. Each day we would fly out to Dogwood and provide the support that Black Watch required. On 8 and 9 November, we carried out routine tasking. We had flown into Baghdad on 9 November to pick up stores and transfer them down to various elements of the Black Watch Battle Group on the ground. During those two days, we had done a bit of overhead observation and resupplied one of the Black

Watch companies that was on the eastern side of the Euphrates River. We were busy and it was interesting work.

On 10 November we flew in to Dogwood to receive a task to pick up a heap of stores and personnel that had landed at Baghdad International Airport. We worked out that it was going to take about three round trips to get everyone and everything back to Dogwood with both aircraft.

The first trip was around 1000 hours that morning. We'd taken an easterly route into Baghdad Airport, landed, picked up what we could on the first trip and returned to Dogwood without any incident. When we landed at Dogwood, I refuelled. While we were taking fuel, the navigator of the Puma suggested that, as we had used an easterly approach already this morning, we should take the westerly route on the next trip. I agreed; on the previous day, we had used the easterly route as well and we didn't want to set patterns in the area. I got the Puma to lead in because it was their idea and it is easier for me to command the flight from the back.

Once we had refuelled, we left Dogwood. Up until now, Keith had been doing most of the flying while I was doing the navigating and getting a feel for the area. It is much easier to load-shed some of the flying to get to know a new area and we figured we would take turns so each of us could become familiar with the region without the added pressure of being in control of the aircraft as well. I was starting to get a good understanding of the area so this time, I jumped on the controls and flew the aircraft north to Baghdad. We had left at around 1100 hours with the Puma in the lead, flying in what we call a combat cruise formation. One aircraft leads and the rear aircraft has a freedom of arc [the rear aircraft can alter its position behind the lead aircraft]. After about five minutes into the flight, we were positioned at the rear right hand side of the Puma as we headed in towards Baghdad. We were cruising at around 120 knots at an altitude of around 50 feet off the ground. The first I knew that we were being shot at was when there was a massive explosion in the cockpit. It is hard to describe but it was as if a puff of mist formed in front of Keith. The mist turned out to be debris from the round as it punched through the right hand Perspex window on his door. At the same time, I could clearly smell cordite from the round in the cockpit as well. In that same instant, I heard a cry of pain. It sounded like it came from behind me and I thought the door gunner had been shot. I figured the round or rounds had come up through the floor and ricocheted around the cockpit.

The old fight or flight syndrome kicked in and my initial instinct was to manoeuvre the aircraft away from the area that I thought we were being shot at from. I turned the helicopter to the south to avoid further contact. As I was moving the aircraft away my door gunner spotted the group of men who had shot at us, and then Keith told us he had been shot. We didn't know how bad it was at first because he is a really stoic kind of guy, but the bullet went through his right bicep and came out under his armpit. The door gunner passed Keith some field dressings and he was able to bandage his arm up the best he could with his left hand while I tried to get us away.

Just as he had finished dressing his arm and shoulder, Keith looked down and noticed that there was a lot of blood pooling in his lap, and realised he had been a bit more seriously wounded than he first thought. He called for another field dressing and tried to stuff it down between his armoured chest plate and his flight suit to stem any bleeding from his chest. He found out later that the round that exited his armpit then went in behind his breastplate and ricocheted off the inside of that towards his chest, but it hit his dog tags before ricocheting off them, and finally lodged in his pectoral muscle. He was a lucky guy. It didn't hit any bones or vital organs. It was a miracle wound. In the end, his injuries weren't that bad and he was back flying about six months later.

It was going to take a lot of manoeuvring to engage the guys on the ground so I decided to head back to Dogwood to get Keith some medical assistance. Some time shortly after the contact, I made a radio call to let someone know that we had just been shot at.

I remember shouting, 'We're hit, we're hit!' hoping that someone would hear our message. There was a chat frequency that we could use to talk between the two helicopters and I used that to send the message. Unfortunately, the Puma didn't hear me because they had just switched over to another frequency to talk to Baghdad at the same time we were hit so they had absolutely no idea that we had been engaged. They continued on their way to Baghdad without any idea what had just occurred behind them.

Fortunately, my transmission was heard by our ground aviation detachment in Dogwood who were our own operations guys. They were able to acknowledge that we had been shot at, which was a massive relief. I was making a number of radio calls on various nets, sending contact reports to the Black Watch Battle Group, while still trying to get hold of the Puma, as well as sending general situation reports as we made our approach back to Dogwood.

As we continued on our approach to Dogwood one significant concern was that I didn't know what damage had been done to the aircraft. I figured that if we were going to come down, I would need to try to put it down in the desert area away from the Euphrates River where there was nobody living, and then evade or try to get rescued from there. Fortunately, everything appeared normal in terms of how the helicopter responded after the contact, and there was nothing on any of the gauges that indicated that it had been hit in any vital areas. We continued on to Dogwood flying in a pretty safe profile so that if the aircraft went down, we would probably survive the landing. Then the Puma came on the radio and were filled in on what had happened. They immediately began returning to Dogwood, too.

We landed back at Dogwood without too many dramas. I started to shut down the aircraft while Keith tried to get himself out of the cockpit. He's a bit of a hard bloke so by the time the door gunner and I got to him, we only needed to lower him down the step out of the cockpit and get him on the tarmac because he'd been able to get himself most of the way out. By the time we got him down, many of the ground crew guys were there and began providing him with first aid. That was the last time I saw him until the end of my tour because I had to head straight over to the operations cell to debrief them on what had happened.

By the time I finished debriefing, the Puma had landed and I spoke with the guys from it. They remembered hearing rounds passing close to the aircraft and looked back towards us on their rear right to see if anything was going on with us. They couldn't see anything and figured that everything was okay. From our discussion, we determined that the gunmen had probably been aiming at the Puma, which by chance gave them the lead they needed to hit us. My door gunner had identified three gunmen on the ground after we had been shot and Keith recalled later that in the moment before he had been hit, he could hear gunshots from outside the aircraft.

After we landed, an engineer conducted an inspection of the entire aircraft and found that it had been hit three times on the right side. Fortunately, none of the rounds had sufficiently damaged the aircraft to affect anything vital, otherwise who knows what might have happened. Having said that, though, one round had almost completely severed one of my controls but had held together for the flight back. The engineer was walking me around the aircraft when a military policeman came over to get the information about the damage for his investigation. Suddenly, while we were going around the aircraft taking photographs, Camp Dogwood came under rocket attack. The three of us soon found ourselves sheltering under the aircraft. We had taken our body armour off as we were climbing all over the aircraft, so we were pretty exposed. I have never felt so exposed in my life. There was one rocket that just seemed to be hanging in the air above us and I knew it was going to come down on us; I could just tell by the sound it made.

Sure enough, it landed only 30 metres away from us and put a piece of shrapnel through the roof of the aircraft, severing a hydraulic line and destroying the hydraulic pump and transmission.

By then, all three of us were lying under the aircraft with hydraulic fluid being dumped all over the ground near us. This happened two hours after I had landed back at Dogwood, and later that day, we came under a further rocket attack. In that first rocket attack, I think I honestly expected I was going to die right then. It's funny, but I didn't think that when the Lynx was getting shot at, but lying under the helicopter waiting for a rocket to land on top of me was the worst feeling I have ever had. When I was flying there was so much going on and I had a lot to think about, but lying under an aircraft in the open waiting for a random rocket to land gave me a terribly exposed feeling. It certainly was an incredible day.

In the second attack, one of the young soldiers was on the phone talking to his girlfriend when the rockets came in. One landed very close to him and he ended up with a bit of shrapnel in the arse. Apparently he said something like, 'Something's happened, I've got to go,' and then hobbled over to the aid post for treatment. In retrospect that was quite amusing. In the end, it all worked out quite well, no one died; but I am grateful for the experience. It was certainly very exciting and interesting. I don't regret getting out of bed that day, and I am grateful that I was able to do my job when I had to.

That night, a replacement for Keith and a new Lynx arrived and we were back flying the following morning. We did a few things for the Black Watch on 11 November and then on 12 November we went up to Baghdad to pick up the General commanding the multi-national division as we had been tasked to take him up to the US Marine Corps base. As we were flying over Dogwood en route for the base, the Black Watch came on the radio to say that the company located on the eastern side of the Euphrates River had been involved in a contact and asked if we could have a look at what they suspected was an illegal vehicle check point run by insurgents. It sounded easy and was on the way, and our job was to look after the Black Watch, not fly generals around, so we happily went to have a look.

I told the Puma to go to a low level and do a pass over the top of the vehicle checkpoint while we stayed at altitude in the Lynx to have a bit of a look at what they would do. As the Puma went overhead, all the guys at the checkpoint shot at it. The Puma went around to the south away from them and we sent a contact report back to Black Watch. I was sitting at around 2000 feet and could clearly see that as soon as the insurgents finished shooting at the Puma, the checkpoint was instantly dismantled. Then they jumped into the three vehicles near by and drove off.

We followed a vehicle that broke off to the east along a road leading to a cemetery. At the cemetery, three guys piled out of the car and started shooting up at us. My head was in and out of the cockpit at this stage as I was trying to pass on grid references and send situation reports back to Black Watch so I didn't see the exact location of the vehicle on the ground when they started shooting. However, the door gunner said the rounds were passing to the rear and the side of our aircraft. He also had a good view of what was happening below us so he was able to engage the guys on the ground. He didn't hit anyone but the rounds hit all around the vehicle, which was enough to stop them shooting at us. They jumped into their vehicle again. The gunner said he saw more rounds coming up as they piled into the vehicle, but I'm not sure where those rounds came from. One of the guys may have let go a few rounds as he climbed into the vehicle.

The door gunner was about to engage them again. I stopped him because of our rules of engagement, and unfortunately we had to watch those guys drive off, unable to do anything to stop them. What we could do, however, was continue to observe the vehicle and send reports back to Black Watch about where they were heading. We needed to head back for more fuel, so I got the Puma to stay over them watching where they were. While we were refuelling, the commanding officer of the Black Watch joined the general in the back of the aircraft and we took off, back on station. One of the companies had been able to locate one of the other vehicles that took off south from the checkpoint and we went to observe them.

They drove up to what turned out to be a mosque. From the air, the commanding officer in the back was able to coordinate a cordon and search of the mosque and brought his guys in. The mufti of the mosque was reasonably cooperative because the guys who had driven into the mosque weren't part of the local community.

In the vehicle, they found a whole heap of equipment like circuit boards, mobile phones and transmitters for making improvised explosive devices. Also, two 155 mm rounds were found in a culvert, which had been discarded by the blokes as they drove into the mosque. The two guys who were in that vehicle were arrested, and we were tasked to take these two back to Camp Dogwood for interrogation. That was a very successful day – it was a turning point for the Black Watch because everything meshed extremely well. They were able to gain the initiative in the area and because of that they didn't have any major problems in that area for the rest of their tour. It was great to be involved in helping to achieve that.

Over the next few months, there were a lot of rumours floating around that I was up for an award, but in all honesty I didn't take any notice simply so I wouldn't get my hopes up. I didn't know I had been nominated for the Distinguished Flying Cross (DFC) until September 2005 when I received a phone call from the Chief of Army who indicated that I had been awarded it. I was very happy but completely speechless! It is a humbling experience because I knew that it hadn't been awarded to an Australian since the Vietnam War. Most pilots know something about the DFC, so to have been nominated for it is quite overwhelming, and to receive it is quite an honour.

If doing what you are trained to do when the situation presents itself is brave, then maybe what I did was brave. However, I don't think of those actions as brave in themselves. At the time I didn't think I was doing anything brave at all. We are all trained to do our jobs, and while what I did wasn't necessarily unique, the situation I found myself in was. Not everyone gets that opportunity to do their job when it really matters. I was very keen about doing my job and doing it well. I had a unique opportunity and in a way, getting a DFC out of it is pretty special. I've copped a bit of flak from my colleagues, but I expected that – I would do the same if someone else was awarded it. They have all been good about it, but they certainly keep me grounded.

Major Scott Watkins is now the Instructor, Aviation at the Combat Command Wing, Puckapunyal. He is married to Karen and together they have two children, Brienna and Lachlan. Major Watkins will receive his Distinguished Flying Cross some time in 2006.

A History of Medals for Courage and Bravery

T HROUGHOUT HUMAN HISTORY, ART AND LITERATURE HAVE made reference to individual and collective bravery, courage, valour, and leadership, however, the origin of actual decorations and awards for courage and bravery is firmly rooted in the military. The awarding of medals for participation in military campaigns and battles can be traced back to the ancient Egyptians and Romans as rewards for particular qualities and virtues on the battlefield. Ancient Egyptians are said to have awarded the 'Gold of Honour' to military leaders for exceptional bravery and valour in around 1400 BC.

The ancient Greeks and Romans were undeniably masters of the military arts. The Romans, who were extremely organised and efficient, embraced the idea of rewarding and distinguishing military merit knowing that these rewards boosted morale and brought a greater sense of pride into their empire. The earliest examples from the fifth century BC are badges that were circular or crescent in shape, which were worn on the breast of the warrior's tunic or fastened to the cheek of his horse. In later periods of the empire, plaques of brass or copper were awarded to officers to decorate them for outstanding feats of bravery in battle. The Romans also produced medallions of bronze or silver that were used as decorations in recognition of military might and valour. Known as *Phalerae*, these medallions generally bore the head of a God such as Mars, Minerva or Jupiter, or the head of an animal such as a lion, and were worn on the warrior's breast along with other marks of distinction.

A History of Medals for Courage and Bravery

The ancient Greeks awarded crowns to their warriors for military valour and prowess. Made of gold, silver, or other precious metals, or of laurel leaves, these crowns honoured individual warriors for their brave and courageous actions. Interestingly, many contemporary medal designs still incorporate laurel leaves as a symbol of military gallantry and brave conduct.

Throughout history, military decorations were designed for and awarded primarily to officers. However, at various stages through- out time, it became important to decorate the valour of non- commissioned officers and other ranks. The first military medals designed as visible rewards for bravery and valour by private soldiers was instituted in Russia by Tsar Peter I during his reign as the Emperor of Russia from 1721 until his death in 1725. Later in the century, during the war against the Turks in 1789, Emperor Joseph II of Austria initiated a Medal for Gallantry as well as a gold and silver bravery medal, which was awarded to men of all ranks who performed with bravery and valour on the battlefield in the face of the enemy.

The first British medals to be issued and formally classed as honours as we understand them today did not appear until 1588, when they were struck by Queen Elizabeth I on the defeat of the Spanish Armada, the 130-strong Spanish fleet that was destroyed as it attempted to attack England. Made from either gold or silver, these medals were fitted with chains so that they could be worn around the neck, over their clothes. Later, in 1643, King Charles I initiated a medal for 'conspicuous conduct' to Robert Welch for recovering the Royal Standard during the first battle of the English Civil War, the Battle of Edgehill. King Charles I was the first British monarch to establish a military medal for courage on the battlefield. Seven years later, Oliver Cromwell issued the first campaign medal that could be awarded to both officers and men. Known simply as the Dunbar Medal, it commemorated the defeat of the Scots Royalists at Dunbar in Scotland. This medal, too, was worn on a chain around the neck.

The first official war medal in the sense that we are familiar with them today was the 1815 Waterloo Medal. It was issued with a ribbon and an instruction declaring that '. . . the ribbon issued with the medal shall never be worn but with the medal suspended on it'. From this time onwards, medals were awarded for nearly every engagement or battle; and by the nineteenth century medals were introduced as honours and awards for gallantry and courage in the face of the enemy or in extremely dangerous circumstances. This formed the foundation for the British and Commonwealth contemporary honours system.

Many nations now have decorations for distinguished military service or gallantry and bravery on the battlefield. For example, in the United States of America, the Medal of Honor is the highest military decoration or honour in that country. First awarded in 1863, it is a decoration awarded by the President to an individual who, while a member of the military, distinguishes himself (or herself) conspicuously and gallantly at the risk of their life above and beyond the call of duty while engaged in an action against an enemy of the United States; while engaged in military operations involving conflict with an opposing foreign force; or while serving with friendly foreign forces engaged in an armed conflict against an opposing armed force in which the United States is not a belligerent party. The action performed must have been one of personal bravery or self-sacrifice so conspicuous as to clearly distinguish the individual above his comrades and must have involved risk to that individual's life. Since its inception, just over 3400 medals have been awarded, and 19 individuals have received this decoration more than once.

In May 1802, Napoleon instituted the *Légion d'Honneur* (Legion of Honour) which is a French Order of Chivalry and was awarded for either bravery in action or for 20 years' distinguished military or civil service in peacetime. It was first bestowed in France in July 1804. This medal remained the ultimate gallantry award until 1852 when the *Medaille Militaire* was introduced to award military personnel for conspicuous gallantry in action. This prestigious order is still awarded in France today.

Examples of other international decorations for bravery, gallantry and valour include the Czech War Cross (1914–1918) and the Medal for Gallantry (1940), the Greek Cross of Valour (1940), the Indian equivalent of the Victoria Cross – the *Param Vir Chakra* (1950), and the Belgian *Croix de Guerre* (1914).

As the highest decorations for bravery, gallantry and valour these awards serve as a public honour to individuals for conspicuous and gallant action, usually in the face of the enemy. Regardless of the nation from which the decoration originates, we can be sure that the recipient has been awarded such an honour for service above and beyond the call of duty.

THE AUSTRALIAN ORDER OF
PRECEDENCE OF HONOURS AND
AWARDS

THE PROCESS OF AWARDING AUSTRALIAN HONOURS DEPENDS entirely upon the type of award itself and has been subject to several reviews since its inception. Most nominations for awards available for military personnel, such as gallantry, bravery, or distinguished or conspicuous service, come from within the Australian Defence Force itself, and each nomination is forwarded through the chain of command to the Minister of Defence. However, any individual or organisation is able to nominate any member of the Australian Defence Force for a bravery award, and these nominations are duly considered as well.

Once such a nomination is received, details are forwarded to the Australian Decorations Advisory Committee who consider all nominations and make recommendations to the Governor-General. A considerable period of verification takes place before any nomination is placed before the Committee. The Committee meets twice a year to consider all verified nominations, and then a list of those people who should receive bravery awards or decorations is forwarded to the Governor-General for the approval of the Queen. Once the Queen approves the list of nominees, the Governor-General's Official Secretary writes to the nominated individual advising them of the proposed honour and asks whether they will accept it. Upon notice of acceptance, the nominees are advised of the Queen's confirmation of their award in due course and asked to keep the matter confidential until the Honours list is published.

This list is published twice a year – the first list is published on Australia Day (26 January) and the second is published on the Queen's Birthday (June).

The investiture is the ceremony in which the decorations are presented to the recipient. It is a very formal and solemn ceremony, usually held at Government House in Canberra. Each recipient (or their next of kin in the case of a posthumous award) is presented in turn to the Governor-General, or on some occasions the Queen herself, while his or her name, rank (if military or other service) and citation is read out to the audience in attendance. The Governor-General attaches the medal to the recipient (or hands the recipient a copy of the commendation in such cases) and finally, they both pose for an official photograph. After the ceremony, each recipient receives a copy of their citation as well as their medal, replica and miniature in a formal folder and box.

In the Australian community, acts of bravery and courage are carried out more frequently than many people probably realise – twice a year these awards are bestowed upon small numbers of people, living or posthumously. Unfortunately for all of us, the greater Australian community rarely hears of these courageous people or their acts. These Australian honours should be a way for the nation to express its gratitude to people who have done something to benefit the country, however general apathy and ignorance mean that the investitures often pass by without any considerable attention.

The Australian Order of Precedence of Awards

The Australian Order of Precedence of Honours and Awards is the official governmental ranking by which orders, decorations and medals are awarded. As a new award is established, the government considers where it should be placed within the existing Order of Precedence. It contains both Imperial and Australian Awards because Australians have been awarded both. However, over time, the Imperial awards will disappear entirely from the list as the current holders of these awards die. Being a list of precedence, the most prestigious awards are ranked higher up the list.

The Australian order of precedence of all recognised orders, decorations and medals can be found in the Commonwealth of Australia Gazette, the most recent of which was published in edition s208, dated Monday, 17 June 1996. There have been a number of additions to the Australian system since then but the updated list is yet to be gazetted at the time of writing.

On the following pages is a reproduction of the list, complete with the postnominals associated with the honour, which are letters signifying the abbreviation of the award's title, which can be listed after the recipient's name. As you'll see, not all awards have post-nominals.

The honours listed in bold are awards that Australians can be awarded as either purely Australian awards, or as foreign awards and honours. Honours and awards listed in the list in bold print are:
- those within the Australian System of Honours and Awards;
- those conferred by the Sovereign in exercise of the Royal Prerogative;
- those within the Order of St John, having been conferred by The Sovereign on the recommendation of the Governor-General; and
- foreign awards.

Victoria Cross	VC
George Cross	GC
Cross of Valour	CV
Knight/Dame of the Garter	KG/LG
Knight/Dame of the Thistle	KT/LT
Knight/Dame Grand Cross of the Order of the Bath	GCB
Order of Merit	OM
Knight/Dame of the Order of Australia	AK/AD
Knight/Dame Grand Cross of the Order of St Michael & St George	GCMG
Knight/Dame Grand Cross of the Royal Victorian Order	GCVO
Knight/Dame Grand Cross of the Order of the British Empire	GBE
Companion of the Order of Australia	AC
Companion of Honour	CH
Knight/Dame Commander of the Order of the Bath	KCB/DCB
Knight/Dame Commander of the Order of St Michael & St George	KCMG/DCMG
Knight/Dame Commander of the Royal Victorian Order	KCVO/DCVO
Knight/Dame Commander of the Order of the British Empire	KBE/DBE
Knight Bachelor	
Officer of the Order of Australia	AO
Companion of the Order of the Bath	CB
Companion of the Order of St Michael & St George	CMG
Commander of the Royal Victorian Order	CVO
Commander of the Order of the British Empire	CBE
Star of Gallantry	SG
Star of Courage	SC

Companion of the Distinguished Service Order	DSO
Distinguished Service Cross	DSC
Member of the Order of Australia	AM
Lieutenant of the Royal Victorian Order (formally MVO 4th Class)	LVO
Officer of the Order of the British Empire	OBE
Companion of the Imperial Service Order	ISO
Member of the Royal Victorian Order	MVO
Member of the Order of the British Empire	MBE
Conspicuous Service Cross	CSC
Nursing Service Cross	NSC
Royal Red Cross (1st Class)	RRC
Distinguished Service Cross	DSC
Military Cross	MC
Distinguished Flying Cross	DFC
Air Force Cross	AFC
Royal Red Cross (2nd Class)	ARRC
Medal for Gallantry	MG
Bravery Medal	BM
Distinguished Service Medal	DSM
Public Service Medal	PSM
Australian Police Medal	APM
Australian Fire Service Medal	AFSM
Medal of the Order of Australia	OAM
Order of St John	*(various)*
Distinguished Conduct Medal	DCM
Conspicuous Gallantry Medal	CGM
George Medal	GM
Conspicuous Service Medal	CSM
Antarctic Medal	
Queen's Police Medal for Gallantry	QPM
Queen's Fire Service Medal for Gallantry	QFSM
Distinguished Service Medal	DSM
Military Medal	MM
Distinguished Flying Medal	DFM

Air Force Medal	AFM
Queen's Gallantry Medal	QGM
Royal Victorian Medal	RVM
British Empire Medal	BEM
Queen's Police Medal for Distinguished Service	QPM
Queen's Fire Service Medal for Distinguished Service	QFSM

Commendation for Gallantry
Commendation for Brave Conduct
Queen's Commendation for Brave Conduct
Commendations for Distinguished Service
War Medals/**Australian Active Service Medal**
(in order of date of qualifying service)
Australian Service Medal 1945–1975/Australian Service Medal/Rhodesia Medal
(in order of date of qualifying service)
Police Overseas Service Medal
Civilian Service Medal 1939–1945
Polar Medal
Imperial Service Medal
Coronation and Jubilee Medals
(in order of date of receipt)
Defence Force Service Medal

Reserve Force Decoration	RFD

Reserve Force Medal
National Medal
Champion Shots Medal
Long Service Medals
(includes Imperial efficiency and long service awards)
Independence and Anniversary Medals
(in order of date of receipt)
Foreign Awards
(in order of date of authorisation of their acceptance and wearing)

Foreign Awards

There are a limited number of foreign and Australian awards that are permitted to be worn on the right breast. The Australian Army list these, subject to approval, as:

United States Presidential Distinguished Unit Citation
United States Meritorious Unit Commendation
South Vietnam Cross of Gallantry Unit Citation
United States Meritorious Unit Citation
United States Navy Unit Citation
St John Life Saving Medal
Royal Humane Society Clarke Medal
Stanhope Gold Medal
Royal Humane Society Silver Medal
Royal Humane Society Bronze Medal

BIBLIOGRAPHY

Bean, C. E. W., *The Official History of Australia in the War of 1914–18*, Angus & Robertson, Sydney, 1942.

de la Billiere, P., *Supreme Courage: Heroic Stories over 150 Years of the Victoria Cross*, Penguin, Sydney, 2005.

Collier, P., & de Calzo, N., *Medal of Honor: Portraits of Valor Beyond the Call of Duty*, Artisan Publishers, New York, 2003.

Coulthard-Clark, C., *The Encyclopaedia of Australia's Battles*, Allen & Unwin, Sydney, 1991.

Dornan, P., *The Silent Men: Syria, Kokoda, and on to Gona*, Allen & Unwin, Sydney, 1999.

Grey, J., *A Military History of Australia*, Cambridge University Press, Melbourne, 1999.

Horner, D. M., *SAS Phantoms of War: A history of the Australian Special Air Service*, Allen & Unwin, Sydney, 2002.

Keegan, J., *The Face of Battle*, Cape, London, 1976.

Keegan, J., & Holmes, R., *Soldiers: A History of Men in Battle*, Viking, London, 1986.

Krasnoff, S., *Where To? For Valour: A true story of Keith Payne, VC*, Shala Press, Queensland, 1995.

Lindsay, P., *The Spirit of Kokoda . . . Then and Now*, Hardie Grant Books, Melbourne, 2002.

Maton, M., *The National Honours and Awards of Australia*, Kangaroo Press, Sydney, 1995.

Murphy, E. F., *Vietnam Medal of Honor Heroes*, Presidio Press, New York, 1987.

Odgers, G., *100 Years of Australians at War*, Lansdowne, Sydney, 1999.

Pearn, J., *Reflections on Rwanda: Selected photo-archive of service with the Forward Surgical Team, the Australian Medical Support Force, UNAMIR II, Rwanda*, Amphion Press, Sydney, 1995.

Review of Honours and Awards, *A Matter of Honour: A report of the review of Australian Honours and Awards*, Australian Government Publishing Service, Canberra, 1995.

Staunton, A., *Victoria Cross: Australia's finest and the battles they fought*, Hardie Grant Books, Melbourne, 2005.

Tyquin, M. B., *Neville Howse: Australia's first Victoria Cross winner*, Oxford University Press, Melbourne, 1999.

Wilcox, C., *Australia's Boer War: The war in South Africa, 1899–1902*, Oxford University Press, Melbourne, 2002.